The Single Trap

ANDREW G. MARSHALL is a marital therapist with RELATE – the UK's leading counselling charity – and writes regularly for newspapers and magazines, including *Mail on Sunday*, *Sunday Express* and *Woman/Home*. His book *I Love You But I'm Not in Love with You: Seven steps to saving your relationship* (also published by Bloomsbury) has been translated into fourteen languages. His most recent book is *How Can I Ever Trust You Again?*

www.andrewgmarshall.com

By the same Author

I love you but I'm not in love with you
How can I ever trust you again?

The Single Trap

The Two-step Guide to Escaping it and Finding Lasting Love

Andrew G. Marshall

BLOOMSBURY

LONDON · BERLIN · NEW YORK

First published in 2009
This paperback edition published 2010

Copyright © 2009 by Andrew G. Marshall
Diagram on page 149 by Bridget Bodoano

The moral right of the author has been asserted

No part of this book may be used or reproduced in any manner
whatsoever without written permission from the Publisher except in the
case of brief quotations embodied in critical articles or reviews

Bloomsbury Publishing Plc
36 Soho Square,
London W1D 3QY

Bloomsbury Publishing, London, New York and Berlin

A CIP catalogue record for this book is available from the British Library

ISBN 978 1 4088 0080 5
10 9 8 7 6 5 4 3 2 1

Typeset by Hewer Text UK Ltd, Edinburgh
Printed by Clays Ltd, St Ives plc

FSC
Mixed Sources
Product group from well-managed
forests and other controlled sources

Cert no. SGS-COC-2061
www.fsc.org
© 1996 Forest Stewardship Council

www.bloomsbury.com

To Kate

Thank you for being my muse and my first reader.

Contents

Introduction

Are you fed up with pretending that citrus-scented baths, moist chocolate brownies and freshly laundered sheets 'seduce the most important person in your life – you'? Has the novelty of curry from the take-away carton and non-stop football long since worn off? You are not alone. There are times when being single makes sense – especially after a painful break-up – but it should be just a stopgap. Humans are social creatures. We have an almost animal need to pair off, that friendship, however good, just cannot satisfy. A loving, sensual and sexual relationship is the best refuge when the going gets tough, a springboard to personal growth and a source of strength that improves our over-all health. In an era of short-term business contracts, fears about personal safety and rapid technological change, we need a partner more than ever before. Yet, it is becoming harder and harder to find the right person.

I've spent twenty-five years as a marital therapist helping people make good relationships. Most of my clients are couples who need help to communicate better and rebuild broken bridges. However, a significant and growing proportion are singles who, try as they might, just cannot find the right partner and divorced people who fear that they will spend the rest of their lives alone. Many have asked me to recommend a book on how to find a loving relationship. So I have read a lot of self-help manuals, but have always drawn a blank. The majority of these books concentrate on game-playing and tricks to make someone fall in love – which is not a good foundation for a lasting relationship. So after years of being unable to find anything to recommend, I finally decided to write one myself and answer the questions that my clients were asking: How can you be open enough to let in love but still protective enough to avoid too much pain, rejection and bitterness? What is the best way to meet people? How do you know if someone is a potential partner or whether lust and wishful thinking have sent you up a blind alley?

I have drawn on scientific research from around the world and my own therapeutic work to devise a programme that will help single people take a fresh look at their search for love, make better choices and find the *right* partner. I start by looking at the changes in our society over the past five years that have made finding love more difficult. It is important to understand these universal pressures. Otherwise, single people can feel ashamed of being alone or, worse still, blame themselves. As you can imagine, this undermines self-confidence and makes the search for love more difficult. Next, I set out my programme to find a loving and lasting relationship. Step One is *Escaping the Single Trap*. This section concentrates on understanding your journey up to this point, your needs and any personal issues that might be holding you back. Whether you have had a series of short-term unsatisfactory relationships or have just finished a long-term live-in relationship – and fear that you will never find anyone else – there is help specially tailored to your circumstances. Step Two is *Finding Lasting Love*. This section sets out the best way to meet a long-term partner and how to move from a successful first date into a committed long-term relationship. Finally, I would like to stress that this is an upbeat book. My most important message is that there is somebody for everybody and my job is to help you find yours.

The Single Epidemic

Chapter One

Why Are There So Many Single People?

Over the past five years, I have noticed a change in the attitudes around being single. Newspapers, reality TV programmes and self-help books have become more and more critical. The scare stories about a generation of single people are getting nastier, the TV gurus' comments more personal and often extremely humiliating. Meanwhile, the advice books have begun to blame people for being alone, that somehow they are not pretty, clever or determined enough to find a relationship. The debate has turned toxic. The result is that many people who are not in a relationship no longer view being single as a natural phase between the end of one relationship and the beginning of another, but somewhere they have become stuck forever. In short, they feel that they have fallen into the *Single Trap*. My aim is to not only take a fresh look at being single but to show how to find a loving and lasting relationship.

When I was recruiting case histories, I invited groups of friends to get together and discuss the benefits, problems and issues about searching for love. However, I met a lot of resistance. 'A few years ago, we'd talk about being single all the time,' explained Anna, thirty-five, 'but we just got bored of the subject and it's not like anything's going to change.' Yet Anna still wanted to talk – but on her own. Not only did people feel unable to truly open up, even amongst close friends, but most felt ashamed about being single. Worse still, some even felt a failure. Yet over the last five years, *all* the relationship problems presented in my office have become more complex and entrenched. It makes no difference whether the clients are married, living together or simply single. Modern life is making relationships more difficult. So my goal in this first chapter is to help you understand the forces at play, learn how to mitigate the impact and most importantly: to stop blaming yourself. The best way to achieve this is to take a step back and look at the facts.

The proportion of one-person households in the UK almost doubled between 1971 and 2001. Singles now make up 31 per cent of all homes. Government forecasts predict that the proportion of solo occupancy will soon increase to 40 per cent – making the single-person home the most common type of household. Contrary to popular myth, it is not just women who are finding it hard to make relationships. The Office for National Statistics report (*Social Trends*, 2007) showed that almost a quarter of men aged twenty-five to twenty-nine lived at home with their parents. The same report revealed that the number of men aged twenty-five to forty-four who live alone has more than doubled over the past twenty years. Even more startling, in a recent survey, seven out of ten Londoners under fifty said that they had dated in the past year – underlining just how few people are in long-term relationships. Despite the popularity, and new-found social acceptability, of internet dating, lunch dates, lonely-hearts columns, speed-dating and old-fashioned introduction agencies, the number of single people keeps on rising. In the same way that more people are on diets than ever before, but the population has never been fatter, there are now more ways to meet a potential partner yet the number of single people keeps rising.

Some of the change is down to well-established trends: easier divorce, people living longer and more social affluence – which gives women the historically novel choice to live alone. However these factors on their own do not explain the changes; we need to dig deeper.

One of the significant changes over the past five years has been the explosion in consumer choice. Where once we could opt for either butter or margarine, there is now low-fat spreads, low salt, organic, buttermilks with added omega 3 or olive oil, no hydrogenated oils and a myriad of other choices. Although making our minds up can be tough, we all buy into the mantra that choice is good. Politicians offer more choice about where to send our children to school or which hospital to have an operation, confident in the belief that this will get them elected. Certainly no choice means no control over our lives, no freedom and no personal autonomy; it would indeed be unbearable. However Barry Schwartz, Professor of Social Theory and Social Action at Swarthmore College in Pennsylvania, believes that unlimited choice is just as bad as no choice and could be at the root of our high levels of unhappiness, dissatisfaction and depression. He got the idea for his groundbreaking book, *The Paradox of Choice* (HarperCollins, 2004), when he went to buy some jeans. He had worn out his old favourite pair and simply wanted to replace them. Instead, he was offered easy fit, relaxed fit, baggy or extra baggy. Did he want them stone-washed, acid-washed or distressed? the assistant asked. While the professor looked at her blankly, she asked if he wanted zip or button fly and faded or regular. It is easy to laugh at an academic out of touch with fashion, but when it comes to dating we are in exactly the same dilemma. The internet provides almost endless choice – with countless dating sites each boasting thousands of members. If you are prepared to travel, there are literally millions of people waiting to meet you. Our gut instinct tells us that this is a good thing – surely, we are increasing our chances of a date. But could our guts be deceiving us?

Why Less Really Is More

When I was a child in the sixties, I was the envy of all my classmates. My grandmother owned a sweet shop. She not only stocked the regular chocolate bars, like the local newsagents or corner store, her shop had rows of jars of boiled sweets reaching up to the ceiling with a ladder to reach the top shelves. There were glass cabinets offering marzipan animals, jellied fruits and individual chocolates from far off places like Switzerland. My grandmother lived in London, so we would only visit occasionally and a trip to her 'Lollipop Shop' – as we called it – was a definite treat. Best of all, my sister and I could help ourselves to anything that we liked. We would start off with our favourites from those Christmas selection boxes which Granny sold loose by the quarter. Next, I would sample the violet creams which were arranged in lines in a special display cabinet and then suck on a mint humbug. However, after half an hour I would no longer be sure what I fancied eating next. On the occasions when I was allowed to play shop, weighing out the sweets for customers and taking the money, I would soon move from indecision to fancying absolutely nothing. Instead of eating more sweets, when faced with unlimited choice, I actually ate fewer. My experience has been replicated in a laboratory study when students were asked to taste and rate a selection of gourmet chocolates. Half the students were given only six chocolates to eat while the other half were given thirty. Not only did the students with less choice rate their chocolates higher but they were also four times as likely to choose chocolate, rather than cash, as a thank-you for taking part in the research. So why were they more satisfied? Professor Barry Schwartz believes that greater choice actually diminishes our enjoyment because we fear that amongst the discarded options is something that we might have liked more.

So what can this tell us about our society's growing number of singletons? Alan, forty-two, used to be a regular in singles bars during the eighties: 'It used to be pointless chatting anyone up too soon in the evening, because people were keeping their options open. The door would open and all eyes would swivel to see who had come in. If it was a regular, you could almost feel the disappointment in the room.' However in the last hour, everything would change. 'People would begin to pair off,' he explained, 'now, if you left it too late – that girl that you'd been eyeing up would be snapped up by someone else. You had to make your move. Often, you'd end up talking to someone who you hadn't really fancied half an hour earlier. I always used to think of this country song "Why do the girls all get prettier closer to closing time?"' The singer was probably joking about the aphrodisiac qualities of beer but he is tapping into a deeper truth. Earlier in the evening Alan was not only comparing the girls against each other but against a fantasy girl who might come into the bar. At closing time, the girls who were actually there would immediately become more appealing. Less choice actually made Alan choose. In fact he is rather nostalgic for the singles bar – which has been largely killed off by the internet. In a way, today's online dating sites are just like yesterday's singles bar. Except there is no closing time – ever.

Not only does unlimited choice make it harder to choose, it makes us believe that somewhere there is the perfect product. Returning to Professor Schwartz and his search for the jeans. The assistant conferred with her colleague to try to decide what he meant by regular jeans, 'you know, the kind that used to be the only kind', and pointed him in the right direction. So far so good, but Professor Schwartz began to wonder if one of the other options would be more comfortable, a better fit and ultimately look better on him. Somewhere in the piles of merchandise was a more desirable pair than the jeans in his hands. Previously when he had bought 'regular' jeans, they had become 'perfect' jeans as he wore the stiffness out of the fabric and they had given a little here and there and moulded to his body. It is the same with contemporary dating. We would like to believe that somewhere there is the 'perfect' partner, a soul mate with whom we can live harmoniously forever more. Unlike with the old-fashioned 'regular' partner, there will be no need for nasty rows or rough edges, but an immediate magical union. In reality, jeans and relationships have a lot in common. There is seldom an instant fit but, over time, we grow into both and before too long we would not wish to be parted from either.

Maximisers and Satisfyers

In the fifties, Nobel Prize-winning economist Herbert Simon decided to look at how people coped with choice; even then consumers had a wide range of products to choose from and big-ticket items – like cars and washing machines – constituted a major investment. He found that the population divided into two categories: the 'Maximiser' and the 'Satisfyer'.

The Maximiser will only settle for the very best. When shopping, the Maximiser might find something that fulfils all his or her criteria – let's stay with jeans – but instead of buying them in the first store will hide them under the rest of the stock. (Heaven forbid that someone else should buy them.) Next the Maximiser sets off to try all the other shops in town, maybe returning and digging out the hidden pair. The Maximiser cannot purchase anything until he or she has looked at all the possibilities. On one hand, it is great to aspire to the best but there are always doubts. Even carrying home the prized purchase, the Maximiser has nagging worries: 'Maybe I should have tried one more store. What if I had travelled into a larger town?' If it was tough being a Maximiser in the fifties, it is even worse with the unlimited possibilities of the internet. Today a Maximiser has more choice and even more stockists. She or he might have the right jeans but maybe someone, somewhere is offering them cheaper. Yet despite all the stress involved, the Maximiser believes anything less than perfect is settling for mediocrity. Meanwhile if a Satisfyer found a good pair of jeans in the first store, he or she would weigh up the fit, quality and price but would choose quickly and decisively. If all his or her criteria were met, the Satisfyer would purchase the jeans – end of story. It might be possible to buy the jeans cheaper elsewhere but the Satisfyer cannot be bothered to look. This is because a Satisfyer aims for excellent rather than the *very* best.

Let me give a personal example that shows the differences between Maximisers and Satisfyers. Many years ago, a friend and I took a holiday in Gran Canaria. Unfortunately we went in the summer – most people opt for a winter break – and the bars were empty. My friend was certain that somewhere on the island, someone was having a better time than us. One evening after the beach, he insisted on trekking across the sand dunes – tall and never-ending – to reach an early evening bar. The journey was hot and tiring and made us feel like Lawrence of Arabia – but without the camels. When we arrived at this celebrated bar, there was only a handful of other clients. My friend knocked back a much-needed drink and immediately wanted to go somewhere else. I wanted to stay and enjoy the views over the sand dunes – which were spectacular – and generally wind down. OK, it was not the best bar on the island, but it was good enough for now. I genuinely could not understand what drove my friend on to the next bar. 'If you get back and someone says: "Did you try X bar? It is the in-place, with all the beautiful people", you'd be mortified if you missed out,' he explained. Obviously, I was the Satisfyer (accepting that we were out of season and making the best of things) and he was the Maximiser (determined to track down the peak experience). So which is best? If Herbert Simon had overheard our conversation in Gran Canaria, he would have been more likely to side with me than my friend. He believed that the amount of time, money, energy and anguish involved in choosing – and in our case getting to the bar – is factored in, that satisfying is the maximising strategy. However, without my friend's drive I would never have reached the after-beach bar in the first place and not only have missed watching the sun sink behind the dunes but also only have seen half the island.

Returning to Alan and singles bars, he is clearly another Satisfyer. 'Many times if I talked to a girl towards closing time, who I'd quite liked earlier but hadn't been a knockout, the chemistry would kick in and we would really click,' he reminisced. 'So I never really thought of it as settling for second best.' Professor Schwartz is probably a Satisfyer too; he had never felt short-changed by just one type of jeans. However his shopping trip made him question his old buying habits and started his journey to his book's conclusion: unlimited choice is turning more of us into Maximisers.

Who Is Most Likely to Find Lasting Love: A Satisfyer or a Maximiser?

With truly important decisions, nobody says: 'I want a "good enough" school for my children' or 'a "good enough" doctor to treat my cancer'. We want the *best* school and the *best* doctor. When it comes to relationships nobody wants to *settle* but to walk up the aisle with the best partner. From time to time, we hear about someone who has been exhausted or disillusioned by the dating treadmill and found someone who 'will do'. Perhaps a bride who has opted for a kind, older man, even though he does not set her heart on fire. Although we can understand the logic at being a Satisfyer and opting for friendship rather than passion, we suspect she is opening herself up to disappointment, becoming attracted to other men and ultimately divorce. Surely with love, we all want to be Maximisers?

However, there is one overriding problem: we might want the best, but how do we know when we have found it? It might be possible to find, for example, the best fridge-freezer. We can consult, say fifty websites, and find the best price. After all, price is easily comparable. Except, we might also want energy efficiency; although this is a statistic that can be compared from one model to the next, how do we trade off the benefits of price with energy efficiency? There are other issues too: capacity, ice-making facilities, design. Although the calculation is hard, there are a limited number of variables to rank before making a purchase. But what about the best school? We can consult league tables, but what about the distance travelled, the after-school clubs, the personality of our child and the facilities in his or her area of interest? What about the personality of their form teacher? Their classmates? Not only are there unlimited variables but each one is almost impossible to call. As for the best doctor, how can we even hope to judge?

So what about the best partner? Especially when searching online or speed-dating, how can we rank the possible choices? The problem is that maximising increases our tendency to judge on the external factors that can be ranked – like looks, height, figure and wealth – rather than internal qualities like character, trust-worthiness, openness and generosity, which cannot. However, these internal qualities are ultimately going to be the deciding factor on whether a relationship is a success or a failure.

Maximising also encourages us to compare – otherwise how do we know if we have the best deal? In some cases, this involves competitive dating between friends but more often we compare the date in front of us with other potential partners. This makes commitment harder, as choosing to walk up the aisle with one person automatically excludes all the other, potentially better, lovers. By contrast, Satisfyers have more trust in their own judge-ment. They are aiming for 'good enough' and each person will have their own way of measuring this. For this reason, a Satisfyer has less reason to compare their beloved. Spending less time looking over her or his shoulder, a Satisfyer is more likely to be contented with their partner and therefore find it easier to settle down.

Another problem for Maximisers is that they are more likely to aspire to dating outside their league. The most beautiful woman or handsomest man might seem like a highway to happiness but we also increase our risk of being rejected. The comic writer and actor Harvey Fierstein has an amusing take on this phenomenon. In his award-winning play, *Torch Song Trilogy*, his lead character advises: 'An ugly person who goes after a pretty person gets nothing but trouble. But a pretty person who goes after an ugly person gets at least cabfare.'

Ultimately, when it comes to love, there is a downside to being both a Satisfyer and Maximiser. Fortunately most of us do not fall squarely into one category or another, rather there is a scale with 'only the very best will do' at one end and 'yeah, sure, anything for a quiet life' at the other. To find out where you fit, look at the test in the exercise section. With unlimited choice driving more of us towards maximising, there is also advice on how to reset your internal thermometer towards the middle.

So what type of person is most likely to find lasting love? At the start, especially when considering an invitation to date or during the first few dates, it is probably best to be towards the Satisfyer end of the scale. This keeps your options open and avoids a snap judgement which can rule out a potentially great partner. When it comes to taking the budding relationship to the next stage, everyone should move towards the Maximiser end and only proceed if everything feels right.

Why It Is Becoming Harder to Meet People

Singles are not the only people who feel isolated and disconnected. This is a general trend affecting everyone in our society. However, single people are probably the modern equivalent of the canaries that nineteenth-century miners took down the pits. These birds were particularly sensitive to carbon monoxide, caused by a blocked tunnel or air shaft, so if the canary perished everybody evacuated. I wonder if the explosion of single people is a warning sign that something is fundamentally wrong with the way that we live today.

The dominant strains in our culture are materialism and individualism, so we stress autonomy, freedom and personal fulfilment – over everything else. The result is that we seem to be losing the social glue that holds us all together. It is not just that we are more likely to be strangers to our neighbours but that we are also less likely to join clubs. Social, sporting and voluntary groups have lost between 10 and 20 per cent of their membership and the remaining members spend less time together – halving over the past two decades. The slack has not been taken up by informal social connections like drinks after work or socialising with friends. Twenty years ago, researchers based at Duke University in North Carolina found that men had, on average, 3.5 'confidants' with whom they could share secrets, but that number has now dropped to just two. A quarter have nobody to confide in, twice as many people than in the 1980s. Women, traditionally thought of as better at friendship, fare only slightly better. According to the study, they have marginally more friends than men but have seen a decline in the number of family members in whom they confide.

Society is growing richer with physical capital (money and resources). The Government is concerned about human capital (education and physical well-being). However, we have lost the dense network of reciprocal and social relationships which sociologists call social capital. This is a combination of the 'Favour Bank' (from Tom Wolfe's book *Bonfire of the Vanities*) where 'you scratch my back and I'll scratch yours' and the traditional idea of 'civic virtue' where you do something for the good of everybody. The phenomenon is highlighted by Robert D. Putnam, Professor of Public Policy at Harvard University, in his landmark book *Bowling Alone*. He writes: 'For the first two-thirds of the twentieth-century, a powerful tide bore Americans into a deeper engagement, but a few decades ago – silently, without warning, without noticing – we were overtaken by a treacherous rip current and have been pulled apart.' He sums up the idea with one striking image: in the past Americans would regularly bowl in leagues, today they bowl less often, with either a few close friends or totally alone.

It's not just that we are spending less time with other people but that the type of social interaction has changed: bonding rather than bridging. Bonding groups have strong links but are more likely to be made of people who are just like us. A good example would be the four characters in *Sex and the City* who meet for lunch and to share news. The key characteristic of a bonding group is that it is exclusive. By contrast, a bridging group is inclusive and open to anyone who pays their dues and abides by the rules. An example would be a golf club, a PTA or one of Putnam's bowling leagues. The ties within the group are weak but the membership is normally diverse. Bonding groups are good for 'getting by', intimate friends rally round when we're in trouble, but bridging capital is vital for 'getting on'. This is because distant acquaintances are more likely to provide a lead for a new job or, more important for single people, an introduction to a partner.

No wonder long-term singles and the newly divorced ask me: 'How do I meet people?' The last twenty-five years have seen the loosening of social ties and the breakdown of many of the organisations that traditionally provided links and support. Although everyone is more alone, stuck in front of computer and television screens, single people are particularly vulnerable. As Putnam concludes: 'Thin single-stranded, surf-by interactions are gradually replacing dense multi-stranded, well-exercised bonds. More social connectedness is one-shot, special-purpose and self-orientated.' For singles, this has meant high-pressure events like speed-dating rather than meeting someone in a casual social setting where it is easier to truly get to know each other.

Summary
- It is important to understand the social pressures and trends behind the single epidemic, otherwise there is a risk of people just blaming themselves for being alone.
- With unlimited choice, it is harder to choose. Not only are we more likely to aim for the perfect partner (not necessarily a problem) but also to be a Maximiser who refuses to consider anything less than the ideal (which lays us all open to maximum disappointment, frustration and even despair).
- Maximisers are more likely to compare themselves with other people. This makes them more likely to feel negative about themselves and their choice of partner.
- Satisfyers find it easier to choose, because they are aiming for a good-enough product rather than the best one. They find it easier to make relationships but risk 'settling' and becoming trapped in unfulfilling relationships.
- The answer is to aim to be somewhere between these two extremes.
- On every measure from voting in elections through to membership of workplace organisations and clubs and societies, we are less likely to be engaged. Everybody has suffered from less social capital – higher crime, vandalism, road rage – but singles are particularly exposed.

Exercises

Maximiser/Satisfyer Scale

Do you choose quickly and decisively or do you need to consider every possibility before taking a decision? You can test whether you are a Maximiser or a Satisfyer by taking the following test. Score your level of agreement with each statement on a scale of one to five. Five means that you completely agree with the statement, one means that you completely disagree and three means that you are neutral.

1 At parties, I find myself looking over the shoulder of the person that I'm talking to – even during interesting chats – in case I'm missing something. 5

2 Dating is rather like clothes shopping. I expect to try on a lot before finding the perfect fit. 3

3 With TV, I often flip through the other channels even though I'm watching something else. 5

4 I am not keen on committing to a night out with friends too far into the future, in case a better offer comes up. 1

5 After going shopping, I often feel less positive about my purchases when I get home. 1

6 I worry that other people get a better deal. On holiday, I like to find out how much other guests paid or avoid such conversations because I'm worried that others paid less and I will feel bad about myself. 5

7 When driving somewhere, I can stress myself out by wondering if there is less traffic on other routes or whether I should have taken a train or some other form of transport. 3

8 I often find myself thinking what would have happened if I had made different choices? Like studying something different or not breaking up with someone. 3

9 No matter what, I have the highest standards for myself. 5

10 I find Christmas stressful because it's important to find the right gifts for everybody. 5

11 On Monday morning, when everybody is talking about their weekends, I often worry that other people have a better time, funnier friends or a nicer family. 5

12 When my insurance comes up for renewal, I will normally consult at least ten alternative quotes. 5

13 I like to find out how things turned out for old boyfriends or girlfriends. 3

14 I find it hard to make my mind up in restaurants and when other people's food arrives often feel they ordered more wisely. 3

Add up your points and discover where you fit on the scale.

Under Thirty-five

You are a Satisfyer. If you find something that works you are likely to stick with it, whether it is a brand of toothpaste or a song on the car radio (a Maximiser would channel-hop in case another station was playing a better song). When it comes to shopping, you consider a manageable number of options and settle for something that fits the bill – rather than the best possible item. As a Satisfyer, you are less likely to suffer buyer's remorse because your identity is not tied up with finding the perfect product at the best price possible. However, there is a balance between not getting stressed-out by choice and taking the easy way out. Many businesses make their profits out of Satisfyers who stay, for example, on the same mortgage rate for years, while the Maximisers have long since switched to a lower rate. You need to be certain that when it comes to the important areas of your life – job, relationship and family – you are not just settling for a quiet life. By maximising in these areas, you could get promotion or more out of your relationships – rather than letting people take advantage and walk all over you.

Thirty-five to Forty-five

Most people fit somewhere in the middle of the Maximiser and Satisfyer scale. In some areas, you will aim for the best and in others you will settle for good enough. This is called 'domain-specific' maximising. For example, you might care passionately about fine wines and look for the perfect bottle to accompany a meal but are unlikely to keep switching internet providers in search of the best deal. When it comes to key areas, like work and relationships, you want to do your best but have realistic expectations of what is possible. By contrast, a Maximiser has not only high standards but expects always to achieve them. As this is impossible, a Maximiser can end up disappointed, depressed and ultimately de-motivated. Be aware that unlimited choice and clever marketing are putting pressure on all of us to tip towards the maximising end of the scale. So do not be tempted to consider more than a manageable number of alternatives – probably around six – as unlimited choice often makes for worse rather than better decisions.

Forty-six Plus

You are a Maximiser. You never settle for second-best and this means that you take a while to come to a decision. In theory, you should be the person most likely to be pleased with your choices. Except, you are often filled with regret. Even if a decision turns out well, you will be disappointed if another option turned out better still. The higher your score, the most likely you are to assess missed opportunities: the job turned down, the holiday not taken, the boyfriend or girlfriend that got away. It is fine to have high standards for yourself, but it is better to concentrate on a few key areas (like job, personal morality and particular interests) than expecting to excel in everything. Finally, try not to compare yourself to other people as this will increase dissatisfaction with your own life. There will always be people ahead but even if life is a competition – which I doubt – it is better to take a long view. This will help you see all your achievements not just one disappointment. Ultimately, you will have a less stressful life if you let go of best and aim for attainable.

Reset Your Maximiser Thermometer

If unlimited choice is turning us all into Maximisers, it is important to concentrate on a few areas to maximise – otherwise we risk becoming exhausted and frustrated. The following exercise is aimed at your purchasing decisions – especially for small-ticket items. Changing your attitude to inconsequential purchases will not only free up more time and energy for important choices but offers a chance to experiment with being a Satisfyer. This is key, as committed Maximisers find it hardest to find and keep partners.

1 Look back at your last significant purchase.
   • How many websites did you consider?
   • How many shops did you visit?
   • What else went into making the decision?

2 Calculate the costs.
   • How long did it take to make your mind up? Even if it is an estimate, put down a figure.
   • How much money did you save? Be realistic with this figure. Instead of the difference between the highest quote and the eventual price, take the saving achieved by maximising – above and beyond that of a regular careful shopper.

3 How satisfied were you with the purchase?
   • Did you have any buyer's regret?
   • Did your effort provide more, less or about the same pleasure as someone investing less time and energy?

4 Did the effort involved justify maximising on this purchase?
   • Think about how much an hour of your time is worth. (If you are self-employed, you will probably have an hourly rate. If you work for someone else, make a rough estimate by breaking down your salary into a daily and then an hourly rate.)

- Compare this figure with the savings achieved by maximising.
- Was maximising a good investment of your time or energy?

5 Next time you make a significant purchase set yourself an artificial constraint.
   - Take three quotes only.
   - Consider only six websites.
   - Look in only two shops.
   - Give yourself only half an hour.
   - The exact constraint is up to you and might change from purchase to purchase. However, set the limit in advance and stick to it.

6 Reassess your purchasing patterns.
   - What were the differences when you satisfied rather than maximised?
   - Did it work out better? If so, in what way?
   - How could you incorporate the benefits into other parts of your life?

7 Make a pact with yourself to:
   - Resist the temptations laid out by the advertising industry. If something really is 'new and improved' your friends will probably recommend it.
   - Compare down rather than up. The lifestyles of the rich and famous will always make you feel inadequate. Instead, compare yourself with your contemporaries or – better still – people less fortunate.
   - Satisfy more than maximise.

Bonding or Bridging?

The idea behind this exercise is to discover how your friendships link together and whether your social capital is from bonding or bridging.

1 Go through your address book and write each family member, friend or acquaintance on a Post-it note.
2 Put your name on a differently coloured Post-it note and stick it in the middle of a blank wall or a large piece of cardboard.
3 Put your best friend closest to you.
4 If you met any further friends or acquaintances through him or her, put them next to your best friend but slightly further out from the centre.
5 Continue until you have put all the friends on the map, showing how one friendship leads to another.
6 If names in your address book come through membership of a club or an organisation, write that down on another differently coloured Post-it and fan the friendships out in the same way.
7 Keep going until all the names are on the wall with the closest friends at the centre and the most distance acquaintances on the rim.
8 Stand back and look at your map of friendship. What are the patterns? Are your friendships all bonding (close and with people like you) or do you have bridging capital too (acquaintances from a wide range of different people)?
9 Are there any key 'connectors', friends who have introduced you to a variety of different people? If so, call and talk to them about friendship. You will find that these connectors approach it differently. They probably phone friends more often, pass on joke emails, enjoy giving parties or belong to lots of different societies. What can you learn from them?
10 What changes would you like to make? How could you make them happen?

Step One:
Escaping the Single Trap

Chapter Two

The Advantages of Working on Yourself Before Looking for Love

There is a central idea in this book. It is particularly important for the first step in finding a loving and lasting relationship but also informs the second step too, all the exercises and underpins my philosophy about relationships. Fortunately, the idea is quite simple to understand. Unfortunately, many people would rather that it was not true. So what is this idea? *Like attracts like.* By this I mean, if we are in a bad place emotionally, we tend to attract other people whose lives are in crisis in some way.

A good example of like attracting like is Christina, thirty-two, whose previous relationship had ended particularly bitterly: 'I was emotionally exhausted from all the fighting and all I wanted was to be held, stroked and made to feel that everything would be all right.' Less than six months after the break-up with the father of her two children, she met Mitchell, who was going through similar problems with his ex-wife. 'The sex was wonderful and I really thought that we understood each other and could really support each other,' she explained. Unfortunately, after a brief honeymoon period, they found that their problems multiplied. 'Once the passion wore off, I found his moaning really frustrating. I would be having an OK day and he'd have a letter from his solicitor and not only would he be in a black mood but his rant would bring up some of the issues about my own case. It was like he was not only scratching his scars but

25

mine too.' When they came to me for counselling, I was immediately reminded of like attracts like. However, when I pointed out their similarities, Christina was quick to distance herself. 'Mitchell is just obsessed with his ex. He just can't let anything drop,' she complained, 'whereas I've made a very really effort to move on.' However, instead of fighting with her ex, she had made it difficult for him to see the children and effectively shut him out of their lives. So although, on the surface, they might have been dealing with the problems differently, in effect they were both in the same place emotionally. Like had attracted like.

Another example is Naomi, who was only twenty-eight when her husband left her. She had thought she had the perfect marriage, so it was a terrible shock. After nine months alone, Naomi decided to start dating again and met 'a sensitive caring man'. At first she thought he was the answer to her prayers but after six months the relationship hit problems. 'He went from calling all the time to hardly phoning and not being available. It sort of fizzled out,' Naomi explained in her first counselling session. My diagnosis was that although Naomi wanted the comfort of a relationship, she was not ready to fully give herself. I suspected that her boyfriend would be in a similar place, that like had attracted like, so I asked her about him. 'His mother was very controlling and he had lots of issues with commitment.' And what about Naomi herself? How did she feel about commitment? 'I didn't want us to move in together or anything, I wasn't ready for that. Just someone to take to friends' weddings or an odd holiday – but he couldn't even cope with that.' Although Naomi felt ready for dating, her heart was still in intensive care. She had unwittingly been drawn to a man who appeared interested but was, in truth, also looking for consolation rather than commitment. If you are still questioning the idea of like attracts like, think about your own experiences. Have you ever needed someone to boost your self-esteem and found someone who, in return, just wanted to use you? What about the time you went out feeling desperate? Did you meet other similarly desperate people? Have you ever met someone who seems to be carrying a lot of baggage and then realised that you have your own issues too?

There is another part to 'like attracts like': how you perceive yourself and how you treat yourself is how other people will perceive and treat you. In other words, if deep down you consider yourself to be unworthy of love, you will attract partners who will treat you as if you are. Jessica, thirty-four, wanted a long-term boyfriend but most of her relationships never seemed to go anywhere. 'I'll meet these guys at parties and we'll click but somehow the relationships always end with me crying in bars,' she explained. So I asked about her most recent boyfriend Bob. 'I suppose I should have known. That first night, when we were back at my flat on the sofa with a glass of wine, he said, "Are you sure you want to do this?" He'd even told me he was not looking for a relationship. But I didn't want him to go. Well, the inevitable happened and we made love. It was good and I developed feelings for him.' In effect, she had known that they were after different things: he was looking for casual sex and she wanted love. However, as she did not treat herself with respect, Bob probably felt that he had the green light to do the same. After half a dozen encounters, he became less and less available and eventually disappeared altogether.

No matter how many times we see like with like, we still hope for exceptions. This is why *Cinderella* is one of our most popular myths. Even as adults, we cling to the belief that someone is going to come along and 'save us', and to save us they have to be 'perfect' or at least 'better' than us. Instead of 'like attracts like', we hope for 'perfect' to reach down and pull us up to his or her level. However, the *Cinderella* myth is actually more complex. In all stories, the hero and heroine have to struggle and overcome obstacles to reach the happy ending. They only attain true union with their prince or princess when they have learnt something important about themselves and grown. In effect, the symbolic fairy-tale marriage is not a hand up but a meeting of equals. From time to time, I counsel couples who at first sight seem to disprove like attracts like. Certainly, Madeline saw herself as Cinderella. She was seventeen when she met her husband-to-be. Edward was in his mid-twenties and seemed much more mature. 'I felt he rescued me from my parents' rows. They used to fight late into the night and me and my sister would lie awake in our bedroom and comfort each other until they finally ran out of energy,' explains Madeline. They married and five years later came to me for counselling. They had started fighting because Madeline was fed up with being treated like a little girl. It soon became clear that behind the grown-up facade, Edward was frightened. Instead of an adult-to-adult relationship, he only felt secure when he was in charge. The more he talked, the more petulant he sounded and the more he looked like a little boy – albeit one dressed up as a knight in shining armour. Inside, they were both probably about the same age.

Although 'like attracts like' is at first sight rather a depressing idea, there is an important upside: if we have our heads screwed on, we attract similarly sorted people. This is why the first part of this book is about working on yourself. Of course, there are benefits to understanding yourself and being aware of why you might have made poor choices in the past. However, the main aim of this section is to help you grow and be truly ready for a committed relationship – both in your head and in your heart. Once you have reached this goal, you will attract other people who are similarly ready for commitment and the chances of a successful relationship will be greatly increased. So how do you start working on yourself?

Why the Journey to a Better Relationship in the Future Starts in the Past

It goes without saying that we tend to date people with whom we feel comfortable – either because he or she is easy to talk to or because we suspect we've found someone special. But what triggers this spark of recognition somewhere deep inside? Why do we feel that we've known this fascinating woman or good-looking man all our lives? The answer is that we probably have. Unconsciously we choose partners who are similar in some sense to our mothers or fathers.

The automatic response to this suggestion is to laugh or protest that our previous boyfriends or girlfriends have been nothing like our parents. Sometimes my clients refuse to even entertain the idea – which is a pity because understanding our emotional inheritance is the single most important factor in finding love. So why are we so resistant? Maybe it wars with the romantic ideal of two soul partners destined for each other, maybe the concept has a whiff of incest but most probably we are only too aware of the fault-lines in our parents' marriage and have vowed to avoid them. 'My father was not only a womaniser; he didn't hide his infidelity and would invite women he was sleeping with to parties. It was utterly humiliating for my mother and I was adamant I wouldn't have a relationship like that,' explains Eleanor, a 35-year-old mother of three. 'I married a man who was sweet, gentle and terribly good-looking and – on the face of it – nothing like my dad. We had two children, and what I thought was a very, very close relationship; we enjoyed each other's company, had sex often, shared the same sense of humour. People used to always comment on how well we got on. Then, quite suddenly, after twenty years, I discovered that he was being unfaithful. I realised almost immediately that there must have been other women; it was like the scales falling from my eyes. I've since heard how he boasted to the whole pub about a woman he was sleeping with.' Despite Eleanor's best intentions she had ended up in the same position as her mother. So what happened? We learn about relationships, literally, on our mothers' knees. We watch how our parents negotiate, argue, avoid confrontation, tackle something head-on, laugh, cry, until it becomes our blueprint for all relationships. In fact until we are old enough to go to school, and become exposed to alternatives, we probably think our family's way is the only one. Even when we discover that not all families are like our own, the lessons from home have been deeply ingrained. For Eleanor this was certainly the case: 'After my marriage ended I went out with someone almost exactly like my husband – attractive, spoilt, feckless – and he was immediately unfaithful.' Falling in love is like casting someone in your own personal play: we search for people to recreate issues we have been unable to sort out when we were children. When we talk about clicking with someone, in reality our two unconsciouses are running down all the possible matches. Eleanor would have been looking for a dangerous and charming man; her first husband, for a woman who could be impressed. Our partners have to speak the same language and want to act out the same scenes, or there is no connection.

It is a lot more complex than women looking for a man like their father and men for a woman like their mother. Sometimes we can end up, over time, playing both our father's and mother's roles. 'My mum and dad believed that "least said, soonest mended" so that when I was growing up, I never heard them argue,' says Sara – who is in her mid-forties, 'the best they could manage was working themselves up into a cool sulk.' When she grew up, Sara found it equally hard to express her emotions. 'My mother was a little better than my father, she would interpret his moods and intervene to sort out my issues with him,' Sara explains. In her first marriage, Sara would play this role for her husband with their children and found herself understanding better some of her mother's frustrations. Unfortunately, her husband died after a long illness. 'Afterwards, I realised that there were lots of things I'd never asked him. Was he frightened of death? How did he feel about leaving us? I didn't really know because we hadn't talked, I'd interpreted.' Several years later, she married again and her second husband could not have been more different. 'He is Italian and is more likely to throw a fit first and ask questions later,' says Sara. 'On one level this is brilliant because everything is out in the open but I find myself saying things my father used to say: "There's no need to be so sensitive" and "Do we have to have a scene?"' In every partnership, it is generally one person's job to bring issues up to the surface and the other's to keep a sense of proportion. In one relationship, Sara had played her mother's role and in the second her father's.

Although many people refuse to find similarities between partners and parents, there is one group who are only too aware: the families of addicts. In fact, researchers have identified four common roles that the sons and daughters of alcoholics adopt to deal with their parents but carry on into their adult relationships. Interestingly, these patterns resonate with many of my clients – even if there is no history of addiction.

Here are the four very different coping strategies:

- Becoming a 'Caretaker'. As children, these people were super-responsible, serious and capable beyond their years, and choose partners who need looking after.
- 'Pleasers' attempt to keep the peace and keep everybody happy, so are desperate to avoid conflict in adult relationships.
- 'Adapters' tune out the problems, soak up the tension and show nothing. As adults they are either very quiet, absent or claim that there is 'no problem'.
- 'Attention-seekers'. When these people were children, they got care and loving by creating problems for everybody else. For example, by staying out late or throwing temper tantrums. As adults, they still create crises and often threaten to walk out or end the relationship over relatively minor issues.

The reason why these patterns are illuminating is that every family faces the same basic pressures: balancing individual against group needs, how to deal with anger and other difficult emotions, how to make decisions, who does what. By providing a more extreme example, the families of addicts can help everyone understand more about what makes their relationship tick.

If you are still sceptical about whether your mother or father has an impact on your choice of partners, look at these four patterns: Caretaker, Pleaser, Adapter, Attention-seeker. Have you ever found yourself falling into one of these roles? Does anyone in your family do something similar? Consider your brothers and sisters and their choice of partners? What connections can you make?

Of course, it is not just the relationship between your parents that shapes your personality but your own personal relationship with each of them. It is here that you can also find clues as to why Mr or Miss Right seems so elusive.

Legacies from Fathers

A man's style of fathering is particularly significant for his daughters – because he is literally the first man in their lives – but it is also important for his sons, who learn about being a man from his example. There are six common types and although many men will use more than one, most have a core style – especially when they are tired or stressed-out. In the exercise section, there is detailed advice on how to improve your relationship (A New Start . . . with Your Father).

Doting

Everybody would like a father that dotes on them and certainly a daughter who grows up feeling adored will have more self-confidence. But there can be a point where doting turns into spoiling. 'While mummy sat on the back seat of the car, I rode up front with Daddy and I always got to choose where we stopped to eat. While I could have anything on the menu, as long as I enjoyed it, Mummy used to have the cheap things. I'd scoff something terribly exotic like Rum Baba for pudding while Mummy would be perfectly happy with just soup,' says Kate, who is thirty-one. However, it is hard to truly grow up if your doting father is always ready to ride to the rescue. Worse still, these women expect every man to treat them like a princess. 'My live-in boyfriend used to bring me biscuits and tea in bed and the whole weekend would revolve round my cravings,' admits Kate. 'But I became so bored that I started having a wild affair with someone who'd just got out of prison and used to clean his gun in bed. I'd never met anybody like him before. Not only couldn't he read or write, he was so unoriginal he couldn't think of a name for his puppy so he called it "dog". I couldn't talk to him, but who needs to talk! Yet I would have died if Daddy had found out I even knew him.' Dads are less likely to dote on boys, and therefore less likely to treat their sons as children even after they have grown up. However, if a son's bad behaviour is not challenged – because Dad thinks he can do no wrong – he too can grow up to be selfish and unable to see anyone else's point of view.

Reasons why this can make you single: It is great to have high standards, but are they so high that almost nobody can reach them?

Turnaround tip: If you behave like a child, a potential partner will automatically slot into parent mode. So next time you are tempted to sulk, throw a tantrum or wheedle – very childish reactions – stop and ask yourself: what would an adult do?

Dangerous

At the other end of the scale from doting dad are the fathers who never grew up themselves. They can be glamorous, exciting and terribly fascinating, but often there is a darker side: some are serial love cheats or have clocked up several wives, while others are dangerous because of drink or drugs. One thing is for sure, these men turn everything into a drama. 'Whenever my friends used to come round, Daddy had to be the centre of attention. He used to disappear upstairs and change into his genuine American Civil War uniform and then strut around the house showing off,' says Beverley, thirty-eight. 'It used to drive my mother up the wall, but I thought it was funny. When I became a teenager, I realised just how much his performance was fuelled by drink. Finally, I understood why he was always so over-emotional.' Beverley has been dating unpredictable men ever since. 'I just don't seem to be able to avoid a challenge. My first boyfriend was the local lifeguard and I was completely captivated by him. He'd be forever standing me up, but the worse he treated me the more I loved him. I thought his moodiness was because he was "strong and silent" but later I caught him in bed with another man. He was just using me to prove something.' Unfortunately, the children of addicts are more at risk of developing an addiction problem themselves than the general population. For daughters of dangerous fathers, it is not just alcohol and drugs that can provide a buzz: difficult men can also be very addictive. The risk for the sons is imitating their father and thinking that bad or dangerous behaviour is the best way to attract and keep women. However, the sons of dangerous men can vow to be nothing like their fathers and grow up to be good husbands.

Reasons why this can make you single: You are attracted to people who nearly always turn out to be bad for you and this has undermined your confidence in your judgement. Alternatively, you are frightened to make a commitment because experience has taught you that relationships are dangerous.

Turnaround tip: It is easy to be angry with these fathers – and you probably have every right to be – however this just keeps the two of you stuck in the past. Instead take a fresh look at both of you. Is his conduct still as bad? Could it be that you are trying to punish him? If so, who is really being harmed by this behaviour?

Dictatorial

Many men still like to be head of the family but there is a fine line between being in charge and being dictatorial. These fathers keep their sons' and daughters' noses to the school grindstone, and bedtimes, friends and chores can easily turn into a battleground. It is not surprising that many children of dictatorial fathers become rebels or grow up wanting to take charge in their own relationships. 'We had terrible fights; he once called me a slut because I wouldn't get out of bed at half-past seven in the morning,' says Sian, a 29-year-old lawyer. 'His favourite phrase was "many a fortune has been made or lost before half-past seven". He would even put a cold flannel on my face to get me up.' It was not just lounging around in a dressing gown that would set him off. 'I'd have to line up everything on my dressing-room table and if I wanted to please him I would rush around and do all that, but as soon as he was gone take great pleasure in scruffing it all up again.' The long-term effect is that Sian's relationships have turned into power struggles. 'To say the men in my life have been controlling is an understatement,' says Sian. 'Sometimes they've been very protective: ready to collect me at three in the morning after a girls' night out, but really just checking up. I once made the terrible mistake of asking a boyfriend who was a recruitment consultant to help freshen my CV for a job I fancied. He picked so many holes that I felt he was trying to turn me into somebody else, and we ended up screaming at each other. Suddenly I had a nasty time-warp flashback – it could have been my father and me arguing over him rewriting my university application form.' Dictatorial fathers want the best for their sons and daughters; although their form of tough love can push their children to the top of the class it can also come across as deeply critical. What's more, these fathers can get so much under their sons' and daughters' skin that they often end up not knowing their own mind.

Reasons why this can make you single: You are either a perfectionist yourself – and therefore have still to meet the 'right' person – or are so frightened of being controlled that you keep people at arm's length.

Turnaround tip: Next time you are faced with a decision, ask yourself three questions. Firstly, what would my father want me to do? Secondly, what would I do if I was rebelling? Just doing the opposite of what he would have wanted is not freedom either. Finally ask, what would I like to do? Another option, especially for women, is to adopt a better father: a healthy older male influence. It could be a mentor at work or a teacher who will take you under their wing and offer positive fathering.

Distant

Traditionally, men have been expected to keep their feelings tightly under control. So many grow up unaware or even embarrassed about their emotions. When under stress, these men hide behind their newspaper, watch TV, or lose themselves in some project in the garden. Whatever the shut-down strategy, these fathers remain a mystery to their children. Other fathers become distant through divorce or because their job takes them away. 'When dad got home, if he was in a good mood or mum reported good school grades he might ruffle our hair, but it was never for more than a few seconds. Perhaps there is a statutory EU minimum for hair-ruffling, which he was determined not to contravene,' says Belinda, forty-six. 'I often wished I'd knocked on his study door and had him explain his complicated filing system; everything had a place and mine was on the other side of that door. He's never told me he loves me, I guess he thinks I know.' The daughters of distant fathers are drawn either to men who find it hard to commit or to men who keep their feelings to themselves. 'I've always felt happier when there was at least one time-zone between me and my lover,' admits Belinda. 'After I stopped dating Americans and Spaniards, I met a guy who lived in the same town but spent most weekends on his hobby of rock climbing. I used to complain that I never saw him, so I dumped him for a guy from work but he was very clinging and I had to start screening my calls.' For men who are distant – like their fathers – it is often easier to make relationships, as many women enjoy drawing out their partners and explaining their emotions to them. Unfortunately some daughters of distant fathers find themselves attracted to men who are so distant that they find it hard to commit to a relationship.

Reasons why this can make you single: Although as an adult you might understand why your father was distant, as a child it will have felt deeply personal. This can leave you worried that nobody will ever truly love you.

Turnaround tip: Concentrate on changing something specific about your father's behaviour – for example: to pay you more attention – rather than reeling off a list of complaints which will probably make him retreat even further into himself. Next, narrow this request down into something as specific as possible. For example, talking to you when you phone the house. Finally, frame it as something positive about the future rather than as an accusation about the past. For example: when he answers the phone suggest chatting for a while before he passes you onto your mother.

Destructive

These fathers cause harm because they have abandoned their daughters and sons or because they are not aware how thoughtless comments can ruin self-esteem. 'My dad is over six-foot-three and he's like a bull in a china shop; he opens his mouth first and thinks later,' says Tara, twenty-six. 'When I was about twelve and beginning to develop curves he caught me taking a tub of ice cream out of the freezer. "We'll have to watch out or you'll put on so much weight that none of the boys will fancy you," he told me. I should have clocked him, and to this day he still denies having said it, but I can trace my weight battles back to that solitary moment. Thinking of my first diet, which I pored over in one of my mother's magazines, the tinfoil packets of carrot sticks and the dry tuna that I used to take to school, it makes me want to weep.' These daughters often choose unavailable men – like married ones – who will end up abandoning them and reconfirming their lack of self-worth. 'In my teens I was anybody's for a compliment,' says Tara. 'I slept with so many boys I got a reputation, but for those few moments I could pretend they cared. These days I'm wiser but I often take something as critical, even when it's not intended to be. When it's cold my boyfriend will say something innocent, like "don't you think you need a scarf", but I will react as if he had said: "your dress is too short and too small". I end up biting his head off all the time – not the most attractive quality.'

Reasons why this can make you single: Experience has taught you that those closest to you are most likely to hurt you. This has left you with a toxic combination of fear of commitment and low self-esteem.

Turnaround tip: New-age philosophies talk about being positive, but all that happens is that we give ourselves a hard time for not pulling off this trick. So try the opposite approach and listen to the critical voice. Once you have heard all it has to say, challenge the exaggerations and distortions. Finally think: 'I can do things that are wrong but it is useful to look back, reflect and learn.' This balanced approach will ultimately make it easier to hear the positive.

Decent

These fathers provide a safe haven for their daughters to experiment with dealing with the opposite sex and provide a good role model for their sons. Unlike the doting father, he knows when to draw the line and not let his children get too much of their own way. 'Whenever I or my sister had a problem, we always knew that we could go to dad,' explains Adrienne, twenty-eight, 'he made us feel he was on our side but would also make us realise that there was probably another side too. Sometimes he was busy, yet he seemed to know when it was something truly serious and he'd stop what he was doing.' A lot of men grow into being decent daddies and have a better relationship with their sons and daughters as adults than they had with them as children. This is partly because they have mellowed with age and partly because they are not so focused on their careers. It also helps that reaching adulthood gives us the chance to forge a more equal relationship. This type of father is also becoming more common as today's dads expect to have a more hands-on approach to being a parent. The impact on the children of decent fathers is generally positive and they grow up to be well-rounded and caring people.

Reasons why this can make you single: For men, you can grow up to be so decent yourself that women prefer you as a best friend rather than a lover. This is particularly hard when you have to watch their hearts be broken by yet another bad boy. For women, you generally make good choices and have good relationships. However, your father is a tough act to follow.

Turnaround tip: It can be as harmful to have a totally positive picture of someone as to have a totally negative one. This is because life seldom comes in black-and-white but in shades of grey. So try and remember times when your father revealed feet of clay and discover a more balanced picture of him.

Legacies from Mothers

We all want our mothers to be pleased with our achievements, partly because we know it makes her happy but mainly because it confirms that she has been a good mother. What's more, if she approves of our life, we feel worthy of her love. For all these reasons, it is harder to be dispassionate about our relationship with our mother than our father, but a closer look can really help understand the past and make better choices in the future. Once again, there are six types of problem mothering, advice on how to cope with the fall-out, plus an exercise at the end of the chapter called: 'A New Start . . . with Your Mother'.

Martyr

Some women have good reason to complain, for example: illness, desertion or destitution has dealt them a tough hand. Before feminism became mainstream, talented women gave up their jobs and resented being stuck in the kitchen. Whatever the reason for their sacrifices, these mothers will not let anybody forget it and use guilt as a weapon. Worse still, their sons – and in particular, their daughters – end up feeling responsible for their good days and bad days. 'I always end up getting edgy if anybody is upset and immediately want to be the peacemaker,' says 28-year-old Cathy. 'At work I find myself taking the blame for a report being late – even if it landed on my desk only a couple of hours before the deadline.' Not surprisingly, Cathy found it very hard to ask her boyfriends for anything. 'I couldn't just tell him I would have appreciated it if he arranged a birthday party for me at a local restaurant,' she confessed. 'Instead, I would drop hints and make suggestions and then get very angry when he didn't do anything.'

Reasons why this can make you single: Your experiences of close relationships have been draining and claustrophobic. So it is not surprising that you are wary of being trapped and find commitment difficult. You either have a tough independent exterior that stops people approaching or have had a series of short-lived relationships that have never truly got off the ground.

Turnaround tip: Understanding your mother's vulnerability is the first step to liberating yourself from the tyranny. Instead of getting angry, which will make her needier and perpetuate a vicious circle, tell her you love her and then laugh together when she goes over the top.

Critical

Mothers want the best for their children, but sometimes their desire for their sons and daughters to succeed comes across as criticism. Their children will often feel that they can never truly please them. 'I have become very critical of myself,' admits Richard, a 33-year-old lawyer, 'it is almost as if I can hear her voice in my head pushing me on. On one hand that has helped my career but I never seem to enjoy my achievements.' Last Christmas, Richard talked to his aunt and got a wholly different take on his mother. 'She had bored her sister silly with all this praise and boasting about me. I just wish Mum had told me.' Richard has had a very up-and-down relationship with his girlfriend. 'I find myself getting defensive about the slightest comment,' he admits. 'I took her to a Proms concert but she didn't seem to be enjoying it. In the interval, she commented that the conductor had taken a piece too fast. I started sulking; I'd gone to a lot of trouble getting those tickets. After I calmed down, I realised I was not responsible for the orchestra's performance and her comment was not an attack on me – but it did spoil the whole evening.'

Reasons why this can make you single: You either keep finding fault with partners, dumping them and hoping that the next will be perfect, or you have become incredibly defensive, fly off the handle at the slightest thing and your partners feel that you are 'too high-maintenance'.

Turnaround tip: If critical mothering sounds familiar, try asking her friends and other family members what she really thinks about you. Your mother probably assumes you already know her feelings or maybe fears praise will undermine your desire to achieve. Next time you overreact to something a potential partner has said, stop and ask yourself if your mother's voice is mixed in there somewhere. If you have a tendency to become critical yourself, examine your standards and ask yourself how many are your own and how many your mother's.

Perfect

Women put a lot of energy into being as good a mum as possible, but for some 'good' is never enough. They have to be super-mum: able to bake, hold down a job and still help out behind the scenes at the school play. Sons can idolise this type of mother to such an extent that other women have a tough job matching up to her. These men can also put potential partners on a pedestal and have 'polite' sex rather than allowing their women to be truly passionate. Meanwhile, the daughters of super-mums can find the legacy equally difficult. Tina, forty-two, started mothering her first husband: 'I felt like I had three children sometimes and with no support, I ran out of energy. I wanted an equal partner.' She is not the only woman who found herself in this dilemma. 'My friends used to joke about my toy boy. I was in my late thirties and he was just twenty-five – blond, blue eyes and very handsome,' says Suzanne, a recruitment consultant who is now in her mid-forties. 'It was a big step inviting him to move in. I had a son and a daughter and I wondered how they would get on. I shouldn't have worried, but he was more like a big brother. I also helped him start his own business but still he wouldn't properly commit. Eventually we split up because I couldn't be his ever-supporting mummy any longer.'

Reasons why this can make you single: For women, you attract the sort of men that need their problems sorting out. Although this is flattering, it is not the foundation for a successful long-term relationship. For men, your expectations can be too high and this makes you easily disappointed.

Turnaround tip: For daughters, if you find yourself behaving like everybody's mother, step back and stop taking responsibility. For example, if you have to nag your partner to get up in the morning, remind him once and then leave it. He might be late for an appointment but he is an adult and accountable for his own choices. At first, it will be hard to hold back but things will get easier, so persevere. For sons of 'perfect' mothers, think about the disadvantages of being so close to your mother. How much does she interfere in your life? Does she have strong views about your girlfriends? Compare your relationship with those of your friends: how does your mother demand more than their mothers? How do you feel about that?

Controlling

Another common example of great mothering that can turn into a problem is the over-attentive mum. It is a short step between looking out for your kids and smothering them; these 'take-over' mums seldom understand the difference. 'She was always ready to fight my battles at school by "having a word" with my teacher or the parents of another kid,' says Barry, thirty-four. 'At homework time, she seemed to be forever peering over my shoulder. She was great but sometimes I felt swamped. Even to this day, I find it hard to let people close for fear of them taking over.' These mums are very likely to have strong opinions about their children's potential partners or lack of them. 'I had been dating Gemma for about six months,' says Michael, who is thirty years old, 'and Mum had told me that if I ever married she hoped it would be to someone just like Gemma. I took this as maternal approval and even considered asking for Gemma's hand. Fortunately, I talked it over with my sister who had quite a different take. Mother had told her that "she could find nothing wrong with Gemma". Ultimately, I decided to trust my own judgement and wait and see.' Mothers who feel confident and secure in themselves do not need to control their adult children.

Reasons why this can make you single: Your biggest fear is being 'swallowed up' and losing control. You find yourself drawn to people who are, in some way, unavailable. They might live a long way away or are already committed to an ex-partner or their work.

Turnaround tip: Your mother might be controlling because she really enjoyed being a parent and finds it hard to let go – even though you've long since grown up. So try helping her find new interests. Explain what you find helpful and what is intrusive and firmly police the difference. Although capitulating might seem easier in the short term, it could encourage your mother to become more controlling in the long term.

Frightened

Many mothers try to hide the effects of their husbands' drinking, gambling or violence. They want to protect their children but end up pulling them into the secret. If they are drinking themselves, or have a mental health problem, these mothers, sadly, provide very erratic child care. 'There was this terrible secret in our family,' says Paula, who is now fifty, 'and although I didn't discover it until I was fifteen, I always knew we were different. My grandmother had committed suicide but my mother never told me. Even now, I don't really understand why she fought so hard to keep it from me.' Paula's upbringing has left her wary of being rejected. 'If I think there is the slightest danger of being dumped I try and get in first,' she admits. 'I almost ended one promising relationship because this boyfriend hadn't phoned for several days. My mind came up with all sorts of possibilities mainly centring round another woman. Before too long, I could see the two of them in the pub laughing at me. Finally, I left a nasty message on his answering machine. Later, I discovered his mother had been rushed to hospital.'

Reasons why this can make you single: For daughters, the risk is that you too will grow up fearful of getting hurt and therefore holding men at arm's length. You can also feel responsible, like your mother, for managing everyone's behaviour. This is not only impossible but sets you up for low self-esteem. Fortunately, this kind of mothering is less likely to make men single. The sons of frightened mothers often become rescuers, which can be appealing to women. However, I do counsel men who are trying to fix women with chaotic lives or who are unable to commit. Alternatively, they can lose interest in a woman once her problems have been solved.

Turnaround tip: If your relationship with your mother has left you with the tendency to overreact, get some distance by imagining what a cool-headed friend might think of your interpretation. Be patient with yourself and do not expect too much too soon, as a difficult relationship with a mother is tougher to overcome than a difficult one with a father.

Racy

Sometimes a mother will try to compete with her daughter and even set herself up as a love rival. 'I often feel under the shadow of my mother,' says Jasmine, who is twenty-six. 'My boyfriends always get on very well with her but I think she laughs too loudly and shows too much cleavage. When I want just a bit of TLC, she is much more likely to give me sisterly advice like: "dust yourself off and get on with it". OK, she is quite cool and doesn't mind me bringing my boyfriends back home, but I never feel comfortable. One night, she brought this man home that she'd picked up at a club and they had noisy sex that kept my boyfriend and me awake.' For both sons and daughters, the risk is that there is a precocious interest in sex.

Reasons why this can make you single: For women, you are at one of two extremes. Either you have thrown yourself into relationships and committed too quickly, often to unsuitable men, or have held back to the point that men imagine you to be cold. For men, you have such a polarised view of women that they seem divided into either Madonna or whore.

Turnaround tip: This type of mothering has a greater impact on daughters, who take the competition personally, than sons, who are just embarrassed. If these problems go back to your childhood, try forgiving your mother. It does not mean sanctioning what she did, but will free you to start an adult relationship with her. For daughters, if the two of you are in competition today, remember it takes two to compete. If you refuse to enter, there is no race. For sons, ask about her relationship with her own mother and the morals of that time. Understanding how attitudes are handed from one generation to another, and why your mother behaves as she does, will help remove any lingering blame.

Unpacking the Effect on You

At first sight, the impact of our parents on our own relationship choices might sound depressing and not particularly romantic. However, I believe that we are not just seeking to recreate our parents' relationship, but something inside us is striving to solve it. I will always remember the advice from my first tutor when I had been despairing about some clients who, despite everything I tried, had the same arguments week after week. My tutor said: 'People make fundamentally good relationship choices.' I was amazed. So why did my clients seem so stuck and why was there such a long waiting-list of other couples with similar problems? She smiled and replied: 'It is up to us to help them discover what made them choose each other and to work together rather than against each other.' Twenty-five years later, I still believe – with every fibre of my body – that we make basically good choices. However, sometimes we do not listen to our unconscious and pass on good prospects; on other occasions we mistake the natural conflict arising from two people sorting out their issues as fundamental flaws. If we held on a little bit longer, before rushing onto the next relationship, we would discover not only someone who is right for us, but a way of making peace with our past too. It is worth the effort. Through counselling, Eleanor, who married a man like her philandering father, became aware of the patterns in her life: 'My new partner, Ian, couldn't be more different. I worshipped my first husband; paid the bills and did all the house-work; I was a doormat. My new partner is very good-looking, but he's quite uncertain and I think we have a more equal relationship. What's more, my daughter is amazed that Ian will break out the Hoover without being asked.'

The Legacy of Divorce

If our childhood provides a template for how we conduct all our relationships – and in particular our romantic ones – just imagine how much more complex the script becomes in the case of divorced families. These children had a front-row seat on the break-up of their parents' marriage and know first-hand about the anger, pain, and sometimes violence that two people who were once in love can inflict on each other. It is not surprising that when these children grow up they have mixed feelings about relationships.

Since the 1970s, when divorce became more socially acceptable, there have been three widespread beliefs. Firstly, children do not thrive when their parents are unhappy. Secondly, if parents are happier, the happiness will trickle down to the children and therefore the divorce is in everybody's interests. Thirdly, and most importantly, there might be some short-term upset for the children but if parents co-operate after the divorce the effect will be transitory. These are the myths but what about the reality? Judith Wallerstein PhD, founder and executive director of the Centre for the Family in Transition in California, studied sixty middle-class families and 131 children over twenty-five years. She interviewed them at eighteen months, five years, ten years and finally twenty-five years after the divorce. Her findings make for some very sobering reading:

- Only one in ten children experienced relief when their parents divorced.
- Eighteen months after the divorce, most were still trying to make sense of what happened.

- Five years on, most children secretly hoped their parents would reconcile – even if one of them had subsequently remarried.
- Ten years after the divorce, half of the children in the sample had been through the experience again after one of their parents' second marriages failed.

However, the most startling effect did not come to light until Wallerstein made her twenty-five-year follow-up. 'Divorce is a cumulative experience. Its impact increases over time and rises to a crescendo in adulthood,' she concludes. While the national debate has obsessed about children's exam results and crime statistics, we have missed the most crucial impact: children of divorced parents find it harder to trust and therefore, as adults, have difficulties making long-term relationships.

In fact, only 60 per cent of Wallerstein's sample had ever married – as one of her respondents puts it: 'If you don't marry, you don't get betrayed.' The comparison with intact families is startling. Here 80.6 per cent of males and 87.4 per cent of females aged between twenty-eight and forty-three get married (General Social Survey). Remember 'intact families' is not just happy families. It includes couples who stay in loveless relationships 'for the sake of the children' and quite a few marriages that are violent or abusive and where divorce would probably have been preferable. What about the children from divorced families that did marry? What was their experience? This is where Wallerstein found another worrying trend: rash and ill-considered early marriages on the rebound from their parents' divorce – with 50 per cent tying the knot while under twenty-five. Sadly, over half of these marriages ended in divorce. In a matched group of intact families only 11 per cent married young and of these marriages only 25 per cent ended in divorce.

So what happens to children when their parents divorce and why is it so hard for them to make good relationships? The answer is simple: they have experienced first-hand just how fleeting love can be. Worse still, unlike the children of intact families, they do not have the benefit of watching their parents disagree in a safe and contained way, compromising, solving differences and making up. These skills are all vital for sustaining a relationship once the first flush of passion and love has worn off. However, the problems go deeper. At different ages, there are particular problems for the children of divorce; understanding them is vital for, firstly, clambering out and, secondly, for finding a partner. So look at the following scenarios and take stock. Your personal legacy will be influenced by your age when your parents divorced, your birth order, your parents' behaviour and, of course, your own personality.

Becoming a Caregiver Child

In many families divorce is such a traumatic experience that it leads to the partial or complete breakdown of a parent's ability to care for their children. Normally this phase lasts for a few months but in others it will continue for years. In these cases, one of the children – normally the eldest daughter – steps into the caregiver role. A good example is Maggie, who is now in her late thirties. Her parents' marriage began to disintegrate in her early teens. She vividly remembers her father telling her of all the things he would have done, 'If it wasn't for you.' When she was sixteen and her father finally left, her mother became seriously depressed. 'On the good days, I'd come back from school and find that she'd spent the day staring at the wall. On the bad days, she'd be in tears. So I started taking her out and walking through the streets in the evening – anything to keep her moving. On winter evenings, when people had not yet closed the curtains, we would look in on all these lighted stages where normal people led normal lives.' When she had finished walking her mother round the town, Maggie would also make tea for her younger sister and then start on her school work. At the weekend, she would help her mother with housework and shopping. Although she still saw her father, she felt alone and responsible. 'It would have seemed like betraying my mother if I'd told him what was really happening, and to be honest I doubt he wanted to know,' she explained. 'So how did you cope?' I asked. 'I kept all my feelings in.' 'So who comforted you?' For a second the confident, outgoing woman who had worked all over the world was stripped away and I could see a lost child. 'My younger sister understood. I didn't have to say anything,' she finally replied. Maggie did not want to admit it, but the answer was nobody.

Bringing up children and running a house involves hundreds of choices. Before divorce, the parent with custody will have been used to talking any problems over with their partner. Suddenly they are on their own. Friends are helpful but not there all the time. The result is that one of the children becomes the on-tap adviser and confidant of their mother or father. Wallerstein found children as young as eight advising their mother on where to live and fathers asking their pre-teen daughters for advice on courting a new girlfriend. It is almost as if divorce has turned an adult into a helpless child and 'parentified' their son or daughter. It is not all bad news. The caregiving child gets immense pride from their exalted position in the household and in some cases, like Maggie's, they can literally save their parent's sanity. However, forever sacrificing your own needs is not a good preparation for the give-and-take of successful adult relationships.

Long-term impact: Caregiver children – particularly the girls – can feel so responsible for their mothers that the two women are bound to each other, sometimes even twenty years after the divorce. Certainly this is what happened to Celia, who is thirty-five: 'We became incredibly close, sharing holidays together and speaking every night on the phone. There have been one or two guys in mum's life over the years. But nothing serious – nobody that has filled the void that Dad left.' Celia is single too, and for the last twenty years her most important relationship has been with her mother. In counselling, Celia began to look back to her parents' divorce and its impact on her own life. 'I feel very responsible for mum,' she sighed and sank into silence. 'What are you thinking?' I asked. ' "How can I leave my mother who has nobody but me?" ' She nodded.

Troubled Adolescence

Family is the scaffolding on which we climb through the different development stages, from helpless baby to independent adult. One of the most difficult times is adolescence, where we start pushing against the rules set by our parents in order to forge our own values and identity. However, parenting has become caught up in the same crisis of confidence in authority as schools, politicians and society in general. Everyone feels uncomfortable setting down absolute standards. Rules seem to belong in some stuffy, authoritarian, patriarchal past. Yet the world remains a frightening and confusing place, and structure is a fundamental human need. This is why 'change your life' reality-TV programmes are so popular. We like to be bossed about and told how to eat properly, discipline our toddlers or dogs and how to clean our homes. Even if, ultimately, we decide to ignore the 'expert' advice, this is still something to kick against.

If even the happiest families have trouble when the children hit adolescence, just imagine the problems for a divorced family. When parents live together, they can find a consensus on rules and standards of behaviour. However, this is harder when parents are struggling to be civil to each other. For intact families the children's adolescence takes centre-stage – with both parents' full attention and steadying hand. Meanwhile, in a divorced family, the ongoing conflict between mother and father is centre-stage. The result is either that their children's adolescence is put indefinitely on hold – like Celia, who still has trouble separating from her mother – or happens in a dark corner, unnoticed by anyone. For this reason, the children of divorce can reach adolescence earlier and with a lot of unresolved anger. In fact, research shows that girls start experimenting with sex younger and both boys and girls have a higher use of alcohol and drugs than their peers.

Long-term impact: 'I started screwing boys when I was thirteen,' explained Josie, thirty, whose parents divorced when she was ten, 'it made me feel wanted.' Unfortunately, she also got a reputation amongst her classmates. 'They called me "tramp" and the "class bike", so when I was offered cocaine I thought "everybody thinks I'm a bad girl, so why not?".' Not surprisingly, Josie had no sense of direction and dropped out of university. She did various jobs and had several dead-end relationships, and from time to time her cocaine use became a problem. 'I would go home with men who I wouldn't have looked at twice if I had not been off my face. Somehow I managed to keep it all together, but I had no idea what I was looking for. Even if I had known, I had no expectation of getting my needs met.' On the morning of her twenty-ninth birthday, she took a long, sober look at her life and decided things needed to change. 'There was not some dramatic revelation. I just decided it could not go on like this any more.' Josie went back to university and moved in with her mother. 'It's been difficult for both of us, but we can approach each other as two adults now – well, sort of. Anyway, we've called a truce. I've stopped hitting my head against a brick wall – because it hurts – and she's done the same. I feel my life is back on track again.'

Becoming a Fully-formed Adult Takes Longer

If the task of adolescence is breaking away from your home, becoming an adult is about discovering who you are, your personal standards and what you want from life, your job and your relationships. Obviously this takes time, but generally somewhere between eighteen and twenty-three, most people develop a sense of their own identity. However the children of divorce are often too frightened to experiment and instead of actively choosing someone, just drift into the first relationship offered. 'I met Sam during my first week at university, we shared a kitchen and soon a bed. Don't get me wrong, he's nice but he's very shy and relies on me a lot,' explains Lauren, who is twenty-five and still with Sam. 'You see, we both found moving away from home a bit of a wrench – so we leant on each other. But while I made friends and enjoyed the experience, Sam withdrew into himself.' They have almost split up on numerous occasions, but Lauren has always stopped short. 'He starts to cry and I cave in. You see, I know the pain of being left. I can still remember what my father was wearing, the leather case with the grease stain, and how my sister tried to bar the way. I couldn't do that to someone else.' It is almost as if some children of divorce do not have the confidence to judge a relationship. Instead of actively seeking the right relationship, they take what is on offer.

Young women whose parents divorced often choose an older man, rather than experimenting with men of their own age. The older man seems appealing for a number of reasons – beyond replacing the father figure lost through divorce. Firstly, older men are less likely to cheat on younger women – and all children of divorce fear betrayal almost as much as they long for love. Secondly, older men are happy to stay at home in the evening and therefore avoid arousing feelings of jealousy. Thirdly, they have already discovered who they are and what they want; this is very appealing to someone who is uncertain about their own identity.

A typical example of an age-gap relationship would be Jonathan and Leah, who were forty years old and twenty years old respectively when they met. 'The age difference was not a problem. She was very mature and I found that we wanted the same things,' explained Jonathan. 'We even have similar tastes in music and he took me to Elton John, Joe Cocker and Tina Turner concerts,' added Leah, describing the start of their relationship. 'We also liked nights in front of the TV and entertaining at home.' I had a picture of an almost scarily mature girl and then it struck me: rather than the usual method of trial-and-error to discover her identity, Leah had simply adopted Jonathan's. No wonder they had similar tastes! However eight years on, Leah had reached twenty-eight and had begun to feel trapped. 'It's like he's stifling me, forever telling me what to do,' she complained. 'But I see you about to do something stupid – like arguing with the boss at work – and I want to step in and stop you,' Jonathan replied. 'But I've got to make my own mistakes,' said Leah. She had started her own journey into being an adult.

Long-term impact: In the same way that gay and lesbian teen-agers have to create their own values, rules and identity – rather than simply adopt those of their parents, the children of divorce also have to experiment to find their own pattern for an enduring relationship. In both circumstances, the journey into adulthood takes a little longer – probably from eighteen to thirty. However by thirty, most people have gathered enough good experiences with boyfriends and girlfriends to counterbalance their childhood experiences.

Overly Self-reliant

Divorce can have some positive benefits – not only do the adults stuck in a loveless marriage get a second chance but their children can learn some important lessons. For example, the need to be self-reliant. Maggie, the caregiver child whom we met earlier in this chapter, became the first person in her family to go to university and she has become well-known within her chosen career. 'I want to make my mark and do something good,' she explained, 'it's a good time to be a woman and I want to make the most of it. If love happens on the way, all well and good. However, I won't be looking for it.' Underneath the professional confidence is a huge fear of being out of control in her personal relationships. She has protected herself by choosing not one man but two who she knew would never commit. 'I'm terrified the relationship is not going to be mutual – any hint that he's losing interest and I'll end it,' she explained. She also told a sad story about visiting a country where she used to work and catching up with an ex-lover. He was now married 'with a beautiful wife and an adorable baby'. However she was quick to point out that the ex-boyfriend had made a pass at her on the trip back to the airport. 'So you see, I wasn't jealous of her,' Maggie finished. The fear of repeating her parents' mistakes has translated into a fear of commit-ment and the expectation that love will continue to elude her.

Long-term impact: The children of divorce believe very strongly in love but they expect to be betrayed. Sadly, the very thing that they want the most and the thing that they fear the most are the same thing. No wonder it seems safer to concentrate on a career instead. Indeed, of the men in Wallerstein's sample who had never married, 56 per cent had not had a serious relationship either. Being self-reliant is a virtue but sometimes it can become a shield which stops potential partners getting close and inhibits falling in love.

The Art of Forgiveness

Whether your parents divorced or stayed together, one of the key tests of being a true adult is having a rounded view of them: being able to acknowledge both their strengths and weaknesses; forgiving their mistakes as well as celebrating their achievements. Carrie, now in her late forties, had a painful childhood. 'I absolutely adored my father but my mother made my life a misery. Dad would take me to works events and outings – while my mother stayed at home. He was interested in my school work, forever praised me and made me feel special. I hated to be left alone with my mum because she used to be really spiteful – pulling my hair and slapping me for the slightest misdemeanour. Sometimes when Dad went to his sister's – who my mother hated – he would leave me behind at home. I used to particularly dread those occasions because Mum would really take it out on me.' As you can imagine, her opinions as a child were pretty black-and-white: mother = bad, father = good. However, as an adult, Carrie found a more balanced view: 'In many ways, I'm angry with my father for not protecting me. He must have guessed what happened. Even when he was around he could be weak and did not like to stand up to my mother. With hindsight, it was strange to take me to adult parties – even back then, it must have raised eyebrows – and what must it have been like for my mother? Later, after my father died, Mum and I became much closer and she told me about the man she loved but who died during the war. Really she should never have married Dad – but they were Catholic and divorce was a mortal sin. I guess she was an unhappy woman. Today she would have asked for help but these things were not talked about in her generation.' Ultimately, Carrie had forgiven her mother. So how do you reach this point?

1 Imagine that you are a lawyer and put together a case for the defence.
   - *Look for mitigating circumstances.* Are you judging your parent through today's eyes and not taking into consideration the prevailing mores of the time? What resources would your parent have needed to act differently?
   - *Why do you think your mother or father behaved as they did?* What sort of childhood did they have? What problems were they up against?
   - *What witnesses – like your siblings or your aunts and uncles – could provide a positive character reference?* You can either imagine interviewing them in your head or, even better, discuss your feelings about your childhood with them. Even without prompting, they will naturally put forward a defence for your mother or father.
   - *List all your mother's or father's good qualities.* It is human nature to take for granted the good things of life and become obsessed by what we lack. So think about the positives from your childhood which someone less fortunate might have longed for. In Carrie's case, she remembered her mother's clean and ordered house, and how she always made sure that her daughter was well turned out.

2 Imagine that you are a prosecution lawyer looking over the case of your favoured parent.
   - *What was your mother's or father's greatest weakness?* If you find this question hard, try turning it round and identifying his or her greatest strength – as normally our bad qualities are the flipside of our good ones. For example, Carrie's father's greatest strength was that he loved his daughter so strongly. Conversely, his greatest weakness was that this left him little energy to love his wife.

- *With your favoured parent, how much is your opinion based on how you would like to see them and how much on solid evidence?* Particularly if one parent was always away through their work or you saw less of them after divorce, it is easy to fantasise and turn them into the perfect parent rather than admit your disappointments.
- *Who would provide a balancing viewpoint?* How did your favoured parent behave towards your brother or sister? If you were their 'favourite', what impact did it have on everybody else in the family? What was the downside to being your mother's or father's favourite? Did you find it hard to break away and do your own thing? Did you feel under a lot of pressure to achieve?

3 How did your behaviour contribute to the problems?
- *Look at all your beliefs about your parents.* Write all these beliefs down the left-hand side of the paper and then find an example to illustrate each one and write that down the right-hand side. Carrie wrote for beliefs: 'My mother was not interested in me.' And for an example: 'She never came to my parent open evenings.' Cover over your list of beliefs on the left side and look at just the examples on the right. What would someone think who is unaware of the hidden belief? Could they guess the hidden belief from the example? Is there a different conclusion that could be drawn from your mother's or father's behaviour? Carrie, for example, admitted that her mother was shy and would be easily intimidated by the teachers.
- *Did you take sides?* It is hard not to be drawn into arguments, and being perceived as on the 'enemy' side will have coloured your less-favoured parent's behaviour towards you.
- *Would you like to be closer to your mother or father, but fear it would mean letting your other parent down?* Even though a divorce happened years ago, it is easy to stay trapped in old patterns. Isn't it time to do what is best for you?

4 Are there any sticking points stopping a better relationship with one or both of your parents?
  - *Write down all the hurtful things that your parent/s did.* It does not matter how trivial they might seem, put down everything that has caused pain. Start with your childhood and work up to the present day. Keep going until you can think of nothing more. Just putting everything down is cathartic.
  - *Cross out anything that no longer bothers you.* This will show what you have already begun to forgive.
  - *What is left?* Sometimes trivial things can hurt as much as major ones. If they still cause pain they should be taken seriously. Consider discussing them with your parents.

5 Forgiveness is not just about the person who caused the hurt but a gift to yourself, too.
  - *Holding on to grudges keeps you stuck in the past.* By contrast, forgiveness will provide the key to a new relationship.
  - *Understand that resentment has a high price tag.* Research has shown that it contributes to higher blood pressure, stomach upsets and depression.
  - *Not forgiving gives someone power over you.* It places you in the role of victim. A more powerful place to be is survivor.

6 What would happen if you discussed what still makes you angry with your father or mother? Although the idea will seem frightening at first, it is important to confront that fear as it is keeping you stuck in the past.
  - *Start with a positive.* It could be some of the things that you appreciate about him or her, maybe something that you have learnt from reading this chapter or just your desire to have a better relationship.
  - *Is there anything for which you would like to apologise?* This could encourage a reciprocal apology.
  - *Explain what is stopping you from having a better relation-*

ship. It helps if you are as specific as possible. To prevent misunderstanding and reduce the chance of the discussion escalating into an argument, try this formula. *I feel . . . when you . . . because . . .*

- *Sometimes just explaining your grievances is enough.* If you receive a full apology, that is brilliant. If your mother or father only offers justifications, listen with an open heart. You will generally learn more about her or him and this deeper understanding might make it easier to let go of past hurts.

7 Make a commitment to a better relationship with your parents in the future.
- *Ultimately the most important relationship is the one that you have now.* Expecting a better relationship is halfway to experiencing one. You will certainly be more likely to interpret future behaviour through a positive lens rather than the old, possibly distorted one.
- *What if you don't know how to contact your parent, they have addiction problems or are deceased?* Try writing an imaginary letter or talking to their gravestone – this can release many pent-up feelings.

A Note for Parents

For parents, reading about the impact of their behaviour on their children is a sobering experience. However, I cannot stress enough that you do not need to be the perfect mother or father – if such a creature exists. Psychologists use the concept of 'good enough'. This means providing a secure loving base but accepting that mistakes will be made. After all, in the outside world children need to be able to deal with both the 'rough' and the 'smooth'. Remember that you are the product of your own parents' relationship, and they of theirs, and so on back through time. Ultimately, blame is pointless.

If you are a recently divorced parent, this chapter will have been doubly difficult to read. However it is important to stress that none of the pitfalls are inevitable and as I have tried to stress, children from even the happiest families can have trouble growing up and finding a partner. Hopefully being aware of the long-term impacts of divorce will make you extra vigilant. If you are still feeling guilty, I would like to stress two points. Firstly, the children of divorce that I have met might have lost out in some ways but they have gained in others, and they are generally more sensitive and aware of other people's feelings. Secondly, I help many people deal with the legacy of parents who stayed together when it would have probably been better to split – like Carrie's parents. Finally, and on a more positive note, this book will help you make a better choice second time around and provide positive relationship role models for your children.

Summary

- Our parents' relationship will set the tone for our own relationships. Even if we want to be nothing like them, it is still a huge influence.
- Our own relationship with our parents – particularly the parent of the opposite gender – will have an impact on our own choice of partner.
- We are part of the first generation whose parents had easy access to divorce. However, the legacy of this revolution is only just beginning to be understood.
- The most important long-term effect on the children of divorce is commitment problems: either rushing in too quickly or holding back too long.
- Although we need to understand the impact of our childhood on our relationship choices, it is pointless to blame our parents. They are the products of their own childhood. It is therefore important to forgive our parents' shortcomings as much as thank them for their strengths.
- A balanced view of our parents is a sign of being a true adult.

Exercises

Understanding Your Personal Legacy

a) Thinking about your childhood, write down your key thoughts about the following questions.

1 Who made the important long-term decisions in your household?
2 Who challenged these decisions?
3 Who made the day-to-day decisions?
4 How were arguments settled?
5 What happened when someone got angry?
6 If you had a problem who would you take it to? Why?
7 Would you get a different response from your mother, your father or other key figure in your childhood? How?
8 Do you find it easy or difficult to trust? Why?
9 How would your parents express their feelings for each other (and, if relevant, their new partners)?
10 How did your relationship with your parents change when you became a teenager?
11 Have you ever felt rejected by either of your parents? Why?
12 Did you feel that one of your parents would try to get you on their side? What impact did this have on you?
13 Did you feel in competition with your brother, sister, step- or half-siblings? Why?
14 What might other people consider different about your family?

b) Put all your answers to one side and then come back after an hour or so and highlight everything that strikes you as important. Do any keywords or phrases appear? What are the themes?

c) Next think about your most important adult relationships, how have you dealt with these themes yourself?

d) What have been the most contentious issues in your past adult relationships? How did your parents cope with these issues?

Unhooking the Past

Detach yourself for a moment:
- Don't be tempted to blame your parents. They are just as much the products of their upbringing as you are of yours.
- Conversely, don't defend their actions either, as too much time justifying their behaviour can stop you from seeing the patterns.

Make connections:
- Find three examples of how you are like your mother.
- Find three examples of how you are like your father.
- If you did not know one or both of your parents find another significant carer whose personality has had an impact on you.

What do you like/dislike?
- Make a list of all the positive and negative legacies from your parents.
- Are there any links between the two? A positive: for example, seeing both sides of the argument, is often the flipside of a negative: for example, unemotional.

When are you most likely to behave like one of your parents?
- Think of an example at work.
- Think of an example with friends.
- Think of an example with a boyfriend/girlfriend.

What are the alternative ways of behaving?
- Brainstorm as many as possible.
- What is missing from your list?
- Maybe ask a friend to come up with other alternatives.
- The last idea or the most outlandish can sometimes be the key.

An example: Paulo came from a family that rarely argued and found himself attracted to confident, outgoing women. However, they would often get extremely angry. He had always tried to appease (like his father did) but this rarely worked and left him ultimately dissatisfied. When we brainstormed the alternatives, he kept finding variations on the same theme: walk away, don't go home, rationalise the argument. Finally, I asked: 'What about getting angry too, or fighting your corner?' It had not even crossed his mind as a possibility. Ultimately, this was the breakthrough in his counselling.

A New Start . . . with Your Father

If you are a woman, improving your relationship with your father is key to improving your prospects with men. For this reason, much of this exercise is aimed at women. However, if you are a man you might like to consider this exercise too. A better relationship with your father will improve your confidence, which will ultimately pay dividends in your search for love.

1 *Assess your relationship with your father*
   - Do you tell your mother significantly more about your personal life and private thoughts than your father?
   - Do you imagine that your father is less interested in these types of information or maybe that it is easier to stick to 'safe' topics?
   - Do you often go through your mother to communicate with your father? (This is especially common with daughter-and-father relationships.)
   - Have you put more time and energy into getting to know your mother than your father?

   If the answer if yes to any of these, you probably treat your father differently from your mother and in some way the relationship will have suffered.

2 *Think of three key occasions, stories or snapshots frozen in time which seem to sum up your relationship with your father*
  • Put as much detail as possible into these pictures. How old are you? Where are you? What can you see? What can you smell?
  • What do these pictures tell you about your relationship with your father?
  • What does it say about his personality?

3 *Reassess your defining moments*
  • Although these memories will have defined your relationship with your father – in both the past and the present – you need to remember that it is just *your* interpretation of events.
  • So find a time *alone* with your father (this is important so there is nobody to interrupt with their memories or tell him 'he's got it all wrong') and ask what he remembers. Be careful not to be judgemental or accuse him. Just ask: 'Do you remember . . .'. For example, Tracy asked: 'Do you remember Monday mornings when you set off for a week of work away from home?' She had always hated the fact that he did not turn back and see her waving. She thought he valued his job higher and could not wait to be off. The truth was very different. 'I hated Monday mornings,' he told her. 'I would focus on putting my key in the car lock rather than see the look on your and your mother's faces. That would have made it even harder. Some mornings my hands would shake as I tried to hold back the tears.'
  • Be ready to ask supplementary questions. How did you feel? What else was going on in your life at that point?
  • Even if he remembers things differently, do not interrupt but keep nodding your head and making encouraging noises, like 'I see' and 'yes'.
  • How do your father's memories change your impression of him?

4 *Assess how your father changed*
- Your defining memories – the glasses through which you will interpret his behaviour – will have happened during your childhood.
- These are normally the years when men are most caught up in their careers – partly because men are more ambitious in their twenties and thirties and partly because they will have felt driven to succeed and provide the best for their children.
- Past about forty-five many men have the weight of 'being a success' taken off their shoulders and can breathe more easily. Meanwhile, you will have started to work and gain insight into the pressures on your father.
- So both you and your father are different people, but all too often your relationship today is still being filtered and distorted by the past.

5 *Make a commitment to a better relationship*
- Try to communicate with open ears, open mind and open heart.
- Make more of an effort – invest as much time and energy in the relationship with your father as you already do with your mother (this is especially important for women, where there can often be a large disparity between daughter/mother time and daughter/father time).
- Spend time with your father alone. (You probably already do this with your mother.)
- Draw your father out. Ask him about his relationship with his own father. What are his greatest achievements? What are his regrets? How has being a father changed him?
- Intimate conversations normally happen when you are doing something else. So ask him to share a skill with you – for example, wallpapering or gardening.

6 *Understand your different ways of communicating*
- There are two ways of approaching a problem. The first is to

talk through all the feelings and wait for a solution to emerge. The second is to take the feelings as given and try to fix the problem. The first places great stress on emotions and the second on rationality. In general, women tend to use the first approach and men the second.

- Both strategies are equally valid but daughter-and-father communication is often hampered because a daughter with a problem expects an emotional response but instead gets a rational one.
- When we share a problem or a piece of news, we are generally looking for one or more of the following: approval, sympathy, advice.
- When Amy, thirty, decided to go freelance, as the first step to setting up her own business, she was worried about her father's reaction. Indeed, after talking to her father she felt judged: 'He asked lots of questions, like he thought I was making the biggest mistake in my life. It seems he has no confidence in my decisions or ability, I felt totally belittled.' In contrast, her mother was approving: 'She was really excited and gave me her full support.' Actually, Amy came away with the wrong impression. Both her parents were trying to nurture her but her father thought she wanted advice, her mother guessed – rightly in this case – that she wanted approval.

7 *Improve your communication*
- Rather than expecting your father to guess what response you need, for example, sympathy or advice, be up-front and tell him.
- When Amy used this strategy, she told her dad: 'I really value your opinions on my business, and your experiences, but I need to know that you approve first.' She was surprised to discover that her father was really proud. He had wanted to do something similar himself but had had a young family and judged the idea too risky. Later, Amy asked her father's advice and he discovered a hole in her business plan.

- Remember your father's questioning and rationalising is partly to help him understand your choices. He will naturally worry – as he wants the best for you – and this is his way of reassuring himself that you will be OK.

8 *If you're still feeling judged*
  - Look at your father's motives, not his style.
  - Ask yourself who is really doing the judging? Sometimes we are so quick to judge ourselves that even the smallest question from our fathers – 'Have you thought about . . .' – can be heard as damning. Are you, in effect, criticising your father for something that you are actually doing to yourself?
  - Tell him the effect that his communication style is having on you. For example: 'I get the impression that you think I'm making a big mistake' or 'I feel you're angry with me . . .'. This will give him the opportunity to either change direction or to correct your reading of his response.
  - Value the rational way. Some men offer their daughters and sons unquestioning and all-embracing support. Although this feels wonderful, it is very similar to how we treat small children. Maybe your father is giving you the compliment of treating you like a grown-up?

9 *Take a fresh look at your relationship with your mother*
  - Mothers have a lot of influence on the type of relationship sons and daughters have with their fathers, so read the next exercise too.

A New Start . . . with Your Mother

In an ideal world, we would have a close relationship with both of our parents. Unfortunately, a lot of my clients find their father a rather distant figure and although they feel closer to their mother, sometimes it feels too close. (If you wonder what I mean by 'too close', see the first two parts of this exercise.) I have paired this exercise with the one before – 'A New Start . . . with Your Father'. This is because our relationship with our father is directly influenced by our relationship with our mother and vice versa.

1 *'I love my mother but . . .'*
  Women get a lot of their identity and self-respect out of being a good mother. So even the slightest criticism of mothers can make us either agitated or angry. Maybe you felt something similar about the suggestion that you might be too close to yours? Be patient with me and answer the following questions:
  • When you were a child, did you feel that your mother sacrificed more than your father?
  • Do you, in some way, see your father through your mother's eyes?
  • Did you become your mother's confidant or adviser over problems with your father?
  • Did your mother ever poke fun at your father over small failings, over-supervise, criticise or not allow him an equal voice on parenting?
  • Do you feel that you hold the responsibility for your mother's happiness?
  • How would your mother feel if you told your father something personal before you told her?
  • Do you discuss your personal problems – with the exception of financial matters – with your mother first?
  • How would she feel if you phoned and just spoke to your father?
  • What would your mother's reaction be if you and your father spent a weekend alone together? Would she be jealous or maybe just uncomfortable – even though she might have done the very same thing herself? (This question is especially relevant for daughters.)

- Do you ever feel that you are siding with your mother because your father did not or does not treat her fairly?
- Is your mother number one in your eyes?

2 *Reassess your relationship with your mother*
- If you answered yes to any of the questions above, you need to reassess your relationship with your mother – even if you felt that she made more sacrifices than your father. Unfortunately men's 'work', like arranging mortgages and insurance policies or fixing things, is less visible to children. Many men continue with jobs they hate in order to support their families or endure long commutes so their families can live in bigger houses or enjoy a better lifestyle.
- Do you feel guilty about answering 'yes' to one of the questions listed above? If so, be reassured that most people agree with at least one of these statements.
- As your mother was probably responsible for the majority of your care as a baby, the bond will be close. However, it should not be so close that your father has felt excluded and therefore less involved in your life.
- In some cases, the relationship between mother and child can become so close that her emotional needs are met by her son or daughter rather than her husband. This is what I mean by 'too close'.
- Alternatively, mothers can become 'too involved' in their sons' and daughters' lives to the point that natural parental concern becomes interfering or controlling.
- Parenting is not a competitive sport. Sadly, some mothers feel the need to be 'number one' in their children's lives.

3 *Give your mother and father equal parenting rights*
- Especially as an adult, you should feel able to have a good relationship with your father without feeling, in some way, that you arc 'letting your mother down'.

- If you spend time with just your mother, you should do the same with your father.

4 *What if my father does not deserve it?*
  - Imagine that you are a detective, new to this case, and interview your father; assume nothing and listen, without prejudice, to his side.
  - Have your mother's opinions been turned into beliefs and, over time, become your hardened facts?
  - What is the proof? Would it stand up in a court of law where the defendant has the benefit of the doubt?
  - In all my years of counselling couples, I have yet to find a regular couple who are not equally responsible for their problems. (See my book *I Love You But I'm Not in Love with You*, Bloomsbury, 2006, for the Three Laws of Relationship Disputes.)
  - Even in cases with addiction and violence, the concept of innocent and guilty is still murky. How much did your mother 'enable' or 'excuse' your father's bad behaviour?
  - Ultimately, nobody knows what goes on in the privacy of other people's marriages. It is both pointless and counterproductive to take sides.

5 *Mothers are wonderful but they are not beyond criticism*
  - When issues are not addressed, they fester and turn a basically good relationship sour.
  - Often everybody is aware of forbidden subjects but they ignore them.
  - This is particularly common in the mother/child relationship where everybody wants to keep things 'nice'.
  - If you were 100 per cent honest, what would you say to your mother?
  - What do you think her reaction would be? What are your fears?

6 *Decide what personality traits you share with your mother*

- If you become touchy around your mother, or her behaviour sets you on edge, write down everything that really gets to you.
- Go down the list and ask yourself: have I ever done something similar?
- Much as we vow at sixteen to be nothing like our parents, we almost inevitably turn into them – the process seems to speed up as we head towards or pass forty.
- Often the things that make us most angry about our mothers are the parts of her that we recognise in ourselves.

7 *Ask her: how can I make your life better?*

- If you feel responsible for your mother's happiness – perhaps she is alone and elderly or suffers from depression – this is particularly important.
- Our general sense of anxiety can send us off in dozens of different directions and waste our energies in something that might be appreciated but is ultimately unnecessary.
- A lot of people worry about asking: how can I make your life better? They fear that the floodgates might open. My experience is that most mothers ask for something small – like regular phone calls.

8 *Remember, ultimately she is an adult and responsible for her own life*

- Do you ever treat your mother like a small child?
- She might find this irritating but does not say anything for fear of upsetting you.
- Does your 'closeness' stop her developing friendships and her own coping skills?
- Does your 'closeness' stop you from developing relationships?

9 *Take a fresh look at your relationship with your father*
- Your relationship with your mother will influence your relationship with your father, so read the 'A New Start . . . with Your Father' exercise too.
- Throughout these two exercises, I have assumed that you are closer to your mother than your father. In some cases, like daughters with doting daddies, it can be the other way round. If this is you, just swap over the exercises.

The Tasks of Divorce: Children of Divorce

1 *Dealing with the loss*
- It is not just the loss of the intact family and its real and symbolic protection, but also the day-to-day presence of the other parent.
- It takes time to come to terms with loss but, when you were a child, your parents would probably have been too wrapped in their own problems or keen to stress that nothing has changed: 'you'll still see both of us', or the positives: 'you'll have two bedrooms'. However, before you can move into the future, you have to mourn the loss.
- If you were not able to do this as a child, it is maybe time to do it now. Write down everything that you have lost through divorce. These could be financial losses, seeing less of someone or losing touch altogether, or lost opportunities. As you start, it might seem hard to think of anything, but one idea will trigger another. My guess is that you will surprise yourself with the number of losses.
- What feelings does this list arouse in you? If it is sadness, accept that this is perfectly natural. Ultimately loss is part of the universal human experience. Nothing is forever, however much we want to believe to the contrary.

2 *Dealing with the anger*

- You have plenty to be angry about. The job of parents is to protect children, not to subject them to pain. There is also an unspoken pact in our society: parents put the interests of their children first. In many cases, one or both parents put their own interests in front of their children's when they get divorced.

- However, as a child you will not have wanted to express this directly to your parents, as this would have hurt them. You will also have been aware of your mother's or father's vulnerability and their neediness. Not wanting to add to their problems, you will either have bottled up this anger or taken it out on some poor unsuspecting person who crossed your path.

- The task is not only to forgive your parents (see 'The Art of Forgiveness' earlier in the chapter), but to forgive yourself for feeling anger. This is probably the hardest part. Accept that you did get angry, look for mitigating circumstances and then look for ways of making amends with anyone who got hurt. A heartfelt apology is often a good way to achieve this.

3 *Dealing with the fantasy*

- One of the ways of dealing with something that is painful and beyond our control is fantasy. The fantasy that 'everything will turn out fine in the end' and your parents will fall back in love again is widespread amongst small children. In the short term, these fantasies can certainly mask a child's unhappiness.

- Another similar strategy is to idealise the absent parent, normally the father, as the symbol for everything that is missing in your life: if only Dad was there, everything would be better. This makes the real day-to-day encounters incredibly loaded and very difficult, as few people can live up to the expectations of perfection.

- Alternatively, the parent that stays behind, normally the mother, reaches a level of sainthood in her son's or daughter's imagination. Again this is understandable: if you have only one parent to rely on – whereas before you had two – you would want them to be perfect. Many mums come a stone's throw away from this goal, but ultimately everybody is human. We all lose our tempers, hold grudges and occasionally make the wrong call. However, if the son or daughter wants to hold on to their fantasy perfect mother, they have either to close their eyes to the truth or to demonise other people.

- When we become adults, we need to separate our fantasies from reality. After all, it is one thing to be angry with a parent for specific incidents of bad behaviour but quite another to be angry with someone for not living up to our private fantasy version of them.

4 *It's not necessarily personal*
  - We are all egocentric – as my mother would put it: 'you think the world revolves round you'. From a child's point of view, everything is personal: 'if he had loved me he would have stayed', 'if she loved me she wouldn't have needed to find me a new Daddy'. As we grow up, our world view becomes more sophisticated and we realise that there are other forces at play, beyond us. However, it is very easy to get stuck in this 'everything is personal' mode and see any rejection through this perspective. So if a father can only make one visit a month, the child thinks: 'If he loved me he would have visited me more.' Even as adults, we can be stuck in the same groove: 'If my father loved me he would call more often/ spend more time with me.' If we can take off the 'egocentric' glasses for a second, we can think of hundreds of reasons why our mother or father might not call. (Including: They might be waiting for us to make the first move.)
  - So next time you find yourself taking all the blame, feeling guilty or taking rejection as personal – take a broader look. Brainstorm all the other possibilities: what are the demands of

that person's work and their family commitments? Remember it is not all about you. What has happened in the past says as much about the other person as it says about you.

5 Taking a chance on love

- Finally, you need to be open to the possibility of success. You do not have to follow the example of your parents. You can find a fulfilling long-term relationship.
- All the research into fear shows that the more that we try to avoid situations that frighten us, the more afraid we become. In effect, the only way to deal with fear of commitment is to take a deep breath and take a chance on love.

Chapter Three

Long Time Single

It is harder today than ever before to find a partner, to settle down and live happily ever after. As I have discussed, trends in our society are sealing us in our personal worlds and making it harder to meet other people, widespread divorce has cast a long shadow and even for people whose parents stayed together there is a legacy to juggle. It is enough to make anyone throw their hands up and admit defeat. Yet every week in my counselling room, I meet couples who have defied the odds and come together to make good relationships. When I draw up their family trees and look at their complex relationship inheritance or hear stories of abuse, I am amazed that they have not only let a partner into their lives but that they have basically sound relationships. By contrast, I meet people who come from happy families but who still cannot find love. So why do some people make lasting partnerships while others feel terminally single?

Our childhood and the world around us are only part of the story. There is a third element which plays a crucial role in whether we find a partner or not. The good news is that it is something under our control: our own attitude. People who find partners have *three* basic mind-sets and by adopting these positive mind-sets, anyone can increase their chances of love.

Become More Optimistic

When looking for love, it is better to be positive. An optimist will happily accept an invitation for a coffee. At the very least it will be fun, and who knows what else? Maybe a friendship, a business contact, or just a recommendation of a great film to see at the weekend. By contrast, pessimists expect the worst: there will be nowhere to park and all the comfy chairs will be taken. Although they might not mean to be, pessimists appear closed off and much harder to know. After all, they expect the invitation to come with a catch: what is he trying to sell or what does she want to complain about? It is not surprising that people like optimists more than pessimists – they are open, friendly and flexible. Better still, they look for what is right rather than what is wrong and therefore are more likely to have a good opinion about us. Ultimately, we like people who like us. Of course, the pessimists will claim that they are more realistic, less likely to get their hopes up (only to have them dashed) and less likely to throw themselves into a foolish doomed relationship. This defensive strategy might stop them from getting hurt but it also keeps love away too.

There is another important difference between optimists and pessimists. When pessimists have a bad date, they draw conclusions that are permanent ('I'm never going to find someone who is right for me'), all-pervasive ('the evening was ruined because I spilt coffee over everything') and personal ('I'm just not beautiful enough' or 'I don't earn enough'). By contrast, optimists, after a bad date, will draw very different conclusions. The problems are particular: 'the atmosphere in the restaurant was wrong'. They are temporary 'I was tired' or down to someone else 'he was not interested'. Most importantly, optimists view problems as surmountable: 'we didn't click on this occasion but I will meet the right guy', or 'perhaps the second date will be better and she'll warm to me'.

There is a final twist to the difference between optimists and pessimists which is particularly cruel. While pessimists put bad things down to permanent causes and optimists to temporary ones, when it comes to good events they swap over. So the pessimist thinks a success is just a fluke. Therefore, on a successful date, the pessimist says 'Wednesday was the club's cool night' or 'I put a lot of effort into researching everything' (temporary and specific reasons). Meanwhile optimists expect the good times to last and think 'I'm always lucky picking places to go' or 'I know how to charm' (permanent and pervasive reasons). Is it any wonder that pessimists often give up and opt out of searching for love?

The following box underlines the differing attitudes to life.

Pessimist	Optimist
I'm ugly.	I'm not looking my best today.
Women don't like me.	That woman didn't like me.
Always.	Sometimes.
Never.	Lately.
I try hard.	I'm talented.
I'm not good at relationships.	I've had some bad experiences.
I can never remember birthdays.	I was busy and forgot.

Can I Change?

Despite all the handicaps in being a pessimist, I'm not suggesting pessimists become optimists and go around spouting uplifting statements: 'today is the first day of the rest of my life'. There are benefits to mild pessimism, judiciously employed. In some professions – like law, where solicitors have to imagine the worst-case scenario – pessimism is a positive advantage. In addition, when things go wrong, pessimists are quick to put their hands up, take personal responsibility for their share of the failure and learn from the experience. By contrast, unbridled optimists just blame other people. In the worst cases, optimists can plunge from one disastrous relationship into another, forever hopeful, but learning nothing. Ultimately, the best place to be is somewhere between mild pessimism and qualified optimism.

So how can you find a point on this scale that increases your chance of finding love? Pessimism is just a way of looking at the world, albeit one so deeply ingrained that it has become a habit. The good news is that habits can be changed. Gemma, thirty-eight, works in sales and slipped into depression after the failure of a six-month campaign to meet men. She had joined an internet dating agency and been set up by friends. One lunch date, in particular, had seemed hopeful. They had a lot in common – books and the theatre – but he had not phoned again. 'I don't know what I want from men,' she complained, 'and I don't know what is good for me.' She sat in my counselling room, defeated, and lapsed into silence. So I asked her about her lunch date. 'Everything I do around men is a failure.' What about the men off the internet? She seemed to have been successful in setting up meetings. 'They're all after one thing,' she replied. I was at risk of becoming depressed too. How could I possibly help? Firstly, I needed to understand the myriad of thoughts that had built into these concrete conclusions. Gemma listed her problems: 'My age is against me, all the decent men can have their pick of much younger women.' 'Having children is a turn-off.' 'Nobody fancies me.' Her language was very pessimistic: 'nobody', 'everything', 'all'. As a typical pessimist, she believed implicitly in her own conclusions. If someone had said to her: 'nobody fancies you', she would immediately have jumped to her own defence. However, because the messages came from a voice inside her head they were accepted as gospel truth.

When I simply repeated her statements back, she started to qualify them. 'OK, not everybody "doesn't fancy me", in fact some of the men have come on strong,' she explained. 'However, there was always a problem: either I didn't like them or felt that they were only offering casual sex.' So a more accurate statement would have been: 'some men don't fancy me'. A small shift but an important one. The next problem was that Gemma was mixing facts and opinions. How did she know that children were a turn-off? Had she done an extensive survey of all men? What about men who had a family and did not want more children? 'I suppose you're right,' she conceded, 'I don't have the pressure of the biological clock although I do have to be back for the babysitter.'

So I asked her to separate out the facts from the opinions. Fact: I have to get back home at a certain time and I'm less flexible about when I meet up. Opinion: I feel that makes me less appealing than someone without responsibilities. Once again, it is a small change but one that lets in a chink of hope. The third problem for pessimists is always drawing the worst possible conclusions. Gemma was no exception. The friend of the friend had not phoned because she was 'too old'. While most things happen for a large number of reasons, pessimists always put it down to just one. So I went through a few alternatives with Gemma:

- He might have wanted a second date but was too busy at work; when things slackened he had felt the moment had passed.
- He might have had a phone call from an ex-flame and decided to try again.
- He might have liked her but only dated blondes.

Gemma smiled and accepted that all my reasons were possible too. When we discussed it further, Gemma admitted that her date had just finished a long-term relationship. Maybe he had been pressurised into the date by her friend and was simply not ready yet? If I had interviewed this man, I would have found a multitude of different and maybe competing reasons for not calling. After all, we are complex creatures. So it is neither realistic nor helpful to put motives down to one damning reason – like 'I'm too old'. Finally, Gemma had built all her bad dating experiences into one catastrophic conclusion: 'everything I do around men is a failure'. I remembered her job. Could she sell to men? How did she get on with her male colleagues? In fact, Gemma had no problems relating to men at work, it was just her personal life. Ultimately, Gemma discovered that she had let some bad experiences, plus her personal interpretations, build up into a hopeless picture. By simply challenging her pessimistic thought-patterns, I had made the problems seem particular to her dates and therefore only temporary. In effect, Gemma had started to think like a guarded optimist.

Summing up, here are some tips on changing your negative mind-set:

1 *Recognise the thoughts.* Often they happen so quickly and are so well-rehearsed, that they pass unnoticed and unchallenged.
2 *Dispute automatic thoughts.* In many cases, personal interpretations of events are accepted as facts, rather than just opinions.
3 *Look for exaggerations.* Have you built a cast-iron case out of a few bad experiences?
4 *Find alternative interpretations.* In particular, ones that are less personal, less permanent and less pervasive.
5 *What conclusions might an optimist draw?* Imagine for a moment that you are an optimist and look at the same information again. How does this change your opinion?

If you need help thinking like an optimist, there is more in the exercise section at the end of this chapter.

Understand and Deal with Projection

The next item on my list of three key mind-sets, which improve the chances of finding love, is rather complicated. However, it is one of the most important ideas in the book and will become increasingly important as we move onto the second step: Finding Lasting Love. So what is projection? Let me tell you a story from my childhood. My grandfather had a cine camera and he would take super-8 films of important family events. My sister and I were particularly transfixed by the moving images of our christenings. My grandfather, and later my father, who inherited the camera when he died, would get all the guests to walk down to the bottom of the garden in groups and then walk back again. Years later, on Sunday evenings, we would beg our father to show the films over and over again. The silent flickering images would be projected onto the living-room wall or, if my father could be bothered to set up the portable screen, onto that. I found these family images and the clues to everybody's relationship completely fascinating, probably an early indication of my future career. If my sister or I needed to go to the lavatory or the kitchen, the only way out of the living room was past the screen and for a few seconds the faces of grandparents, aunts, uncles and cousins would be projected onto our faces. I tell this story because it illustrates one aspect of projection. When someone responds in an over-the-top way to us – either positively or negatively – it probably says more about them than us. We have unwittingly become the blank screen onto which they have projected their opinion of someone else or some feeling that belongs to them. Often the less someone knows about us, the blanker we are to them, and the more likely they are to be able to project their needs, emotions or expectations onto us.

A common example would be someone who had a difficult relationship with their father, projecting that role (almost his face too) onto their boss. Although repeatedly rebelling against a superior, or an overwhelming need for approval, might seem a work problem, it is often acting out old family dynamics – with colleagues standing in for brothers and sisters. This same process happens a lot with celebrities and public figures. Princess Diana became such a potent icon because we seldom heard her, just saw photographs or film of her arriving at a premiere or a hospice. We could project our needs onto her too. This is why Diana's friends found her public image so at odds with the woman they knew; the image had been projected onto her and therefore said more about us than her.

The psychological term 'projection' was invented by Freud, who used it in a very specific way. He discovered that his patients would first deny unpleasant feelings – or something that contradicted their image of themselves – and then further distance themselves by projecting the negatives onto someone else. The classic example would be a man who had hidden homosexual tendencies. Particularly before gay liberation, this man could have had a secret hatred of himself. Of course, he would deny those feelings but he could go one step further and project his hatred onto gay men in general and might even go so far as to beat one up. The colloquial term for this kind of projection is dumping. For example, we might be angry with someone at work who never stops talking, not just because it is irritating, but because our colleague's behaviour reminds us of our own failure to listen. However, it is not just negative things that belong to us that we project onto others, they can be positive things too. In counselling, my clients project all their hopes onto me and turn me into – in their mind – someone all-powerful and all-knowing. In the short term, this is not a problem. My clients feel hopeful, their problems feel more manageable and they start to make progress. I will talk about this more in a moment. However, the important thing to stress is that *everybody* is projecting all the time – both favourable and unfavourable characteristics, behaviours and attitudes. So not only do we need to be aware of our own projections, but what other people might be projecting onto us.

When it comes to courting, our natural tendency to project goes into overdrive. On the first few dates, this new man or woman is a blank screen onto whom we can play out our dreams, our fears and the bits of ourselves that we don't really like. Sometimes projection can help make a strong initial connection and sometimes it can hold us back. Take Claude, a 34-year-old gay man, who agreed to be interviewed for this book. We had met in a bar and although it was quiet, he attracted appreciative glances. So I wondered why Claude was single. 'My father was very domineering, he did not like music or people coming round to the house,' he explained. 'I'm thirteen years younger than my brothers and sister – who left home early – and I was an unplanned mistake who stopped his freedom.' It soon emerged that Claude did not consider himself attractive. So where could his poor self-image have come from? 'Dad called me "Cockroach" – it was supposed to be affectionate, but I'm sure that you get the picture. As a young man, my father had been very handsome. You should see the pictures. But as he grew older, he ended up looking exactly like me. It's quite uncanny. Although, I didn't go through the gorgeous stage.' It is clear that Claude's father had projected his ambivalence about his loss of looks onto his son and made him into the ugly one. 'What do you think if someone is attracted to you?' I asked him, aware of the hungry eyes of some of the other clientele in the bar. 'If someone likes me it's strange,' he replied. 'I probably think that they have poor taste.' 'That there is something wrong with them?' He nodded sadly. Not only was Claude struggling with the projection from his father but he, in turn, was projecting his own sense of being damaged goods onto his dates. It is not surprising that Claude has had only two relationships – the longest of which had lasted only six months.

Another example of projection is Samantha, thirty-three, who came to see me after a series of unsuccessful relationships. 'Men are so false, they pretend to be great and I'm suckered into thinking this one might be different, but you know what? They all let you down.' Samantha had no trouble making relationships – in fact she quickly became involved – but none of her relationships seemed to last. She thought the problem was her dates, and wanted me to offer advice on how to change them, but I suspected that she was projecting something onto these men. Samantha explained that the relationships started very well. 'We have lots in common, we like similar things and we laugh a lot. But actually they're putting on a show and, slowly but surely, I discover that actually they are quite selfish or spend too much time at their mother's – you get the picture?' It soon emerged that Samantha was desperate to be in a relationship and have a family. She tried not to let her fantasies get in the way and remain level-headed but actually she was projecting an ideal man onto these dates. No wonder she liked them so much at the beginning. But her new boyfriend could not remain a blank sheet – over a few dates she would get to know the real person – and end up feeling deceived. In many ways projecting positive qualities can be just as problematic as projecting bad ones.

With projection influencing how we behave towards other people, it is not only important that we understand how it works but learn how to deal with the results. In my experience, whether handled well or badly, projection moves through five phases: recognition, exaggeration, distortion, confusion and resolution.

The Five Phases of Projection

Using Samantha as an example, this is what happens as we progress from a first meeting through to knowing someone well:

1 *Recognition*

Something about a stranger encourages us to project our desires, our expectations or something about ourselves onto them. While I was counselling Samantha, she was dating a new man. Her eyes were shining as she talked about him. He was a businessman and although he was younger, 'believed in commitment'. I have put the last part of her description in quotation marks because at this early stage of counselling, I had no means to know whether this claim was true or not. I had only Samantha's version of their first few dates. However, the glowing reports were probably a projection: she had wanted him to behave in a certain way and had interpreted his behaviour to fit those expectations. Yet it is more complex than the boyfriend being just a blank screen. The projection needs to stick – rather than slide off. Think of it as a hook provided by the boyfriend. Although I was sceptical about the long-term potential for this relationship – considering Samantha's track record – some part of this man was fed up with the single lifestyle too. Either consciously or unconsciously, he had provided a hook for the projection.

2 *Exaggeration*

Next, you notice and exaggerate the behaviour that fits in with your beliefs. Through Samantha's eyes, her boyfriend staying over on Saturday night and not leaving until after supper on Sunday showed not only that he was keen but the relationship was getting 'serious'. Alternatively, he could have had nothing better to do or being a single man really appreciated a hot home-cooked meal – but Samantha could not even consider this option. Every positive scrap of evidence was being exaggerated.

3 Distortion

The longer that two people spend together, the better they get to know each other. There are also more dates or social/business encounters to provide information about character and intentions. During this phase, events that do not fit are downplayed or ignored. When first describing her boyfriend, Samantha had mentioned his ex-girlfriend and small child in passing but said they 'lived the other side of the country' – and therefore 'were not an issue'. This is clearly a distortion of the truth.

4 Confusion

There comes a point where it becomes harder to reconcile what we would like to believe and the evidence. The result is confusion and we feel uncomfortable that the other person does not behave in line with our projections and expectations. Samantha was upset because her boyfriend had disappeared off to the West Country for the weekend to visit his son. Her tears seemed to say: 'If he is so committed to this relationship, how can he abandon me?' Other information began to emerge about her boyfriend. Previously she had described him as a businessman but now he had been downgraded to self-employed builder. Later in our session, Samantha complained that she was being given 'mixed messages'. On one hand, he had disappeared for the weekend, but on the other, had been jealous of her going out with friends. 'It was like he cared what I got up to, but he had no right to tell me what to do,' she said. Samantha was truly in the confused phase.

5 *Resolution*
Ultimately the differences between projection and reality can no longer be resolved. In Samantha's case, the relationship ended after six weeks. She decided that he had been leading her on and did not want a relationship after all. But how much had been her projection and how much his behaviour?

So What is the Alternative?

It seems rather unfair to build someone into the perfect potential partner and then beat them up for something that they never claimed to be. So my work with Samantha aimed to break her destructive patterns and provide a model for constructive projection. As I explained earlier, my clients arrive expecting that I will have all the answers. Not only do they project onto me all their hope but in some cases will regress to being like small children, unable to make any decisions, because they have also projected their capable adult decision-making skills onto me too. In this *recognition* phase, I am also providing a hook. I am trained to be the 'good father' and to provide empathy and understanding. During the *exaggeration* stage, anything that I suggest will be treated as if written on tablets of stone. All my clients' successes between sessions are put down to my wisdom rather than their coping skills or determination. When I get things wrong or make mistakes – after all, therapists are human beings too – these will be overlooked or forgotten during *distortion*. In the next phase, *confusion*, my clients have to reconcile their image of me as the fountain of all knowledge and the dawning realisation that they are the true experts on their life – after all, they live it while I only observe for an hour a week. Finally, in *resolution*, they discover that they had the skills to solve their relationship problems after all – they were just hidden or had been sabotaged. I am no longer a sage but a human being, with flaws as well as strengths. They have taken back the projection. They no longer need me. We shake hands and say goodbye as equals. If Samantha had met her boyfriend after she had completed her counselling, her *resolution* phase could have been different. Instead of rejecting him for not being perfect, she might have weighed up his good qualities and his failings and found that the former outweighed the latter.

I cannot stress too strongly that everybody is guilty of projection. However, people who make successful long-term relationships – probably unconsciously – project fewer expectations with less vigour, and therefore have less distortion and confusion to unravel. Finally, this makes it easier to reach a balanced and well-considered resolution. To help build on your knowledge of projection and provide skills on how to deal with it, there is more in the exercise section at the end of this chapter.

Comfortable with Commitment

This is the third and probably hardest of the mind-sets but it is crucial for crossing over from being single into a settled relationship. When I talk about the need to embrace commitment, many of my single clients become angry. Mia, thirty-two, is typical: 'I have no problem with commitment whatsoever. I'm ready to settle down. It's the men out there. They're all committed commitment-phobes.' When I looked at Mia's relationship history, she had indeed thrown herself into several relationships. The most recent was with someone she had met through work. 'We started off arguing all the time – because we had fundamentally different attitudes to everything – but this developed into a strong attraction. I started enjoying his company and he told me about his unhappy relationship.' They soon started a passionate affair and every time he was in town, Mia would drop everything and make time for him. She stopped seeing other guys and would write several times a week. 'He emails back occasionally. The most recent one was a complaint about his girlfriend. I tell him we'd be so good together – I'd marry him in a shot – but he seems frightened of making a lasting commitment. How long can I hold on? I need some sort of sign.' On one hand, Mia appears comfortable with commitment, but on the other she had chosen someone who lives in another country (and visited her town only three or four times a year), who is already in another relationship and, on her own admission, holds different beliefs. It does not seem a recipe for success. So what is really happening here? When I first started training as a marital therapist, I tended to take my clients' words at face value. However, I was working with a man who kept saying how much he valued his freedom, how he didn't love his wife, how he couldn't stand living with her any more. I will always remember the wisdom of my supervisor. She interrupted my report on the case: 'How long has he been coming to counselling?' Five weeks, I told her. 'His mouth might say he doesn't want to save the relationship, but week after week his legs bring him up two flights of stairs to your office.' From that moment on, I started listening to my client's legs rather than his lips, challenged his desire to leave and the couple eventually solved their differences. I share this story because lots of singles talk about being ready for commitment but end up sabotaging their prospects in one of two ways. I call these 'Blowing hot and cold' and 'Over-committed'.

Blowing Hot and Cold

Everyone has used this strategy at some point in their life – especially when young or inexperienced and find themselves too deep into a relationship too quickly. However, you should be concerned if you recognise a repeating pattern or if this description fits your most recent relationship.

- At the very beginning, it feels safe to blow red hot as you are still trying to win over the other person or because there is some sort of safety net. For example, falling for someone on holiday or someone about to leave the country.
- As the relationship continues, you give off all the right signals about commitment and, at the time, probably mean them. However, the day-to-day reality of being in a relationship leaves you feeling hemmed in, overwhelmed and wanting to pull back.

88

- You begin to pull away and become frosty.
- Once in the coldest part of this cycle, even reasonable requests for intimacy feel like demands and need to be resisted.
- At this point, you will value 'space' and 'time for myself'.
- In the worst cases, the fear can turn into panic attacks and you literally feel the need to flee.
- More often, you will erect artificial barriers to intimacy. For example, turning off your mobile, not returning phone calls or being unwilling to plan into the future as this is perceived as 'putting pressure on'. Instead, you stress the advantages of being 'spontaneous'.
- Sometimes the barriers are physical. For example, taking a job assignment in another city.
- In other cases, the barriers come from another relationship. These might be socially acceptable – like problems with child care or caring for an elderly relative. However, more often, people who blow hot and cold run more than one sexual relationship at the same time.
- Nostalgia for past relationships can be a strong factor too. In comparison with your feelings about your current boyfriend or girlfriend, issues with your ex seem insignificant. This old relationship is stone-cold dead, and therefore it is safe to blow hot again.
- If there is too much distance, too many barriers or the other person shows signs of leaving the relationship, your approach will change. What you are about to lose increases in value and you turn up the heat again.
- The other person feels positive, and he or she becomes committed again. The courtship tips back into the hot phase. Although you promise 'this time it will be different', nothing has fundamentally changed.
- The whole cycle will repeat again and again – sometimes for years on end.
- These 'Blowing hot and cold' relationships normally end bitterly – although usually it is your partner who suffers the most.

Sometimes there are so many barriers and excuses that the relationship simply ceases to exist. In other cases, you simply disappear or meet someone else who, at the time, seems the perfect partner.

- In effect, this kind of relationship is like a dance – with the distance between the two partners carefully maintained. If your partner steps forward, you step back. When they retreat, you move forward again.

When looking at the behaviour outlined above, it is hard to understand how anybody would put up with it. However, there is one kind of potential partner who seems to thrive – at least in the short term. This is someone who uses the other dance which guards against true intimacy: Over-committed.

Over-committed
This is the hardest of the dances to self-diagnose – after all it is easier to listen to our words than to examine the more subtle messages from our behaviour. So read the following questions with an open mind.

- Would you describe yourself as very romantic and often make big gestures – like turning up unannounced in a far-away city?
- Do you fall in love very quickly and commit yourself without really knowing someone or giving them a chance to prove that they are truly worthy of your devotion?
- What is your reaction to negative information about someone? Do you tend to minimise it? For example: He's married – that could change. She flirts with everyone – it doesn't matter, she's going to be mine.
- Have you fallen for men or women who were unavailable, seldom available or made themselves unavailable using the techniques outlined in 'Blowing hot and cold'?
- Looking back at past relationships, did you know about the problems but believed that either you could cope ('It doesn't

matter, I don't need that much attention') or could easily change the other person ('He just needs to get more in touch with his feelings' or 'She just needs to believe in herself')?

- Do you make yourself totally available to your beloved – right from the start? By this I mean physically, emotionally and sexually.
- When you become more emotional and open, have you ever found that your beloved becomes more distant?
- Do your boundaries come down in direct proportion to the barriers put up by the other person?
- If you totalled up the hours spent on your last relationship, would you have spent longer talking about your beloved with friends, thinking about him/her or doing activities that link to your beloved (listening to their favourite music or writing poetry) than actual face-to-face time with him/her.
- Have you thought that a relationship could be better if only . . . (put in your personal idea)? This normally involves spending quality time together – for example, a romantic holiday – with all your energy going into making this happen. If you have managed to pull off one of these special events, did it make that much difference in the long term?
- Do you find yourself putting most of the effort into keeping the relationship going? Have you turned yourself inside out to be truly accepting and understanding, but somehow it never seems enough? Did the other person make you feel that you were forever bothering them?
- When a relationship ends, do you take a disproportionately long time to recover?
- Can you find yourself still holding a candle for someone, even years later?

Most people will have answered yes to one, maybe two of these questions, but if you found yourself nodding as you went down the list it probably means that you do favour this kind of dance. In therapy, people who are 'over-committed' discover that they were more attached to a fantasy version of their beloved than the real person they dated. This was certainly the case for Mia, whose beloved was already involved with somebody else: 'I didn't really love him, but what I thought he could be.' In effect, she had been projecting her dreams onto him. Once she realised that she had been mourning not for what she had lost but some fantasy of how it might have been, she found it easier to move on.

Sometimes people use both of the dances that avoid true commitment. Jackie, who is now twenty-nine, met Rob in her mid-twenties on a holiday in Greece. In this relationship, she was 'blowing hot and cold'. The attraction was instant and the couple spent twenty-four hours together non-stop: 'We did all that goofy stuff like building a sand-castle together on the beach, champagne picnics and we stayed up the whole night cuddling and kissing. But all too soon, his boat had to leave the island where I was staying. It was the perfect holiday romance.' Although they exchanged addresses, Jackie did not really expect a relationship. 'He lived in New York and I had a demanding job. However, we started writing and telephoning, and he suggested flying over to visit. I was very flattered and being reunited at the airport was like something out of a movie. I was on such a high but it did not stop me noticing that he was a couple of inches shorter than I remembered. He expected me to live in a thatched cottage rather than a small one-bedroom flat, but we had a great time. It was strange to have him under my feet for a week, having to entertain him all the time, and as I still had to work, it was exhausting. Don't get me wrong, I was dreading him leaving but looking forward to doing what I wanted again.' There were also times when Jackie wanted a bit of private space. 'I would suggest that he took a bath, so I could catch up on a report for work, but he'd keep calling for me to come and scrub his back.' Rob was ten years older than Jackie and had inherited a lot of money from his parents, so was in the position to make grand gestures. 'When on the last night together, he suggested a cruise round the Caribbean – all expenses paid – I wanted to put the brakes on. It was all moving too quickly and I didn't like the idea of "being bought" so I thanked him but declined.' Despite her reservations, the relationship continued for another two years. Jackie paid for her own trip to New York and Rob came back to the UK on a couple of occasions. However, Jackie kept on being ambivalent about making a commitment. At one moment she would be on a high: 'My first trip to the States, I tried to sit as close to the front of the plane as possible. Somehow I thought that would get me that little bit nearer to Rob's arms again.' The next, she was feeling hemmed in and hiding behind work commitments. When Rob was not around, Jackie would miss him and send out all the signs that she wanted the relationship. When he was there, she was not so sure. 'It was hard for Rob when I turned chilly. He'd be all concerned and ask if anything was the matter. I wanted to scream: "leave me alone".'

In her next relationship, Jackie became 'over-committed'. On this occasion, she managed to avoid all her old feelings of being trapped or hemmed in and threw herself wholeheartedly into the relationship. So how did she overcome her fears? This is the sad part, she didn't. She chose someone who was not truly available. Jake lived only an hour's drive away. The sex was incredible. There was only *one* problem: Jake's profession. He was a dog breeder with rows and rows of runs in his back garden. The dogs provided endless excuses for not seeing Jackie: a bitch would be about to give birth, staff shortages meant Jake had to work extra shifts, visits from prospective owners, or he was too busy hand-rearing a pup that had been rejected by its mother. Jackie explained how Jake would put up other barriers: 'He'd never want to make another date straight away. It would be a couple of days before I'd catch him in or he'd call back – so there was never any continuity. I kept thinking it would all be great if we could spend some proper time together. I tried to get him to come to my birthday weekend and meet all my friends – but on the Saturday afternoon he had last-minute problems and I lost my temper. So he not only opted out of the party but coming down for Sunday lunch with my mum and sister.' However, it was not all bad and the relationship lasted for three years. 'He was a really caring guy. Lots of insight and well-read too. He introduced me to some great books and music. If only he could have met me halfway.' Unfortunately, Jackie had been keeping the relationship alive by sheer force of will. (She had even persuaded her best friend to buy one of Jake's pups, so she could let him see what 'fun' her friends were and integrate him further into her life.) Certainly, Jackie had been committed but to a man who showed no sign of committing himself – or indeed fulfilling quite a lot of the basic requirements of a true relationship. In effect, the commitment had been all on Jackie's part. It took several weeks of counselling before Jackie could understand that although she wanted intimacy – a basic human need – she was equally frightened of getting it. Instead of facing up to this dilemma, she had been involved in a complicated dance round the problem. With her lips, she had been all for a relationship, but her choice of men had stopped her from having to deal with the reality. In a sense, she had had her cake but did not have to eat it!

What about the Partners of People who 'Blow Hot and Cold' or who are 'Over-committed'?

It takes two people to make a relationship, so it is important to look at the kind of people who make up the other halves of these partnerships.

- From time to time, I see couples who both blow hot and cold and take it in turns to want to be close or to retreat. These relationships are seldom satisfying but the highs when both partners want to be together (normally in the making-up phase after a horrible row) can be addictive and provide enough hope to keep the couple going through the lows.
- I have met couples who were both 'over-committed'. However, this combination is extremely rare. On paper, it should be a match made in heaven. Two people who want to be everything to each other and together all the time – what could be better? However, this intense togetherness can only work if

each person submerges their personal needs and identity for the sake of the relationship. This is not a problem in the short term but generally the couple ends up 'loving but not being *in* love' and the sex either dwindles away to nothing or is dull and dissatisfying.

- The most common combination is 'blowing hot and cold' and 'over-committed'. Unfortunately, 'blowing hot and cold' will soon feel trapped (and retreats) and 'over-committed' will be anxious that they are going to be abandoned (and become more demanding). Generally these kinds of relationships last somewhere between three months and three years and normally end with 'blowing hot and cold' disappearing. However, this combination can last longer – normally with breaks – because 'blowing hot and cold' tends to return with promises of trying harder.

So Why Do People Fall Into This Pit?

Human beings have two basic but contradictory needs: intimacy and independence. We are social creatures and need the emotional and physical support that comes from a loving relationship – whether from a partner, friend or parent. However, we also value our autonomy and need enough freedom to be ourselves – rather than be crushed by the expectations of other people. It is a hard balancing trick: if you are too independent, you have no relationship; too much intimacy and you lose your personal sense of identity. In successful relationships, both partners are responsible for some of the intimacy and some of the independence. However under stress, people get polarised and one partner will push for more time together and the other will retreat into their work, watching TV, the computer, the pub or an all-consuming hobby.

Psychologists believe our response to intimacy is based on our childhood experiences. People who had a 'good enough' childhood will find it easy to get close to someone else (secure attachment) but not feel that their sense of themselves is at risk. They make up 56 per cent of the population. Meanwhile, people who had bad childhood experiences will find it hard to trust other people (avoidant attachment). Not surprisingly, they prefer to keep people at arm's length. In a mild form, it involves guarding personal time inside a relationship. In the mid and more extreme forms, it either means becoming a loner or more likely – because intimacy is a basic human need – swinging back and forth between intimacy and independence (in other words blowing hot and cold). Twenty-five per cent of the population have some degree of avoidant attachment. The third category is people who felt unfulfilled as children and as adults can never get enough love. This is called anxious attachment. These people worry because their partners seem reluctant to get as close as they would wish. In the mild form, this is the half of the relationship pushing for more time together. In the middle, it is someone who dismisses their own needs and puts everything into the relationship. In the far end, this becomes 'over-committed'. This category accounts for 19 per cent of the population. So where do you fit in? Look at the quiz in the exercise section on attachment styles in relationships, work and social situations.

How to Feel Comfortable with Commitment

When I explain that the roots of our attitude to commitment are in our childhood, a lot of my clients become depressed. As Jackie said: 'How can I change that?' But this attitude underestimates the healing properties of a good relationship. The physical and emotional bond of a lover is the closest thing to that between a mother and her baby. So in the arms of our beloved, we can re-experience our first relationship and, in many cases, repair or enhance our attitude to intimacy. It is never too late to change. Perhaps, at this point, I should talk from personal experience. Until I reached thirty, I would be best described as avoidant attachment (kept people at arm's length). This was partly because I was concentrating on my career, but mainly I feared losing my personal independence. The best way to describe it was an irrational fear of being swallowed up. I finally made sense of this feeling when I interviewed an expert on twins. She had been studying their parenting styles, especially girls whose twin had been a boy. (My mother is a few minutes younger than her twin brother.) According to the expert, because girls mature quicker than boys, the girl twin is normally in charge of her brother and likely to boss him about. As mothers, these girl twins continue to be very 'in-charge' – especially of their sons. Of course, my mother did not want to swallow me up but this is probably what it felt like to a small boy! So the following steps to becoming comfortable with commitment are informed by both personal and professional experience.

1 *Accept where you are starting from:* Our culture places a lot of stress on freedom, independence and pleasing yourself. The news is full of theft, violence and terrorism and so it is harder than ever before to trust other people. However, we often make it worse by pointing the finger at ex-partners rather than accepting our own commitment issues. If you recognised yourself – even if only in a mild form – in either 'Blowing hot and cold' or 'Over-commited', congratulate yourself. Owning up to a problem is halfway to solving it.

2 *Aim for small changes:* Once people accept that a certain type of person is bad for them, the temptation is to go for the complete opposite. For example, Jackie felt under pressure from Rob flying in from New York, so decided to choose someone who would be laid-back, like Jake. However the dynamic of the relationship was the same – commitment problems – she just played different roles. Think of commitment as a continuum with a hermit at one end and someone who brings a removal van on the second date at the other. Instead of flying to the far end – which will freak you out and probably be too far in the other direction – aim to move a little more into the middle.

3 *Be up-front:* The third part of this book concentrates on meeting new people, so there will be more later. However, in a nutshell, the idea is to avoid the extremes of your old behaviour. For avoidant attachment, this could mean returning messages at your earliest convenience – rather than days later. For anxious attachment, this could mean stopping pushing for some of the events that you imagine will promote intimacy – like sleeping over or taking a holiday – and waiting for the other person to bring them up. In addition, I advocate what I call 'Showing the Owner's Manual'. After a couple of dates, mention your particular pattern. This does not have to be a big conversation, ideally it should be over in a couple of sentences. After all, you are just showing the manual – not trying to sell! For example, 'I just thought I'd warn you that I like you, but sometimes I can come on a bit strong. So please tell me if I start moving too quickly.' Alternatively: 'I'm really enjoying going out with you, but I thought I should make you aware that I have had some bad experiences in the past. So if I seem to hold back, let me know and I'll tell you if it is just my natural reserve or whether I feel things are going too fast.' Remember this is not a confession, a detailed explanation or a relationship history. You are making the other person aware of your issues, and more importantly, giving them permission to ask questions in the future.

4 *Monitor your progress*: Our attitude to intimacy is deeply ingrained, so do not expect too much too soon. However, you will be amazed at how much better it feels even just a few steps further towards the centre of the scale. You can start with friends – where the stakes are lower – so if you have avoidant attachment ask a friend to come and stay. If you previously felt that your space was invaded after twenty-four hours – aim for thirty-six. If you have anxious attachment, you could try lengthening the time between calls to your best friend. You

might find, once given the opportunity, that he or she will initiate more calls.

5 *Find a level of intimacy which feels comfortable for you:* There is no right balance between independence and intimacy. I have met couples who have vowed never to spend a night apart and I know others who would go crazy without business trips or occasional weekends away with mates. Each couple needs to find what works for them.

Summing up the Three Mind-sets that Promote Relationships

There are three qualities that make it easier to climb out of the *Single Trap* and find a partner: optimism; the ability to deal with projection; and feeling comfortable with commitment. These mind-sets are closely interrelated and improvements in one aids progress in all. Being optimistic about a relationship makes it easier to commit. When someone stops projecting, they are less likely to push either all responsibility for intimacy or for independence on to their partner. This, in turn, makes commitment less of a stumbling block. Even a small improvement, therefore, sets up a virtuous circle: where one step forward makes the next easier and that in turns helps with the next and so on.

Single Life Today

There are times in everybody's life when being single makes sense. During an intensive time of study or a leap up the career ladder, moving to a new city and putting down roots and, most commonly, after a relationship break-up. For example, Sophie, fifty-two, has been single for four years since the messy break-up of her marriage. 'There's nobody in my life at the moment but I'm not looking. I put a lot of energy into my work and one of my sons has just bought his first flat. So I've been helping him furnish it and move in. I'm always busy. To tell you the truth, I'm rather enjoying pleasing just myself. I can decide what to watch on the TV, what pictures go on my wall and if I want to just read, there is nobody to tell me I'm being selfish. I still do many of the things that I did with my ex-husband – like going to galleries, the theatre and the opera – but I either go with friends or by myself. I might be alone quite a lot but I'm not lonely.' Sophie has found a good resting-place for now between the past and the future. Being single might be easier today – and that is something we need to celebrate – but I am always struck by how hard it still remains. Lorna is thirty-eight and has recently married, but she shudders when she looks back. 'I don't think people in relationships understand how exhausting it is to be single – especially for women. You have to ruthlessly plan your social life or you can be left looking at a long empty weekend of nothing. The weekdays are not too difficult. I'd be tired after work or I'd take an aerobics class; alternatively, it would be a girlfriend's birthday and a group of us would go out for a meal. However, Friday night to Sunday night belonged to my friends' boyfriends, partners and husbands – so it could be an empty dull void.' Lorna went on to contrast married life today with the past. 'If it's a nice Saturday morning, we can be totally spontaneous and go out for a drive and walk on the downs, maybe a pub lunch too. Beforehand I'd phone my single friends on the off chance – but they would probably be busy – or my mum. It was particularly depressing when her social life was better than mine.' Before she married, to fill the weekend void, Lorna would do things that she later regretted. 'I would agree to go out with guys that I didn't really fancy – or even like. I'd open a bottle of wine on Friday night, get melancholy drunk and phone ex-boyfriends. Don't get me wrong, this did not happen all the time. There would be weeks, months when I'd be strong and focused, but suddenly it would all slide and I'd be opening pillow-sized bags of pretzels and doing things that would make me hate myself.' It was clear that Lorna did not want to talk any further. Anushka, thirty-two, was more forthcoming about her sex life: 'I have all these excuses: "I've been working hard", "I've had that nasty row with my eldest daughter and need a bit of TLC", "It's Valentine's Day", and I'll let myself sleep with someone I don't *really* know. Sometimes, it would be fun, but more often just plain tacky. Somehow, in my mind, the excuses make it OK, but who am I really fooling?'

On the surface, single men have it easier than single women. Even today, it is easier for a man to walk into a pub on his own and football and other sporting occasions provide plenty of casual contacts. However beer is at the centre of each of these activities and while filling the empty hours many men develop a drinking habit that repels potential partners.

Coping Strategies That Can Backfire

Although much of the stigma of being single has disappeared, it still remains tough. Worse still, many of the tricks that single people use to take the edge off what Lorna calls the 'void' make things worse. In effect, these coping strategies fill the hours – and therefore work in the short and medium term – but often become a trap.

1 *Friends as Surrogate Partners*
Balancing the needs of your partner and those of your friends is always difficult, especially if your relationship is still at the courting/dating stage. Carol and Alice, both in their mid-thirties, have been flatmates for three years. 'Alice was not just someone to go out with – but more importantly someone to stay in with on a Saturday night,' explained Carol. 'But when I met my future husband, who liked clubbing, I felt that I was betraying her by leaving her behind. When she came too, she felt like a gooseberry, and anyway she doesn't like noisy places.' Often it seemed that Alice was subtly trying to under-mine Carol's relationship, but she stuck to her guns and put her boyfriend first. This is important during the early days of a relationship – which I call 'Blending' – where each potential

partner has to let their barriers down. Normally, there is a lot of lust, passion and love – which helps – but unless a couple spend enough time alone together it is impossible to build up the trust necessary to let someone truly into your life. Unfortunately, I counsel many single people who use their commitment to a circle of friends to keep potential lovers at arm's length. Although it is annoying for friends when you have less time, it can ultimately be in everybody's best interest. Shortly after Carol met her future husband, Alice started going out more and married eighteen months after her friend. As well as friends as surrogate partners, I have met single men and women who have used their children – taking them out for an evening in a fancy restaurant – and their aged parents. Whoever takes the surrogate role, the effect is the same. This relationship takes such precedence that budding love affairs are starved of oxygen and never truly get started.

2 *Comfort Dating*
To ward off feelings of loneliness, some people ensure that they always have a love interest – even if it is nothing very serious. Women who comfort date often choose an older man who will take them places and entertain lavishly. Men choose women who perhaps have children and are pleased to lay an extra place for Sunday lunch. Comfort dates are just something to be going on with; a bit of light-hearted fun until something better comes along. In some ways, there is nothing wrong with this strategy – especially if the other person knows not to take things too seriously. However, relationships seldom stand still, simple affection grows into something stronger and someone gets hurt. Alexandra, thirty-seven, had been seeing Leo, fifty-two, for four months. They had been to the theatre, spent a Bank Holiday Monday by the sea and shared a bed together. 'One Sunday morning we had a long cuddle. It felt really nice to be held,' explains Alexandra, 'but he seemed tearful and after a bit of coaxing confessed: "I know this is not forever but

please let me stay around until you find someone else." It was like he was holding up a sign saying "kick me" and I felt so ashamed of myself. I'd been using him and it made me feel all dirty inside.' This comfort-dating relationship had becoming damaging for both partners' self-esteem.

The gay world has a twist on the casual but repeat rendezvous, except their version skips the date part and heads straight to the bedroom. It's called f**k buddies. Over the past five years or so, this phenomenon has spread to the heterosexual world too. In effect, two consenting adults enjoy straightforward recreational sex; there are 'no strings' but a friendship to add an extra layer of intimacy. It sounds fine but often works better in theory than in practice. 'Toby was involved with someone else but we had our Wednesday nights – when he was supposed to be at his Spanish class,' explains Phoebe, twenty-eight. 'Our relationship was all about the sex – it was like a work-out between the sheets. It got my pulse racing and put a smile on my face that lasted to the weekend.' However, sex has a way of binding two people together and Phoebe found she was enjoying chatting and sharing a bottle of wine as much as lovemaking. 'I found myself resenting the fact that he didn't call, that we never went anywhere – he was frightened of being spotted with me. In short, I started acting like his mistress.' Phoebe had fallen in love and became embroiled in an affair that lasted eighteen months. Although comfort dating and f**k buddies might seem a harmless way to fill the void, it can leave everyone with even more emotional baggage.

3 *Living Behind a Shield*
Although it makes sense to take time out while recovering from a painful break-up, some people are so traumatised that they choose to opt out permanently. Liza is in her fifties, I've known her for about ten years, and over that time she has never mentioned a partner or even an interest in one. In fact, she has often told me that women over fifty are virtually invisible and,

as a writer, she enjoys the chance to watch without being observed. Indeed, I think of her as having a sheet of Plexiglas between herself and men. She talks to them and they talk to her but there is a barrier that stops the unspoken communion that builds attraction and desire. So has she truly retired? 'I've been writing in a bar close by where I live; the food is cheap and good quality and there's a quiet corner in the organ loft – it used to be a church. Normally, there is nobody up there, but a few weeks ago I saw this guy reading a book – at a table at the opposite end,' Liza explained. 'Being curious, I peeked a look at the book – something about science – when he went down to get another drink. The next two times that I went in, there he was at the same table with the same book. It felt too much of a coincidence. The third time, he was not there. I was deep in a screenplay and when I looked up from my laptop, he was there at the table next to me. I was so startled that I looked down immediately. When I left, I thought about saying something – "Still reading the same book"? – but he buried his face in his paperback.' As Liza told the story, I could sense, for the first time, her longing to connect. There had probably been count-less other men who were interested but who Liza did not notice or she was too shy to encourage. As it turns out, Liza had a bad experience – a relationship with a man who became violent – and her top priority has been safety. She dare not let her Plexiglas defence down – in case she gets hurt again. This strategy has been a great success, she has remained safe but alone. In fact, it had become so much a part of her that she was not aware of it. She was probably even a little shocked that I thought she had retired from love. If you recognise your own behaviour here, there is advice in the exercise section.

4 *Something to Fill the Void*

There are many ways to distract yourself from the pain of isolation. The most common choice is long hours in the office. This is not only socially and culturally endorsed, but our jobs can provide personal fulfilment and a way of making sense of our lives. The common goals of teamwork are also very bonding and provide the illusion of intimacy. However, it is only a shadow intimacy, as anyone who has left a company and returned a few days later to pick something up can attest. All too often, work becomes an excuse for an empty private life: 'I'm too tired and too busy.' Other ways of numbing ourselves from the void include: comfort eating, long hours in front of the television, alcohol, compulsive shopping, gambling, recreational and prescription drugs. It goes without saying that when we are numb – cut off from our feelings, intuition and common sense – that we make foolish relationship choices.

Ultimately all these coping strategies are ways of distracting ourselves when reality gets too depressing or too frightening. It is a natural human reaction: we do not like pain. However, pain has real benefits. It tells us when something is wrong with our lives. It tells us when it is time to make fundamental changes. If we do not listen to the lessons of pain – and choose to distract ourselves – we set up a vicious cycle where one bad choice and one bad relationship delivers another. The nineteenth-century German philosopher Friedrich Nietzsche would go even further: 'The worst sickness of men tends to originate in the sentimental way they try to combat their sickness. What seems like an easy cure, in the long run produces something worse than what it's supposed to overcome. Fake consolations always have to be paid for with a general worsening of the original complaint.' What this means for single people is that the original problem of being alone – not so difficult to overcome – is hardened into a mountain of obstacles. In effect, distractions and coping strategies make us pessimistic, frightened of commitment, and more likely to dump or project blame onto other people.

Summary

- One of the biggest handicaps for people who have been single for a long time is directly under their control: their own mindset.
- Pessimists consider set-backs to be all-pervasive, personal and permanent. Meanwhile optimists view them as temporary and down to specific circumstances, so therefore easier to overcome. Optimists find it easier to make relationships because they are open to new ideas and new people.
- Feelings that we find hard to accept and difficult family relationships are often acted out in a different arena, by projecting them onto someone else. Although everybody uses projection it comes to the fore on dates.
- Projection allows us to channel all our hopes and dreams onto strangers and turn them into our fantasy made flesh. When we get to know the real person, we feel betrayed: they are not the person that we imagined. In the meantime, we overlook their good qualities and may reject an appropriate partner.
- It is often easier to talk the talk of commitment than to follow through and commit. One way to deal with this contradiction is to blow hot and cold about the relationship (and to blame our partner for making us behave in this manner) or by becoming over-committed to someone who does not truly return our feelings (and blaming them for the lack of commitment).
- What we imagine protects us from the pain and the void of being single often makes it harder for us to find a loving relationship.

Exercises

Pessimistic Thoughts – First Aid

When something bad happens, or you are under stress, it is easy to slip into an automatic pessimistic reaction. This exercise is aimed at stopping this destructive pattern. Find something that will snap you out of your negative frame of mind. Some people have a rubber band round their wrist and ping it. Another idea is to keep a card with the word STOP written in large red letters in your wallet or bag. When you feel yourself falling into old patterns, bring it out and look at it. Finally, you could have a bell to ring. The choice is up to you but find anything that will bring you up short.

Next, remember the three golden rules:

1 It's not what happens but how I deal with it.
2 I can't control adversity but I can control my reactions to it.
3 I will look for the positives, which I can build on, rather than concentrating on the negatives, which I cannot.

When the crisis is over, you can then get out a piece of paper and start challenging your thoughts.

Challenging Pessimistic Thoughts

1 *The first job is to recognise the thoughts*. This is hard, as they are always second nature. So take a piece of paper and write down everything as it comes to you. Do not censor yourself, write everything no matter how stupid or unimportant it seems.

2 *Look at what you have written*. When I do this exercise with clients, the first surprise is that there is always less than they expect. Often our thoughts, trapped in our head, spiral out of control and become endless versions of the same thing. Writing everything down stops this from happening.

3 *Separate facts from opinions.* Facts can be proved. Facts stand up in court. Anything that involves interpretation is opinion. For example, 'I made a fool of myself on the date.' What is the evidence? Fact: I made a joke about ten useful things to do with a dead cat. Fact: She has a cat. Opinion: She thinks I'm insensitive and stupid. Another example: 'I had a real pig-out and blew my diet last night.' What is the evidence? What is a pig-out? Fact: I ate a large packet of crisps last night. Opinion: I am a glutton.

4 *What are the consequences?* This will help you understand how your pessimistic interpretations of events translate into behaviour. Make up a grid with the headings: facts, opinions, consequences. Transfer your thoughts onto the grid. For example:

Facts	Opinions	Consequences
I ate a bag of crisps	I'm a glutton	I abandoned my diet
My joke went down badly	I'm insensitive	I did not ask for a second date

5 *Argue with yourself.* Look for alternative opinions. What is the case for the defence? What is an exaggeration? For example: the dieter could remember the last five days when he or she stuck to the sensible eating plan; the man could remember the jokes that his date did laugh about. Put the alternative opinions onto your grid and add alternative possible consequences.

Facts	Opinions	Consequences
I ate a bag of crisps	I've stuck to my diet up to now	Keep going
	I will occasionally have slips	Build treats into my diet
My joke went down badly	She liked my other jokes	Phone her
	I need to think before telling a joke	Be more careful next time

Try to come up with as many different opinions as possible as each of them will suggest another alternative outcome and many of them will be optimistic.

Gratitude Diary

When you have been single for a while, it is easy to become preoccupied with what you are missing and forget about the benefits of what you have. This can lead to unhappiness and even depression. Conversely, if you can keep hold of the positives, you will be more optimistic and more likely to achieve your goals. This is where the gratitude diary comes in.

1 *Buy an attractive notebook.* Find something that is a joy to have by your bed, on your desk or in your briefcase.

2 *Make a contract with yourself to fill it in two or three times a week.* Sunday night, when you are looking back over the past week and forward to the next, is a good time.

3 *Start each entry with 'Today, I feel grateful for . . .'.* Normally these small moments pass us by, but writing them down keeps them fresh and stops us forgetting.

4 *Aim for five items a day.* Find something that came directly out of your recent experiences. For example, 'someone gave up their seat on the train' or 'I had a call from an old friend'. If you find it hard to come up with five items, go for something enduring like 'the view from my bedroom window' which otherwise you might take for granted.

5 *Try using these five headings.* Friends and family (for example, the enduring support of a sister), work (the chance to

travel or meet someone interesting), the wider community (a great delicatessen near where I live), something beautiful or sensual (walking home through the park or the smell of freshly roasted coffee), something intellectually stimulating (a great debate at the water-cooler, an interesting book or great music).

Projection, Projection, Projection

When you meet someone new and have a strong reaction – either positive or negative – try out this exercise. It also works with casual acquaintances – perhaps a colleague at work – whom you dislike but cannot put your finger on exactly why.

1 *Recognition*
Take a long dispassionate look at this stranger. Does he or she remind you of anybody? Maybe their face, a quirk or the way they move? What about their behaviour? Next think about the behaviour or attitude that grates and then take a deep breath. Could the same criticism be levelled at you?

2 *Exaggeration*
Once you are aware why this stranger provokes such a strong reaction, watch and double-check that you have found the right reason. Could there be anything else to add? In particular, look to see if you are 'dumping' on him or her.

3 *Distortion*
This is the most important phase. Look for evidence that the stranger is not like your mother, brother, sister. When you feel persecuted, for example, by her loud voice or his demand that you repeat something at work, tell yourself: she is not my mother or he is not my brother.

4 *Confusion*

Repeat the above part of the exercise on a couple of separate occasions, so you create a longer and longer list of contrary evidence, and you will soon be surprised that you ever thought that stranger was like your family member or reminded you of yourself. In effect, you have stopped projecting.

5 *Resolution*

Finally, look back at what you can learn about yourself. If you have been projecting your feelings about a family member, it is probably time to reassess your relationship with this person. Consider talking over old gripes or challenging their behaviour today. If it something that you dislike about yourself that you have projected onto a stranger, how could you work on that facet of your behaviour? Do you need to be easier on yourself? Do you expect too much?

What Is Your Attachment Style?

This quiz highlights the differences between the attachment styles, offers insights into how other people approach the same issues and some targeted advice for your personal style.

1 *How do you feel about your work and your colleagues?*
   a) I am satisfied with colleagues and the level of job security.
   b) I do not feel truly appreciated by my colleagues and often feel that I deserve promotion.
   c) My colleagues are lazy and some of them are not very good at their jobs, but I feel that my job is secure.

2 *Which of the following best describes your work pattern?*
   a) I can work well both alone and as part of a team.
   b) I prefer working with other people and get them involved in my tasks.
   c) I work best alone.

3 *What is your work/life balance like?*
   a) I get more pleasure from relationships than from work.
   b) Problems with my love life sometimes interfere with my work.
   c) My work life is more important than my love life.

4 *You have a new work colleague who within hours of arriving has told you all sorts of personal information. How do you react?*
   a) I like people who are up-front but I would not respond in a similar manner until I got to know the new colleague better.
   b) I like people who self-disclose and I would respond by telling her/him everything about myself too.
   c) I do not like people who behave like this and would never dream of telling work colleagues such private information.

5 *Which of the following statements best describes your feelings about yourself?*
   a) Although I have my bad days, I generally have fairly good self-esteem.
   b) I have low self-esteem and can never get enough compliments.
   c) People see me as confident and in control but they would think differently if they saw the real me.

Mostly a)
Secure attachment. You are generally comfortable being close to other people and have few issues about trust. Congratulations, you are well-placed for the next part of the programme.

Tip: If you did not answer a) on all the questions, look at whether you were more likely to answer b) or c) on the rest and read that section too.

Mostly b)
Anxious attachment. Being close to other people is a very attractive proposition for you, but some people find that you come on too strong. You have a tendency to disclose lots of information about yourself and later wonder if it was a good thing. When it comes to intimate relationships, you find that you can never get as close as you wish and worry about the other person betraying you. In the past, you have often become too committed too soon and got your fingers burnt. The result is that you can try too hard or, worse, imagine slights when none was intended.

Tip: Look before you leap and weigh up if someone is truly worthy of your love or interested in your friendship. Next time you catch yourself about to commit, step back and observe. See if you can double the time you normally take to fall for someone or decide to become friends. Slowing up a bit will help improve your judgement.

Mostly c)
Avoidant attachment. You find it difficult to trust other people or to allow yourself to depend on them. You are nervous when someone gets too close and often your partners want more closeness than you feel comfortable with. In past relationships, you have blown hot and cold. This is because one half of you really wants to be in a loving relationship, but the other half is rather scared.

Tip: Be wary of the messages that you give out during the first stages of a new relationship. A heady combination of lust, the excitement of the new and the hope that it will work this time makes you appear more committed than you truly feel. Try not to set up patterns that will make you feel cornered in the future. For example, if you phone every day the other person will expect and come to rely on frequent contact. So keep asking yourself: Am I writing cheques that I might not be able to honour? Also look at the next exercise on 'Lowering the Shield'.

Lowering the Shield

A shield might protect you from pain but it can keep out good things like love and affection.

- We are programmed to like and protect things that appear vulnerable, like puppies and kittens. By contrast, something that appears invincible – like a tank – does not provoke the same warm feelings.
- Picture your shield. What is it made of? Bricks, or something that you can see through? How high is it? Up to your knees, your neck or over your head? How thick is it?
- Over the next few days, be aware of your shield and when it lowers and raises. How do you react under stress? How do other people react to your behaviour?
- With a clearer idea of your defences and how they operate, you are ready to make some changes. Next time that you feel threatened, take a deep breath or count to ten and then imagine lowering the shield a bit. Where do you see the shield now? What difference does this make to your behaviour?
- Think about what could help lower the shield further or make it more transparent. At work, for example, you could ask for help with a project, admit that you have a problem or simply buy time to think through all the implications and tackle them calmly.
- Remember, even small changes will pay dividends.

Chapter Four

Recovering from Previous Relationships

There are two different kinds of people who end up feeling that they have fallen into the *Single Trap*. The first have had plenty of relationships but few, if any, have reached the point of setting up home together. In effect, they have spent most of their adult lives either living alone or with flatmates. The second have been married or in a long-term relationship (three years or more) for most of their adult lives but following divorce, bereavement or relationship breakdown are single again. Many of these people have not been on their own since their teens or twenties, their confidence has been knocked, dating has changed out of all recognition and they fear that they will never find a new partner. The previous chapter concentrated on the problems of the first group – long-term single. This chapter looks at the issues facing the second group – newly single. However, I would recommend that everybody reads both chapters. The previous chapter introduced important ideas – especially projection – that inform the rest of the book. This chapter explores the break-up of a relationship and the long shadow that it casts. Although of prime importance to someone who has recently ended an important relationship, there is useful information for anyone who has ever loved and lost. This chapter also has advice for people suffering from unrequited love or who have difficulty moving on and explains the importance of grieving.

The Importance of Proper Endings

After a break-up, someone being attracted to us is a great confidence boost and the excitement of new love can temporarily lessen the heartache of past rejection. So is it any wonder that friends advise us to 'get back out there', 'there are plenty of other fish in the sea' and 'you can do better'. However, jumping too soon into a new committed partnership, without grieving and learning from the past one, takes all the issues from one relationship into another. In many cases, by the time people reach my office there are multiple relationship problems to unpick. Ella, a woman in her thirties who ran a PR agency, desperately needed help. Her marriage had recently ended, her father had died six months previously and she had also ended a long-term affair. 'Men keep making passes at me,' she explained. 'The father of one of my daughter's friends had been advising me about sorting out my father's estate. Suddenly, he put down the paper and put his hand on my knee. "Let's take a break, there's nobody in." And we ended up in bed. I didn't really want to but I couldn't think of a reason not to. The final straw was this elderly cancer specialist who'd sought advice about setting up a clinic in the town, he made a pass too! I turned him down but I felt so angry.' There had been an overlap between Ella's marriage and her long-term affair, which in turn had only just finished when she started her casual sexual relationship. Three separate sets of pain is hard enough – but all Ella's relationship problems had become one tightly wound bundle and she was completely overwhelmed.

The other danger of love on the rebound is simply repeating the same relationship, with the same arguments, but with a different partner. We all know friends who fall for the same type of man or woman over and over again. From the first time we meet their new partner, we know the script – from passionate kisses to bitter recriminations. We might try to warn our friend but somehow they are blinded by passion and can never see the similarities. Looking through gossip magazines, it is also striking how many celebrities fall for the same type of lover, even the same look, time and again. I call this phenomenon: Identikit partners. The faces might change but the same relationship repeats again and again.

Justine certainly had a type: bad boys. They were drummers in bands, installation artists or actors. Many of them were too fond of smoking marijuana and all of them lived in flats with coffee cups that had not been washed. Justine would find herself clearing up their flats and trying to organise their lives. On reaching thirty, she decided that she was in a rut and made a conscious choice to change. 'One New Year, I wrote a list of what I wanted from a man,' she remembered, 'and top of the list was that they must be sane and fertile.' She did find just such a man – he worked in an office and lived a nine-to-six sort of life. On the face of it, everything was perfect, and they had two children together. However, Justine had not really learnt from her previous relationships – or indeed her relationship with her father who had also been creative, chaotic and had drink problems. 'I started to find my husband so boring,' she explained, 'he'd moan about the state of the house, how long I'd spent on the sofa, and we'd argue about money. One night, I had a horrible realisation: he was nagging just like I would in my past relationships and I was telling him to "chill" – just like my boyfriends had told me.' Justine was indeed in another identikit relationship, but this time she was the chaotic one and her husband the sensible one.

At the other end of the scale from loving on the rebound are the people who find it hard to love again – sometimes even years after a relationship officially ended. Author Leonie Frieda had been divorced for seven years when she wrote: 'The feeling of being married, if only in the abstract, still hampers my ability to let anyone too close and I am, frankly, lonely. I even beg my children to watch movies with me in my enormous bed, in the same way that they used to beg me. I seem unwilling or unable to allow full access to my heart. It's as though the seat next to me is taken, even though there is nobody there.' As far as the courts and her ex-husband were concerned the marriage might have been over, but Leonie was still stuck in the old relationship. Popular songs and poetry are full of stories of love that is strongly held but not returned. Sometimes, the beloved does not even know of their admirer's existence or mistakes the passion for mere friendship. However, most commonly, the beloved did once reciprocate but now rejects the love. Whatever the background, people suffering from unrequited love still cannot move on – even though they know the situation is hopeless.

What love on the rebound and unrequited love have in common is that the relationship has not reached a proper ending. To learn, to recover and to move on properly, we need to go through a grieving process. In effect, someone who loves on the rebound is trying to skip the grief, while someone suffering from unrequited love has become stuck with their grief. So how do you reach a proper ending? How do you mourn for your loss?

Five Stages of Grief

These were originally outlined by the Swiss-born psychiatrist Elisabeth Kübler-Ross who wrote the seminal book *On Death and Dying* (Simon & Schuster, 1969). She had been working with terminally ill patients in New York and noticed that they moved through five stages: denial, anger, bargaining, depression and acceptance. Although Kübler-Ross's prime aim was to help doctors approach the dying with sensitivity and understanding, her stages have been appropriated wholesale into bereavement counselling. In my opinion, this is a pity. Five stages make grief appear easier than it is in reality. Stages suggest phases of a journey, something manageable to work through one bit at a time. If only it was that simple. In my experience, it is perfectly possible to experience all the emotions in Kübler-Ross's five stages in one day. For me, grief is more like a pack of wild animals: sometimes lying low in the forest, sometimes stalking and occasionally going for the throat. However, over time these beasts can be approached, tamed and house-trained. With that note of caution, the five stages *are* useful for coming to terms with loss – whether through death, divorce or relationship breakdown – because they show that our feelings are natural, healthy and very human.

Here are the five stages:

1 *Denial*

The first response to bad news is numbness: 'No, it can't be happening to me.' Denial is like a buffer against the shock. It provides us with a breathing space to collect our thoughts, our coping strategies and gather our supporters.

2 *Anger*

The evidence is impossible to ignore. Finally, the truth dawns: 'Oh yes, it really is happening.' The next emotion is anger: 'Why me?' 'What have I done?' Generally, there are two kinds of anger. The first makes complete sense – after all, we are very hurt – and is normally aimed at our partners (for betraying our love and trust) and ourselves (either for our mistakes or not spotting the seriousness earlier). I call this kind: rational anger. The second sort of anger, however, is completely different. Although we need to be angry, we dare not show it to our partners (especially if we are trying to persuade them to stay). Instead, the feelings are dumped onto someone else. For example, the person who told us that our partner had been cheating, the other man or woman in the triangle, or our partner's family for 'encouraging' the break-up. I call this kind: irrational anger.

3 *Bargaining*

All the anger has changed nothing. So the coping strategies begin. As children, we learnt that demanding something seldom brings what we want. So we tried asking nicely, being on our best behaviour or volunteering to do something in return for having our wishes granted. In many ways, grief turns us into small children again: not in control of our destiny. So it is not surprising that we regress and try to strike a bargain: 'just let me live long enough to see the birth of my grandchild', 'please stay for my fortieth birthday celebrations' or 'let's make wild passionate love and pretend everything is OK'. Bargaining is fine in the short term but all it does is postpone the inevitable.

4 *Depression*
Still nothing has changed and we sink into depression. However, it is important to stress that depression can be a healthy part of mourning. If we can allow depression to teach us – rather than blank it out with drink, chocolate and other coping strategies – it will become a vital part of our recovery. There are two elements to depression. The first, Kübler-Ross called reactive: a natural response to loss. The second is preparatory and is linked with the part of depression where people retreat into themselves and want to do nothing but pull the duvet over their head or sit silently on the sofa. Shutting down and retreating from the clutter of everyday life allows us to concentrate our brain power into problem-solving. In effect, we need to imagine an end before we can cope with it and breaking down the problem is a necessary part of building something new.

5 *Acceptance*
Once the anger and the depression has been worked through, we come to the reward. We might not want the relationship to end but will finally accept the inevitable. Although there was hope in some of the previous stages, it has been a flickering candle and easily blown out; during acceptance the flame shines brightly. Sometimes there are set-backs – like visiting somewhere that provokes memories – but generally we spend more time looking into the future than remembering the past.

These Stages of Grief are equally applicable whether you wanted to end the relationship or not – but each party experiences them slightly differently. If you instigated the break-up/divorce, the denial stage is probably longer. For Carrie, fifty-six, who ended her thirty-year marriage, it was like waking up from a long sleep: 'I remember looking round the family dinner table one Christmas and knowing I could not do this for another year. Suddenly, I realised that I had been fooling myself. My husband would never change and the relief, it flooded through me. It was only then that I understood just how sad I had been.' Like many people who wanted a divorce Carrie was surprised by the depression that followed. 'My husband did everything to hold on to me. But in the end, I just thought – you can have the house. I want to be free. So I thought I'd be celebrating my decree nisi but when it arrived in the post, I just sat at the bottom of the stairs and wept.' Although she had longed for the divorce, she still needed to mourn. 'I was down for a long time – like there was a barrier between me and the rest of the world. But I suppose that it had to happen, I'd been really pumped up with adrenaline from all the fighting and when it was over I deflated quicker than a balloon.' Eventually, Carrie was able to look back at this period of depression as valuable. 'I suppose I needed to lick my wounds and it was probably better to stay at home and recover than to go out partying.'

For the person who is left, the anger often lasts longer – especially if their partner has been unfaithful – and the ensuing depression phase involves a greater sense of being betrayed. Mark, twenty-eight, speaks for a lot of people: 'I would have done anything for Francesca but it was never enough. I just think of those hours retiling the bathroom, lining up the patterns, and afterwards all she said was "nice". I lost it but she just stood there calmly and said, "You can't guilt me into staying." When I think about her with anybody else, I have this knot inside my stomach and I fear it's never going to go away.' In some ways it is harder to grieve when you have been divorced, rather than bereaved, as the rejection is more personal and the ending less final.

What Holds People Back?

The stages are not a simple ladder to climb one rung at a time. There will be times when you find yourself retreating back into denial or bargaining – this is perfectly normal. Sometimes you will think that you have reached acceptance only to hear some news – like your ex has someone new – and feel cast back to the bottom of the ladder. However each time you slip back, the fall will be softer and the climb back easier. The main problem is getting stuck in either the anger or the depression phase. Here are some of the most common scenarios that make the recovery process tougher:

Not Wanting to Hurt the Other Person

Breaking up is a dirty business, and sadly it is impossible to do it painlessly. Sometimes the partner who wants to leave will hold back the news until after an important event – like a holiday together. However, once the other party finds out, this just increases the pain or provides another thing to be angry about. Returning to Liza, the writer who had trouble recovering from an abusive boyfriend, she had tried to keep things civil. So she included his name on round-robin emails which told friends when her plays were being performed. Naturally, he turned up to watch them. When I questioned whether this was wise, Liza replied: 'He won't think that he's a friend, because I kiss friends on the cheeks and I made a pointed decision not to kiss him.' I doubt he would have registered such a subtle rejection.

Tip: Ultimately, it is kinder to be direct with your ex. Otherwise throw-away comments to ease the pain – 'who knows what the future brings' or 'maybe one day' – can be misinterpreted as hopeful.

Trying to be Friends Too Soon

Nearly every couple that I counsel who decide to separate vow to stay friends. This is a laudable goal – especially if you have children – but hard to pull off. Mark and Francesca had been at university together and had a large circle of shared friends. 'It seemed natural to invite her to my birthday celebration at a local restaurant,' says Mark, 'except I got upset because she wouldn't sit next to me. She sat near the door and left straight after the cake. It sort of ruined the evening.' They originally separated because of Francesca's affair, and when that ended, Mark helped her move into a new flat. When Francesca had a problem with her boiler, he would drop everything and fix it. 'It took me a long time to realise that while Francesca was making a new life for herself, I was looking for signs that we could go back to the old one.'

Tip: It is a big leap from lover to friend and it is impossible to make the transition overnight. So take a three-month break before meeting up again. If you have children, contact is inevitable, but keep it down to factual exchanges about your kids.

Fighting Over 'A Matter of Principle'

This is normally a sign that one or both partners is trying to punish the other and looking for the courts to prove their 'goodness' and their ex-partner's 'badness'. This is nearly always a dead-end and only increases the pain. It is far better to be rational, try to solve old arguments and contain new ones. This is especially important when there are children. Victoria and Scott would argue about the drop-off time for their six-year-old daughter. 'If I don't get her back on the dot,' explained Scott, 'Victoria goes off the deep end, but I don't want to spend my special day with my daughter constantly looking at my watch. It's my time and, within reason, I should be able to bring her back when it suits.' Victoria, of course, saw things differently: 'She needs her routine. Not Daddy bringing her back at all hours and being tired and grumpy the next day. If I phone and ask where they are, Scott gets huffy and hangs up.' Unfortunately, neither partner was prepared to budge and their arguments moved from time-keeping to the amount of access.

Tip: Arguments are easier to resolve if you deal with one issue at a time. To stop yourself moving on to another problem, before finishing the first, put an elastic band round your wrist. When you are on the phone to your ex-partner and feel the temptation to say 'and another thing . . .', ping the band. The small moment of pain will distract you for long enough to break the habit. Afterwards make a note of your issue and think of bringing it up another time. Often, however, it is not really that important.

Obsessing

The relationship might be over but one partner is determined to stay in the life of the other – if only at a distance. This includes behaviour like phoning and hanging up, driving past their home or meeting up with mutual friends in order to elicit snippets of information. Danielle, twenty-nine, went even further: 'I would Google him to see if there was anything new, I knew his email password so I'd read his mail and I'd do other web-stalking-type stuff.' She worked at the same company as her ex – albeit at different branches – and so shared a staff Christmas party. 'It was like a military operation. I spent weeks dieting, exercising and shopping for the "look what you're missing" dress. You should have seen his face. We ended up back at his place and it was incredible. Except the next morning, nothing had changed. I'd thought it was make-up sex but for him it was break-up sex.' Ultimately, obsessing takes up so much energy there is no room in your life for anything else.

Tip: Next time you feel the need to 'check up' on your ex or indulge in other obsessive behaviour, stop. What is the feeling that you are trying to prevent? Is it anger or depression? What is your fear? Remember, these distractions are holding you back from healing and the opportunity to reach acceptance.

Revenge

In this scenario, there is no shortage of anger. Except one partner is using it to bypass the depression and head straight for acceptance. Typical strategies include sleeping with your ex's best friend, spreading rumours, smashing up prized property or refusing access to the children or a shared pet. 'I thought if only I could hurt Callum as much as he hurt me, I'd feel better,' explained Kate, twenty-nine. She had found that he was selling his house and posed as a possible buyer. 'I was deliberately only available when he was at work so that I would be taken round by the estate agent. When she was on her phone, I tore up a couple of pictures, rearranged the fridge magnets into a swear word and poured mouthwash onto his mattress – so it would look like he'd peed in his bed. I went home cackling – even though he will have guessed that it was me.' Although Kate claimed the revenge made her feel good, with a little probing she soon admitted that it made her also hate herself.

Tip: Revenge not only encourages the other party to reciprocate – which further pumps up our anger – but binds us to our ex for even longer. So next time you're tempted, try the opposite and do something nice – like returning some treasured possession. In the long term, it will make you feel better.

Hopeless Devotion

Even though the relationship is dead – or without any viable future – one half is still holding on with both hands. These people get a perverse pleasure from the tragic elements of lost love, for example: re-reading old love letters, playing songs that remind them of their beloved or watching weepie black-and-white movies. 'Our love was pure, a shining beacon in the mediocrity of everyday life,' explained Cassandra, fifty-two. 'Halfway through our first week-end together, we were sitting at a pavement café – it was the first sunny day of spring – and he said "I can't imagine not being with you". I knew I'd never heard truer words and we toasted them with champagne.' However, six months later, her lover's firm posted him back to Egypt. Cassandra wanted to follow, but discovered he had a wife and children. It was a tough blow and her friends were initially supportive, but six years later have lost patience. Especially if the relationship was reasonably short-lived, it is better to learn from it and move on.

Tip: In therapy, I often find people with hopeless devotions are more attached to the fantasy of perfect love than the real flesh-and-blood person. So how do you move on? Make a deal with yourself not to feed the fantasy. Stop listening to 'special songs' and put treasured items in a drawer or into the loft. If you start day-dreaming about 'if only' scenarios, divert yourself by doing something vigorous like scrubbing the kitchen floor or occupy your brain with a crossword puzzle.

Five Practical Ways of Moving On

After looking at endings in theory and how they can go wrong, here are some simple practical steps through the grief process. I have illustrated them with an example from my case book.

1 Find an Explanation for the Relationship Ending

Graham, twenty-six, had been constantly obsessing about why his girlfriend of four years had split up with him, taken him back, cheated on him and finally finished the relationship for the second time. The pain had become so bad he told me: 'I could drive off a cliff just to get away from it.' Throughout our session, he kept coming back to the same question: 'How could she do it to me?' Especially as he believed: 'I did everything to make her happy.' It became clear that until we could answer this central question, Graham was stuck. 'Graham and his girlfriend Martina's backgrounds could not have been more contrasting. His parents had been happily married for almost thirty years. Her father had been an alcoholic and her mother had mental health issues. Graham's grandmother summed up the situation very neatly: 'lovely girl, but can't bring herself to settle down.' Martina's most revealing comment about her relationship was to Graham's mum: 'the bubble is going to burst'. Although his mum tried to reassure her that her son was 'not like that', Martina's life experience told her differently. If Martina's base-line was mildly pessimistic, Graham's was wildly optimistic: 'I could see what she could be.'

After much discussion, Graham decided that the relationship ended because 'we wanted different things'. Contrasting her casual infidelity with his fierce loyalty, he finally admitted: 'we had different values'. From this point onwards, when Graham found himself worrying about the relationship – for example, asking: 'Why was it always me who would text first to say "I love you"?' – he had a built-in answer. This allowed him to deal quickly with random thoughts about his ex, rather than spiralling down into obsession or depression.

2 Give Yourself Time

Nobody wants to accept this ingredient for healing. We all want to put the pain behind us as quickly as possible; surely a weekend should be enough? Unfortunately, recovery always takes longer than we expect. Graham needed ten months to find enough distance to understand his relationship with Martina properly. Like a lot of people who have been through a painful break-up, Graham had dated someone for a few weeks. Fortunately, he recognised that he was not really interested in this new girl, although she was keen, and he ended the relationship. Not only is it unfair to use someone else as a temporary 'feel-good' fix or as a 'security' blanket but the inevitable second break-up will bring even more pain. Looking back over twenty-five years of counselling people through marital break-ups, the cases with the most debilitating pain involve someone throwing themselves into a rebound relationship. The inevitable crash seems to triple the sense of failure, isolation and depression from the first break-up.

3 Check and Double-check that Enough Time has Passed

Obviously there are no hard-and-fast rules to when you are ready for a new partner. It depends on both the length and seriousness of your previous relationship. However, in general, I advise waiting a year. There is something very therapeutic about passing all the important anniversaries: first birthday alone, their birthday, Christmas etc. If you are having trouble coping, or are not good at waiting, look at what you have learnt. No experience, however wretched, feels quite so bad if you can find something positive. Graham was startled when I asked him about the benefits of his break-up but with a little prompting came up with four answers: he had got to know himself better; he would take future relationships more slowly; he had become stronger; and, finally, that he would stop letting people take advantage of him. As Graham admitted: 'I will often do something for somebody else, even if I don't fancy doing it myself.' Previously he had been very happy to collect people for away squash matches – even though it never seemed to be his turn to be offered a lift. With this knowledge, Graham found a more equitable arrangement with his squash team. Admittedly, he would much rather have had Martina than these personal insights, but Graham had begun to transform his past and put down foundations for his future.

4 Bring New Things into Your Life

If you keep on doing the same old things, you will have the same old life. Starting new interests or pastimes has two clear benefits: firstly, it provides a temporary up-lift and secondly, it fills time which could otherwise have been spent obsessing about an ex. Relationships are very time-consuming and one of the worst side-effects of a break-up is the loneliness of endless empty weekends. Rather than making late-night drunken phone calls to a former lover, or starting a new 'comfort' relationship, fill the gap with something positive. Graham had already begun to learn to ride a motorbike and used his Sundays for long rides. He also decided to start playing the guitar. Before beginning my programme, he had not seen these interests as part of his recovery. Neither motorbikes nor guitars are likely routes for meeting women, but this is absolutely the point. These interests are just for you. Something you have always wanted to do but have not had the time or money for before. In this way, you will be nurturing yourself rather than rushing around looking for someone to provide the quick fix of a new romantic relationship.

5 Learn when to Listen to the Voice in your Head and when to Distract Yourself

Even with an explanation for your break-up and incorporating the other 'moving on' steps, you will still be ambushed by thoughts about your ex. Graham was making good progress and had certainly stopped wallowing in the past. However, he arrived at our fourth session complaining that he had spent most of the week thinking about Martina. None of his usual distraction techniques – like going for a motorbike ride – had worked. In these circumstances, I normally find that the internal voice is there for a reason. In other words, it is trying to tell us something – unfortunately the message is normally overwhelmed by a lot of over-analysing.

As we talked over the week, Graham explained that Martina's mother had died. He had been trying to decide whether to text his condolences to Martina or not. What would happen if he did? If she texted back, it would just open up the old wounds and if she did not reply, he would be depressed. So Graham decided to do nothing. I probed further, was there anything else? He was worried that Martina might have a few drinks on Saturday night, get maudlin and call him. (It was how they got back together after their first break-up.) What were his options? He decided to switch off his mobile on Saturday night. Graham's internal voice had, indeed, good reason for communicating. For advice on sorting out the important questions from just obsessing, see 'How to Listen Effectively to Your Inner Voice' in the exercise section.

Boost Your Self-confidence

If the end of a significant relationship has undermined your self-confidence – or maybe it was never great in the first place – it will take time to get back onto an even keel. The following eight stages, taken gradually, will stop the rot, provide a more balanced picture and aid recovery.

1 *Stop putting yourself down.* It is amazing how many people litter their conversation with phrases like 'this is probably not a good idea' or manage to both arrive somewhere and dismiss themselves with: 'it's only me'. Listen to other people's conversations and gather more examples, then commit to exorcising them from your vocabulary.

2 *Don't compare yourself.* There are always people who seem to find life easy and radiate confidence. But you can never know

what is really going on their heads – they might just be good actors. Conversely, there might even be people who envy you! Ultimately, comparing yourself with others is a dead-end so concentrate on your own journey.

3 *Reframe your thoughts*. Change the negative into something more positive. Instead of 'I can't . . .' or 'I won't . . .' (for example, trust anyone ever again) substitute 'I choose to . . .' (spend time with my friends at the moment or take up a foreign language).

4 *Imagine what you want rather than don't want*. We often know what we're trying to avoid – like being lonely – but have a more hazy idea of what we're aiming for.

5 *Set small and realistic goals*. Change is frightening and fear makes us close up, retreat and consider ourselves failures. In contrast, small and easily achieved steps bypass fear and help us feel successful.

6 *Be patient*. Nothing of any value is achieved overnight.

7 *Don't give up*. There will always be obstacles. The difference between people who make it and those who fall by the wayside is that the former look for a way round the problem or simply try again.

8 *Accept yourself, warts and all*. Don't confuse confidence with being perfect. (For more help, see 'Four Steps to Raising Your Self-esteem' in the exercise section.)

Whenever I counsel people who have come out of a long-term live-in relationship, who are despairing about ever finding love again, I remind them that they already possess some vital skills. They have learnt how to make allowances for another person and have opened enough space to let another person into their life. If they have done it once, they can do it again. In many cases, I discover that they have already started to make new relationships, but have dismissed them because they have not gone the full distance. This is a mistake . . .

The Joy of Mini-relationships

Our society believes that the longer a relationship lasts, the better it must be. However, our obsession with 'happily ever after' and 'till death us do part' makes us overlook the benefits of relationships that are measured in months rather than years. When one of these relationships ends, the people involved often dismiss it as not important or something that happened on the rebound from a serious partnership.

Kara, a 27-year-old marketing executive, is just one of my clients who has benefited from re-evaluating a short-lived relationship. 'I'd been dating this lovely sensitive man for about five months and I really thought "this is it". He worked with problem kids and really knew how to listen, all my friends liked him, but suddenly he became distant and that was it.' Kara's feelings of failure were compounded because her husband had mysteriously disappeared two years previously. Beyond one brief phone call, from the other side of the world, she had no proper explanation about why her marriage had ended. Through counselling, Kara stopped thinking of her relationship with her ex-boyfriend as a 'rebound' and turned the experience into a learning opportunity. 'I decided to call him and have a proper conversation about what had gone wrong. Later, he sent me a wonderful long letter and I suddenly realised this is exactly what I had wanted from my ex-husband. It was very healing and I feel I've really moved on.'

Many other clients talk of the benefits of new ideas and interests gained while getting to know someone. 'I can't have been out with Anthony on more than two dozen dates,' says Rebecca, a 42-year-old teacher, 'but during one of those long conversations when you first meet someone I told him about my ambition to learn to meditate. He was a member of a local Buddhist centre and took me along to a lunch-time session.' Although the relationship with Anthony did not last, she still attends the Bodhisattva Centre. 'It has really helped centre me and I would never have had the courage to attend on my own.' While short-term relationships invariably bring new experiences, many partners in committed relationships are wary – and even hostile – if their other half pursues new interests.

Even when these relationships have little potential for marriage or living together, they are still valuable. Jody, fifty-five, enjoyed the company of Javier, a fifty-year-old hotel manager, but she foresaw obstacles. 'There were three things wrong with him: he had a shocking record collection, was about to be transferred to St Petersburg and, worst of all, he was Spanish,' she explains. 'My late husband had been Spanish and it seemed too painful to return over old ground.' Nevertheless, Jody decided to go ahead and enjoy Javier's last three months in England. 'It was wonderful to taste proper Spanish food and speak the language again; and actually it didn't bring back that many painful memories. I learnt that Spain is a big part of my past and just because my husband died, I don't have to cut myself off from it.'

Looking at successful but short-lived relationships, I discovered that they had several qualities in common. They happen at times of rapid personal growth – for example after a divorce or during an adult education course. With one or both halves changing, the focus is on enjoying the moment – rather than planning for the future or arguing about the past. The cornerstone is always good communication, not just hours of talking but a real emotional honesty. 'I dated this woman who had a great bullshit detector and I bounced all these ideas about myself off her,' says Bruce, a 39-year-old electrical engineer. 'She would tell me what sounded true and when I was just fooling myself.' This openness contrasts with a lot of courting relationships where people present just their best side. To understand this phenomenon, and differentiate from simple dating, it is important to name it. I opted for the term 'mini-relationship' which suggests all the best qualities when two people share their lives, yet still recognises that they seldom last.

But if mini-relationships are so beneficial, why do they end after a few months? Unfortunately, the foundations of a mini-relationship and a committed one are very different. The first is about healing and growth and the second about stability and longevity. People in mini-relationships need to be flexible and experiment with being someone different. Bruce even spelled this out at the beginning of his mini-relationship: 'I told her I needed the relationship to find out who I was.' Many of my clients become different people and what attracted their short-term partners might no longer be there. Bruce's short-term partner, Sylvia, admitted: 'To find that a big strong man needed me was very appealing and I suppose it boosted my confidence too. But after a few months, the passion subsided as he no longer needed me. However, we have managed to keep a friendship and that feels good.' Although it is possible – through intensive discussion – to effectively jack up a mini-relationship and install a new under-carriage, my advice would be to think very carefully. The temporary nature of a mini-relationship is one of its greatest strengths. Bruce certainly found this: 'I didn't have to worry that she would use some of the stuff I told her against me at a later date.' Managing a healthy termination is crucial; trying to go past the relationship's natural sell-by date only causes bitterness and spoils a positive experience.

When my clients understand the concept of mini-relationships, some worry that they have had too many. I am only concerned if someone has been too busy helping their partners heal and ignoring their own needs, or keep facing the same problems without achieving any change. However, most of my clients discover that each mini-relationship has brought a small amount of healing. As many relationship issues stretch back to childhood, it is only natural that several mini-relationships are needed to overhaul the problems.

Think back over the relationships since your break-up. Have you had a mini-relationship or mini-relationships? What did you learn from it? My guess is something that will help in your search for lasting love. However, until you silence your inner critic, which has been listening to wider society's message that long-term is good and short-term bad, you will find it hard to recognise your progress.

Summary

- Love on the rebound compounds the problems of recovering from a break-up.
- When a relationship has truly broken down, it is better to stop striving for an unrealistic ending and make a good job of accepting a real one.
- There are no short-cuts through grief: it takes time, but ultimately you will reach acceptance.
- Some of the things that prevent people from healing and moving on include: trying to be friends too soon, fighting over children or a matter of principle, competing with an ex, and being vengeful.
- Although other people finding you attractive can increase your self-confidence, the most enduring confidence comes from self-knowledge.

Exercises

How to Listen Effectively to Your Inner Voice

1 Write down everything.
   As the thoughts pop up, write them down: no censorship, however ludicrous. Don't try to answer anything, just move on to the next thought. This is what Graham came up with when I did this exercise in one of our sessions.

   Why sleep with someone else?
   How can she be so nasty?
   How can she blame me?
   How can you say you love someone and not mean it?
   Why say something like . . . I didn't used to love you but I love you now?
   Can I ever trust someone again?
   Can I ever talk to someone again?
   How can I have the same feelings for someone?
   All I want is to be happy.
   I used to be so easy-going.

2 Turn statements into questions.
   Sentences like 'All I want is to be happy' and 'I used to be so easy-going', encourage us to feel stuck and hopeless. Instead, turn them into questions:
   How can I be happy?
   How can I be easy-going again?
   Immediately, we have a task and can begin to look for solutions. The second benefit is that you will no longer feel passive or a prisoner of your feelings.

3 Go back and start answering the questions.
   Now the questions are on paper, rather than going round in your head, they are more manageable. Certainly, Graham

found he could answer, in seconds, what had been troubling him for hours. His answers follow the questions.

Why sleep with someone else? She wanted to and didn't think about me.

How can she be so nasty? It is easy to blame someone else.

How can she blame me? See above.

How can you say you love someone and not mean it? Just words.

Why say something like . . . I didn't used to love you but I love you now? See above.

Can I ever trust someone again? Yes.

Can I ever talk to someone again? Yes.

How can I have the same feelings for someone? I don't know but I hope I can.

4 Some questions will need greater thought.
Often underneath all the worry about the relationship ending will be larger questions that tap into larger issues.
In Graham's case they were:
How can I be happy?
How can I be easy-going again?
Graham had answered the previous questions almost spontaneously, these final two took greater thought. Eventually he came up with the following.
Riding my motorbike.
I will meet someone else someday.
There are times when it is OK to lose my patience.
It is part of not letting people take advantage of me.

If you need help, try phoning a friend to talk it over. A lot of people are reluctant to ask for more help, fearing that they have already bored friends by endlessly talking about their ex. However, there is a big difference between rambling on about the past and tightly targeted questions like these.

Doing a Relationship Detox

1 If you have had a lot of short-term relationships, this will help you get off the dating merry-go-round for a while. To take stock, select a picture of each person that you have had a serious relationship with and spread them out in front of you. At first sight each of your X files will seem very different. Most people don't have a type and will have dated people with different looks, jobs and backgrounds. The secret is to uncover the underlying similarities. Here are some common themes:

   • *Extreme dating.* They were all difficult but you enjoyed the challenge or drama of never knowing what to expect.
   • *Comfort dating.* They wrapped you in cotton wool and admired you greatly but, ultimately, they bored you.
   • *Trophy dates.* They impressed your friends but ultimately there was no chemistry.
   • *Wounded birds.* These dates brought out your protective side and make you feel strong, needed or important.
   • *Knights or ladies in shining armour.* They promised to solve your problems or look after you but ended up being controlling.
   • *Social dating.* You might have liked your date, but the real meeting of minds is with her or his family, children or network of friends.

   Be aware that going for the opposite type is not moving on, it is normally playing the same dilemma from a different angle. For example: if you have been cheated on in one relationship, playing fast and loose in the next.

2 What issues keep on coming up over and over again? Is there something that your dating history might be trying to tell you? Rather than jumping into the relationship – and possibly acting out the same problems again – is there another way of tackling these issues?

3 Avoid dating for between three and six months – depending on how stuck you feel. This is especially important if you have a low opinion of yourself. Use the time to repair the damage; this could be reading self-help books, going on a retreat or taking an adult education course. A good way of boosting self-esteem is doing some voluntary work. Offering to fix the guttering for an elderly neighbour or volunteering for a kids' adventure training holiday will not only divert your attention from your own problems but the praise and thanks will make you feel better.

4 Finally break the general patterns: seek new hobbies, interests, go out with different mates or simply change your route to work.

Four Steps to Raising Your Self-esteem

1 *Building on firm foundations*
Look at the following headings:
A part of my body that I like.
An aspect of my personality that I value.
A past achievement.
An aspect of untapped potential.
Get a piece of paper and write down *one* thing under the following headings and then add beside it *one* thing that your best friend would write. Finally add *one* thing that an ethical advertising agency might use to write a contact advert for you. As this is an ethical advertising agency, they can exaggerate but will never tell lies.

If you cannot come up with something for one of the headings, don't worry as this exercise will take some time. Put the paper to one side and ask your best friend to help. The ethical advertising agency will be the hardest but trust that the ideas will come and when you least expect it, they will pop into your head. Ultimately, you will have twelve compliments to boost your self-confidence.

2 *What one thing would you like to change about yourself?*
Close you eyes and really picture what life would be like if you got it. What would you see? How would it feel? Expand the picture and walk around in it. What can you smell? What can you taste? What can you hear? What can you touch? Indulge all your senses.

3 *How can you make this happen?*
First of all make sure that your goal is framed as a positive. For example, instead of 'stop being shy', reframe as 'I want to be happy talking in front of strangers'. Next, ask yourself: How will I know when I have achieved this? It could be 'When I speak up at a meeting at work' or 'When I ask a question at a public lecture/ talk.' Once you have a goal, ask yourself: How could I go about it? For example, reading the agenda for the next staff meeting so that you are fully prepared or researching an author who is coming to your local book festival so you could ask something during the Q&A session. Finally decide what the first step would be. For example, booking a ticket for the talk or volunteering to be co-opted onto a committee at work.

4 *Reward yourself*
Every time you make a small step on the road to your goal, make a note of your achievement and give yourself a reward. It could be a piece of chocolate, spending Sunday morning in bed watching a movie or treating yourself to a gadget or some other luxury. However, it is important to celebrate your successes.

Chapter Five

Getting Ready for Love

When helping clients through my programme, this is often the point where they feel overwhelmed and risk sinking even deeper into the *Single Trap*. Some doubt that they will *ever* find a lasting relationship. However, this is when the hard work begins to pay off. We have reached the positive tipping-point, when the heavy lifting of the last few chapters will begin to pay dividends. There are three key tasks to complete before you are ready for love. The good news is that you have already completed the first task, you are halfway through the second and have probably made a good start on the third. So what are these tasks? They are:

1 Understanding the past.
2 Clearing away current obstacles.
3 Knowing what to look for in the future.

To both recap on how far we have travelled and to help prepare you for the final part of the book, I will share an in-depth story from my case book.

Understanding the Past

At the present point in her journey, Sandy – an attractive 41-year-old with three children in their mid- to late teens – felt exhausted and overwhelmed. She had been divorced for six years and had had a series of relationships that ranged from disappointing to disastrous. She sighed and said to me: 'You must think I am really screwed up.' Actually, I admired her honesty and readiness to look at the messy bits of her life. I could see that underneath the slightly brittle exterior was a resourceful and loyal woman who would make someone a great partner. Sandy had grown up in an all-female household. Her mother was a beautiful but rather vague woman who seemed to be forever in front of a mirror getting ready for her husband's return. Sandy had a younger sister, and a grandmother who lived with them. Her father, a businessman, was away during the week and although he returned on Friday night, spent a lot of the weekend on the golf course. She described her father, who died a few years ago, as: 'jealous, good-looking and lovely'. One of her strongest childhood memories was looking out of the window on Monday mornings: 'it seemed like he was leaving me'. In her father's absence, Sandy was in charge and would fix things round the house. It is not surprising that her expectation was that 'men are always going to leave'.

When listening to Sandy's story, I had been struck by how she saw herself in very black-and-white terms: the 'nice school-girl' who at sixteen became the 'aggressive shoplifter'; in her marriage, 'the happy devoted mum' who felt moulded by her husband (frequently away) and became a 'good-time girl with a hangover who couldn't get out of bed in the morning'. Sandy's last two relationships seemed, on the surface, to be completely different. As she said: 'I have a different personality with every man.' The first man had been very laid-back and this brought out the opposite in Sandy. 'I'd got crazy jealous because he didn't seem to care and I became very insecure. So I'd do terrible things to get his attention, like sleeping with other men and hitting him.' The second man was incredibly jealous and would go through her mobile phone checking her messages. 'I didn't really mind,' said Sandy, 'that was the sort of thing I used to do. So I understood.' Unfortunately, he would also get drunk at parties and accuse other men of paying her too much attention. On one occasion, he got into a fight with six bouncers outside a night-club and the police were called. As Sandy explained: 'I became like one of those terrible women you see in TV documentaries about binge-drinking screaming over and over: "don't do it, don't do it".' He had promised to change and Sandy was thinking about letting him back into her house and her life. Why? 'With a jealous guy, I can be laid-back. No paranoid mornings or waking up drunk, I can be OK,' she explained. These might have been two different relationships but the dynamics were the same. In one relationship, Sandy played the 'jealous' role and in the other, the 'innocent' one.

When Sandy finished her story, I helped her look at how the pieces of the story fitted together. By understanding her relationship with her father, she began to make sense of her behaviour and stopped feeling, as she put it, like a 'freak'. She also began to question her own black-and-white thinking. Finally, she was ready to accept that she was not 'bad', but someone with a difficult childhood who had made some poor choices – a much greyer interpretation. We were ready for the next phase of 'Getting Ready for Love'.

Clearing Away Current Obstacles

Sandy was using her relationships to prop up her poor self-image. Indeed, the former boyfriend begging for a second chance had done wonders. 'I don't think he realised how much he loved me until it was too late,' she said with a half-smile, probably entertaining private daydreams about saving him from his demons. However, relationships are difficult enough without the added strain of propping up low self-esteem. What's more, there are other, and better, ways of feeling good about yourself. It was as though a lightbulb had come on above Sandy's head. 'A new boyfriend might make me feel attractive, and good about myself, but it only works in the short term. If he doesn't phone, or we have an argument, my self-esteem drops through the floor. So really a new relationship is a rather high-risk strategy.'

In fact, there are millions of other ways of improving self-esteem. For example, walking the length of Hadrian's Wall, having a painting accepted for a local art exhibition, running a half-marathon, getting an Open University degree or just simply shopping for an elderly neighbour. It is all a matter of taste and interest. Sandy had already gone back to work, expressly to improve her self-image, and had found a responsible and interesting position – an achievement for someone who had been out of the job market bringing up children. Our goal was to find other interests or projects to build on this positive development.

For Graham, the 26-year-old recovering from a painful relationship in the previous chapter, his obstacle was that people took advantage of him. Although Graham was a joint business partner with his brother, he would often be treated like an employee. After some discussion in counselling, Graham took a stand over something quite small – consulting each other about lunch breaks – but it made a fundamental difference to their relationship and helped Graham value himself as someone whose opinions should be consulted and taken into consideration. This was the final piece of the jigsaw and a few months later Graham started dating again: 'She is a really nice girl. I can't tell you the difference. Instead of me doing all the running, she's just as likely to phone up and suggest doing something. When I had to cry off one Sunday, because we were giving the business a thorough cleaning, she offered to help out. It was brilliant.' For other people, the current obstacle is even more practical. Patricia is my partner's cousin and we were invited round to her house. I was immediately greeted by two boisterous spaniels who leapt all over the place. She had a small gate between her hall and the open-plan living room, the sort used to stop small children falling downstairs. She closed the gate, keeping the spaniels in the hall, and we sat down for a beer and a chat. I could tell from all the hairs on the sofa that the dogs were allowed up there, but I was not prepared for the anarchy that was about to be unleashed. The dogs had been whimpering to be let through and Patricia could not concentrate on our conversation, so she removed the gate. Now it was impossible to talk as the dogs were bouncing all over us, trying to lick our faces. I like dogs, and have one myself, but these spaniels were impossible. Patricia had asked me over because she was interested in my work with single people. She had just, inadvertently, shown me her current obstacle. 'How do your boyfriends feel about your dogs?' I asked. 'They hate them,' replied Patricia. 'I had one who preferred to rent a hotel room when we wanted to make love.' She showed me her bedroom and although there were two dog-baskets, the spaniels slept with her. Worse still, the male dog sometimes got aggressive with men who shared the bed. I am not an animal behaviourist but these dogs were out of control. From one look at my face, Patricia could tell what I was thinking. 'If you guarantee me that I'll find a man, I'll learn to train my dogs,' Patricia said. 'There's one thing I can guarantee,' I replied, 'if you don't train the dogs you'll *never* get a man.'

However, for most people the obstacle is an attitude – normally so deeply ingrained that they are not really aware of it. Here are five of the most common ones:

1 *Love as a Saviour*
   The power of love to solve our problems runs through most fiction and movies. Edmund White, one of America's foremost contemporary writers, probably best sums up this idea in his autobiography *My Lives* when he describes a returned smile from his beloved: 'For a moment I'd imagined I'd been pro- moted into a higher order of humanity by this lap-swimming, Latin-reading blond giant.' He was no longer an awkward teenager – with an unresponsive father and a desperate mother – but one of the chosen. Although love can help us temporarily forget our problems, there is no simple, lasting, transforming fix. We remain ourselves, which if you really think about it is ultimately rather reassuring.

2 *You Have to be Fabulous*
Behind all the cosmetics, gym and beauty culture is one message rammed home in a thousand oblique ways, so that nobody actually has to articulate it: buy this product, work that body and you too will be supremely loveable. Yet in the muddy trenches of everyday real love – twenty-five years of counselling people with relationship problems – I am regularly reminded that ordinary couples fall in love, struggle and reclaim love; plain couples too; even downright ugly ones. Yet reading the life stories of famous men and women celebrated the world over for their beauty, you discover time and again that perfection does not guarantee love. It's all down to character, truthfulness and true grit. Of course, if you belong to the small proportion of the population who have never worried about their appearance, it is worth getting advice on new clothes or a haircut. If going to the gym makes you feel great – go. But for everybody else: don't put off looking for love until you are five pounds lighter, have saved up for that outfit or had that make-over. Recently, a friend showed me a picture of herself taken ten years before and said: 'If only I'd realised how fabulous I looked.' Don't wait for ten years to pass and look back, you are good enough today!

3 *Comparison Culture*
Our society has become obsessed with making comparisons. Half the pleasure of an exotic holiday is not going there, but making friends envious. All too often, partners are not valued for themselves but for how they make us appear. Worse still, we look at someone whose partner has the qualities currently in demand and wonder what he or she has that we lack. Instead of worrying about other people's opinions, concentrate on what you consider loveable.

4 *The One*
This belief is almost beyond rational, but perhaps love is the triumph of belief over reality. In this world view there

is just *one* perfect person out there for us. What if they are out tonight and we miss them? What if they have already fallen for someone else? Worse still, what if they are not returning our calls? It is enough to put even the sanest person under intolerable pressure. Trust me, there are lots of potential partners waiting to meet you. I can speak from personal experience. After my first partner died, when I was in my thirties, I thought I'd never find love like that again. In my forties, I fell in love again. It is different, but just as good.

5 It's Everybody Else's Fault

It is very easy to look around and complain about other people's behaviour. However this is just a defence mechanism that stops us looking at ourselves. In therapy, I often discover that my clients are guilty of the very same behaviour themselves. An example is Georgia, thirty-eight, who arrived at my office and declared: 'When I meet a single man over thirty, I ask myself: What's wrong with him?' 'Why should there be something wrong with him'? I asked. 'If he was any good, some woman would have snapped him up,' she replied defensively. It took several weeks before she opened up and admitted that she felt that there was something 'wrong' with her and that it was making her single. This was an important breakthrough: instead of being scornful and dismissive about possible partners' failings – something that she could not change, Georgia had begun to look at herself – something that she *could* change.

Having cleared away the obstacles – whether from attitudes, emotional issues or lifestyle – we can move to the third part of 'Getting Ready for Love'.

Knowing What to Look for in the Future

Rebecca is thirty-eight and desperate to find love. She admits: 'If I'm forty and still single, I'll throw myself under a train.' However, her record with men is poor. Her most recent serious boyfriend was Adam, a 42-year-old TV producer. He was exciting and great company, but totally unpredictable. His work meant he would phone up at the last minute and cancel. 'He would totally mess with my head. For example, he'd claim that he had to go to Manchester but would be spotted at a neighbourhood bar on his way to football. When I told him I knew, he just laughed. I didn't mind so much the cancelling, just that I could not trust him.' They had started dating two days after he split up from his previous girlfriend who had helped him through cancer, which had thankfully gone into remission. 'On the very day that he cancelled on me for football, I discovered that he had fixed up to go out with her too – as friends,' explains Rebecca. Despite feeling extraordinarily let down, Rebecca continued with the relationship for another six months. 'He was older and sensible and sometimes told me truthful things. Like, just because I don't phone, it doesn't mean I'm not thinking about you.'

The boyfriend before that was called Daniel. They had been friends for many years but dated for nine months. 'He is the step-brother of one of my sister's ex-husbands – it's sort of complicated. He was really vulnerable and very sweet but he had all these demons. I tried to save him, but I couldn't and he has slipped further into depression and alcohol problems.' Another boyfriend, Harry, was a tour guide on an overland truck journey that she had made through South America. They had paired off during the trip and seen each other on and off since he'd returned to London. 'He was a loner and fiercely independent. He would ignore me during the day, really cold and rejecting, but cuddle up to me in the evening round the camp fire. Later, he explained that he thought it wrong to give me special treatment during the day – because it would be unfair on the other clients. I just wish he'd told me at the time, so I could have understood.' Rebecca explained that Harry's mother had left home when he was thirteen and his father had met another woman when Harry was fifteen and moved out too. After that, Harry had lived alone. So it was not surprising that he found it hard to trust someone enough to let them get close to him. Rebecca's first relationship had been at twenty during a university exchange in America. Jay had been another exciting and glamorous lover but he had also two-timed her. Finally, her longest relationship had been with Alexander. They had dated for two years when Rebecca was in her late twenties: 'He worked in IT and he was really normal. His parents were still married and lived in Dorset. However, I was least into him of all my boyfriends. That's probably why it lasted longest – because I was relaxed and grounded. The problem was that I had no desire. He was really patient and I saw my doctor but nothing really worked. I thought I could really trust him but he cheated on me and dumped me.' Shortly after his relationship with Rebecca ended, Alexander had got married.

To help Rebecca process her relationship history and learn what might work better for her, I drew up a Relationship Tree where each lover is represented by a branch and the observations about the relationship are clustered around like leaves (see the diagram opposite).

Rebecca's name was written on the trunk and each of the boyfriends was associated with adjectives or short descriptions. At the end of the session, I wrote Rebecca's overarching need at the roots of the tree. We will come to that later. But what was Rebecca's reaction when she saw her past mapped out like this? She immediately saw some important themes: 'I've tended to choose exciting men – but actually they have been either unavailable or untrustworthy or very distant, or all three.' The only exception had been Alexander who was very safe (until she had driven him away); however he was so safe that there was no real attraction. Rebecca had recognised the two extremes of her dating pattern. In the future, she decided, it would be better to aim for somewhere in the middle.

Remembering the central concept for this section of the book *like attracts like* (if you are in a good place you will attract people in a

alone since 15

cold

distance

depressive

alcoholic

American

distance

best friend

Harry

lack of trust

Jay

Daniel

ex-girlfriend around

husband material

untrustworthy

no desire

Adam

Alexander

cheated

cancer

Rebecca

marriage and children

similarly good place, if you are ill at ease with yourself you will attract people who are equally uneasy). What else could Rebecca learn about herself? She immediately grasped the idea: 'I can see the match with Daniel as I've had problems with depression and while he had problems with alcohol, I had problems with food.' Fortunately, she had sorted out her borderline eating disorder and had not attracted that kind of man since. This discovery increased her confidence and she admitted that killing herself if she was still single at forty was 'too dramatic'. However, it did lead her to the overarching need (to put on the roots of my diagram): marriage and children.

So Are You Ready?

Before we move on to the final part of the book, which looks at how to find love, it is worth pausing to take stock and checking that you have completed the three phases of 'Getting Ready for Love'. Do you feel that you understand your past relationships? Have you cleared away the current obstacles? Do you know what kind of man or woman to look for in the future? To these questions, I would add one more question: Do you feel bitter, angry or resentful? If the answer is yes, you may need some time out from relationships. So consider 'Doing a Relationship Detox' in the exercise section of Chapter Four. In the long run, it will be worth the extra effort. Take Mike, who is thirty-eight and had a string of unsatisfactory relationships after his wife left him: 'One night I was flicking through all the profiles on an online dating site and thinking of signing up but I had this sudden thought: What's to stop the same thing happening all over again?' So he decided to stop, analyse his behaviour and find a different approach. 'I had been seeing friends of friends or women I met through work not because I wanted a partner but to get out of the house and ease the loneliness. So after watching ballroom dancing on the TV, I decided to take lessons. Just to relax and have fun. They were a great crowd and although one woman was interested, I was only lukewarm and worried that if things went wrong it would make classes awkward. And anyway she started to put on all this pressure – invitations to dinner and "wouldn't you like to go to see this movie". I began to feel that we ought to be lovers even though it was not something that I really wanted. It reminded me that this was how I drifted into my marriage. I didn't want to let my wife down! Anyway, this woman and I remained friends and occasional dancing partners but then six months later I went to a big ball and met this gorgeous woman. The rest, as they say, is history.' In effect, Mike had understood his past relationships, cleared away his current obstacles and discovered the type of relationship that he really wanted. However, Mike had the benefit of therapy to probe deeply and bring hidden patterns up to the surface. In order to help you achieve something similar, I need to help you find a way down into your unconscious. This is easier if approached at an angle, rather than head-on, so the next section might seem odd, but be patient.

Unlocking Your Secret Love Agenda

From the beginning of time, mankind has been fascinated by stories, not just as entertainment but as a way to make sense of the world. What is most extraordinary is that the oldest surviving manuscript – found by the explorer Henry Layard in 1839 under a mound of sand in the desert of Mesopotamia – would be instantly recognised today. *The Epic of Gilgamesh* is about a society threatened by a great evil. The source is traced to a distant underground cavern and the hero, Gilgamesh, arms himself with a mighty axe and sets off to save mankind. When the hero meets the evil mastermind, Humbaba, they have a series of taunting exchanges. Gilgamesh is captured but somehow overcomes extraordinary odds, makes a thrilling escape and kills the monster. Gilgamesh has saved the world and can return home triumphant. Although this story was found in the remains of one of the earliest cities built by mankind (biblical Nineveh), we are still watching it today at our local multiplex – for example, as the latest James Bond movie.

So what has all this got to do with being single? There are two important insights. As every culture, throughout all time, has told the same stories, these plots offer an extraordinary insight into what it means to be human and the problems that come with that territory. (I will go on to explore this idea more in a moment.) The second insight is that as soon as we are old enough to focus on pictures and understand words, we are told stories by our parents. We are literally introduced to the world around us through stories and remain mesmerised for the rest of our lives. And it is not just movies, books and TV drama; documentary-makers, historians, journalists, the producers of 'reality shows' like *Big Brother* are all using the same building blocks to help us process millions of disparate and often contradictory bits of information into one coherent and compelling narrative. In the morning news conference, the editor will even ask his team: What is the story? When we meet friends and catch up on each other's news or gossip, we are trading stories. Every new experience – whether good or bad – will be fitted into a much bigger story: our autobiography. When we meet someone new, we become a character in their ongoing life story – and whether we like it or not, how we are perceived will be coloured by what type of story they are constructing about their life. This is why understanding the stories that we tell ourselves, and others, is a direct route to our unconscious.

One of the most effective ways of decoding stories is using the ideas in a book called *The Seven Basic Plots* by Christopher Booker (Continuum, 2004). The author believes that understanding stories provides an insight not only into our own lives but helps us understand the world around us. So what are these seven basic plots?

1 *Overcoming the Monster*
Ordinary life comes under a terrible shadow. A young hero emerges who overcomes extraordinary odds, defeats the mon-

ster and emerges a wiser, stronger and more mature person. Society as a whole has benefited and everyone is safe again.

Examples: The Epic of Gilgamesh, Jaws, Star Wars, Jack and the Beanstalk.

Who might use the plot?: Someone who has come out the other side of a damaging relationship or an addiction problem (where the monster is in some way their own behaviour).

2 *Rags to Riches*
An ordinary person, dismissed by everyone else, takes centre-stage and is revealed to be someone very special. This is perhaps one of the most popular plots.

Examples: Cinderella, Pretty Woman (in effect, *Cinderella* for the 1980s), *Cocktail* (this Tom Cruise movie puts a man into the Cinderella role), *The Ugly Duckling, Aladdin* or *Jane Eyre.*

Who might use the plot?: Anyone who feels that love will transform their lives but is waiting for someone to come along and raise them up or inspire them.

3 *The Quest*
A hero or heroine learns of a priceless goal, worth any effort to achieve. He or she leaves home and sets off on a perilous journey. Whatever happens on the way, whatever distractions, the story cannot be resolved until he or she reaches the goal.

Examples: Lord of the Rings, The Odyssey, Watership Down.

Who might use the plot?: Anyone who has been actively looking for love – the ultimate priceless goal in many stories – rather than waiting for someone to 'save' them.

4 *Voyage and Return*
Rather than deliberately setting off on a quest, the hero finds himself or herself in a strange world and has many thrilling adventures but eventually decides to return home again. Generally, the hero has not been outwardly changed by their adventures.

Examples: Alice in Wonderland (Alice falls down the rabbit hole and later wakes up and considers it all a dream), *The Wizard of Oz* (Dorothy is blown to Oz by a hurricane but does at least learn that there is 'no place like home'), *Gone with the Wind, The Tale of Peter Rabbit.*

Who might use the plot?: Someone who has been on a lot of exciting or horrifying dates but remains basically the same person.

5 Comedy

This is a particular plot – not just a funny story – and is instantly recognisable today as the genre of movie called romantic comedy. The roots, however, go all the way back to Ancient Greek drama. Two true lovers are separated by either circumstances (traditionally parents who disapprove of the union) or misunderstandings between the lovers. Things go from bad to worse and it seems the lovers will never come together. At the last moment, the obstacles are overcome, and not only are the couple united but their families and their community celebrate.

Examples: The books of Jane Austen (who revolutionised the genre by introducing the idea that the obstacle might partly be the character of the hero(ine) not just outside forces), *The Importance of Being Earnest, Some Like It Hot, Notting Hill, My Big Fat Greek Wedding.*

Who might use the plot?: Anyone whose love story has hit a stumbling block will look for ways to overcome the obstacles created by other people or the misunderstandings arising from not truly knowing each other's feelings.

6 Tragedy

This plot has been called comedy with an unhappy ending, and the shape of the two story types are remarkably similar. In both plots, a wider society is under a shadow because someone is thinking only about themselves and their own needs or opinions. In tragedy, it is normally the hero(ine) who is causing the problem. He or she has some good qualities but also a fatal flaw. Although things might go well for a while, eventually the obstacles get greater and greater. Unlike in comedy, these problems are not overcome. The hero fails to learn or change until it is too late and meets an unhappy ending (normally death). However, society learns something and is cleansed by the experience.

Examples: Othello (there are many of the misunderstandings of a traditional comedy, e.g. dropped handkerchiefs, but they are not resolved and the hero murders the heroine), *Madame Bovary, Anna Karenina, Bonnie and Clyde.*

Who might use the plot?: Anyone who gets a perverse pleasure out of a doomed love affair, and certainly falling for a married man/woman follows this plot, with the heroine/hero nearly always ending up alone.

7 Rebirth

A dark shadow has been cast over the hero. For a while, danger might be comfortably remote but eventually it consumes everything, until the hero is almost experiencing a living death. However, at the very last moment, the hero is redeemed by someone traditionally considered less powerful, perhaps a child, an old man or a woman, and everybody lives happily ever after.

Examples: *A Christmas Carol* (Scrooge is saved by his compassion for Tiny Tim), *Beauty and the Beast, The Secret Garden* (the spoilt children are redeemed by nature and the boy from the village – considered to be closest to nature – and they eventually redeem their father/guardian), *Sleeping Beauty, The Snow Queen.*

Who might use the plot?: Someone who wants to save their beloved – normally from themselves – but more likely bad habits, debt or emotional problems.

It seems extraordinary that just seven plots can cover all the different permutations that writers can dream up and life throw at us, but it is true. In fact, when a film or a book is disappointing or just seems to end – rather than have a proper resolution – it is generally because the author has tried to break away from these seven basic plots. As Christopher Booker explains, these 'stories present to us what amounts to a kind of ground map of human nature and behaviour, governed by an absolutely consistent set of rules and values. These values, like the archetypal structures which shape stories, are programmed into our unconscious in a way that we cannot modify or control.'

When it comes to real life, it is possible to view events through several different plots at the same time depending on your perspective. The woman who has fallen in love with a married man might look through 'Rebirth'. Her beloved is under the spell of a witch who does not truly love her husband and is therefore ruining his life. She has come along to redeem him and make him truly happy. Meanwhile, the wife would probably view events through 'Overcoming the Monster', with the mistress cast as the monster. The husband might initially be in 'Comedy' and certainly many farces are focused on a man trying to keep his wife and mistress apart. However, from the perspective of people outside the triangle, it will probably be a 'Tragedy'. So look over the seven plots and think about your own autobiography. Did you ever feel that you were living out a story? If so, which ones? If you keep on seeing the same plot-line – over and over – or you expect love to conform to one in particular, this is a useful insight into your subconscious. There is more in the exercise section.

One of the most important messages in Christopher Booker's analysis of the seven plots is that stories provide a guide on how to live. By analysing what heroes need at the beginning of a story, what they gain through their adventures and why some stories turn into tragedy, we can learn what makes the good life. So what are the lessons coded into all stories?

1 At the beginning of every story, the hero lacks something.
2 The hero is in some way unbalanced.
3 In a Comedy, what the hero lacks is in some way represented by the heroine. He has to learn her value so they can be united and become one balanced whole.
4 In a Tragedy, the hero keeps on becoming more and more unbalanced until nothing can save him/her. The hero ends up alone or dead.
5 In The Quest and Overcoming the Monster, the prized object, defeating evil or lessons learnt on the journey will balance the hero.
6 In Rags to Riches and Rebirth, the hero emerges from the shadows and either society or the hero himself/herself has a more balanced view.
7 The story ends happily when everyone, and society in general, has reached balance.

So what do I mean by balance? This is where I need to bring in the theories of Carl Jung, one of the founding fathers of psychology, who studied myths and legends and believed that, like dreams, they offer an insight into the dark corners of our minds. (After all, these stories survive and thrive because they resonate strongly with something inside us.) Jung concluded that a happy and fulfilled person is in touch with two very different parts of their psyche: the animus (inward-looking) and the anima (outward-looking).

Animus	Anima
Strength	Compassionate
Discipline	Intuitive
Self-control	Sensitive to the needs of others
Firmness	Understanding
Rationality	Able to see the whole picture

Traditionally, the qualities associated with animus have been seen as masculine strengths and those of anima as feminine ones.

However, it goes without saying that men can be sensitive and women can be rational. This is the genius of Jung: rather than falling in with the prevailing stereotypes at the beginning of the twentieth century, he believed that both genders had to be in touch with both sets of qualities to achieve balance.

How Finding Balance Can Help You Find Love

Stories demonstrate the problems that arise when people become unbalanced. For example, tragic heroes are gripped by the animus part of their psyche and so obsessed with their own needs that they are unaware of the chaos that they are spreading. Othello is consumed with jealousy and so rational (animus) he cannot see the false logic presented by his rival Iago, who is feeding him lies about his wife. With the animus firmly in control, Othello is so shut off from his anima (able to see the whole picture) that he cannot recognise those qualities in Desdemona either. Therefore, Othello cannot achieve balance and the play ends with a pile of dead bodies.

In a story with a happy ending, like *Beauty and the Beast*, the strength, discipline and self-control of the Beast is trapped until Beauty arrives with her compassion, understanding and the other qualities associated with the anima. At the beginning of *Pride and Prejudice*, Elizabeth is too in touch with her animus (rationality and self-control) and therefore unable to access her anima (compassion). Therefore, she unfairly judges Mr Darcy, who is awkward in social situations and therefore not at his best at the ball. In all these stories, balance is finally achieved and everybody can live happily ever after.

It is all very well for Jung to say that we should all be in touch with both animus and anima but many of the virtues are contradictory. How can you be rational *and* intuitive or firm *and* sensitive? Indeed, throughout myths, legends and popular movies there are few characters who start out balanced: Merlin in the

Arthurian legends, Gandalf in the *Lord of the Rings*, Athene the goddess of wisdom in *The Odyssey*. Interestingly, these are all solitary characters who have no need for another half because they are already complete. It is difficult for ordinary mortals to balance the qualities of anima and animus, so we have traditionally 'projected' the anima onto women and the animus onto men.

Returning to the specific issue of being single, stories tell us that we need a partner to feel complete and to become balanced. Think how many fairy-tales, myths and legends end with a wedding – symbolising the coming together of the anima and animus. Stories also point out where someone caught in the *Single Trap* might be going wrong. Starting with men, Martyn is a 32-year-old whom I counselled about a string of intense relationships that ultimately went nowhere. When we looked at the patterns, we saw that he always fell for women who were very needy. 'Their lives are often a mess and I can see what should be done and sort everything out. But although they are grateful, the relationship always fizzles out and turns into a friendship,' he explained. In effect, Martyn was so compassionate, intuitive and understanding – in touch with his anima – that he was unbalanced, and at an unconscious level his girlfriends felt that he had nothing more to offer. Another man who found it hard to make relationships was Luke, twenty-eight: 'I've come to the conclusion that women prefer bastards to nice guys.' In counselling, I quickly discovered that he was so anxious to please and sensitive to the needs of the women he dated that he found it hard to articulate what he wanted. 'I'd much rather do what pleases them.' I knew from my female clients that this is fine up to a point but makes it hard to get to know the real man and, worse still, women consider this behaviour 'weak' and therefore unattractive. Once again, Luke was too in touch with the anima side of his psyche. Other men with this dilemma include those who are too close to their mothers or divorcés who become over-bonded with their daughters. In both these examples, the men have achieved a sort of balance with the anima – except it is a twisted, dark version that is ultimately unhealthy.

Turning to women, what happens if they are too connected to one side of their psyche? A woman who is controlled by her anima will become too considerate, too compassionate and so sensitive to the needs of her man that she will put up with even abusive or disrespectful behaviour and could end up trapped in an unhappy marriage. If these women had strength, firmness and rationality (animus), they would walk away. In contrast, many women who have been single for a long time are unbalanced towards the animus. Certainly, Karen, thirty-eight, came across as hard, brittle and a little self-obsessed when I interviewed her. She told me about a relationship with Brian, a long-distance lorry driver whom she'd been dating for three months, that ended on his birthday: 'I hadn't seen him for a week because he'd been delivering in Europe. I'd fixed a birthday supper, candles – the whole thing – but when I met him at the door with a kiss, he grabbed my boobs. I was fuming. I had a nice evening planned and he just seemed to want sex.' Karen had a very fixed idea of how Brian was going to spend his birthday: starting with a glass of champagne with a strawberry inside – 'I thought we could slip them into each other's mouths' – followed by light conversation about his trip with their starter, her news over the main course, he would open his present before dessert and then they would glide magically towards the bedroom. This determination to be in control and the discipline not to skip straight to lovemaking – Karen did find Brian very sexy – is typical animus. If she had been more in touch with her anima, she might have considered Brian's wishes – after all it was his birthday. She might also have seen the bigger picture: he had spent a week on the road and had probably missed her terribly. Instead Karen was so furious about her ruined plans that she picked a row and Brian stormed out without his present. There is more in the exercise section, for both men and women, about achieving a balance between anima and animus.

So, summing up, stories are about the conflict between our personal needs and the co-operation needed for us all to live reasonably peacefully together. However, at this point in the history of mankind, the developed world has tipped towards the animus. Many modern stories are simply a diversion – they have been detached from real meaning – or just stop abruptly with no proper conclusion. Meanwhile, there is an epidemic of singletons because of the breakdown of social capital – as discussed in the first chapter of the book – and because we all place less store on the values of anima.

However, it is not all bleak. By working through the ideas in this section of the book, you will not only have learnt important lessons about who you are and what you need, but also opened yourself up to a better kind of relationship. The final section of the book looks at how to find the right person.

Summary

- It is important to check that you are truly ready for love before searching for a mate.
- Knowledge gained about yourself is vital for knowing what kind of partner you need and what kind to avoid.
- There is an added bonus to working on yourself: when you feel better you will attract other people who also feel good about themselves.
- Stories are like dreams: an express way to our unconscious. So understanding what types of stories you tell and which ones you like will unlock your secret love agenda.

Exercises

Drawing Up a Love Contract with Yourself

- This exercise should not be rushed – take your time.
- You might want to come back over the next few days and add extra points. I suggest carrying around a small notebook to jot down thoughts as they come into your head.
- Do not feel constrained by the numbers below. They are a guideline. If you have one good answer under each heading that is enough. It is also fine if you come up with more answers, especially for the lessons learnt. However, if you have a long list under the last two headings, go back and select the most important ones – you will have a clearer goal that is easier to achieve.

What I have learnt along the way:
1
2
3
4
5

One change I should make:

What I need:
1
2
3

What I should avoid:
1
2
3

- Try to make your answer to 'One change I should make' something practical and positive. For example: 'Learn to sing', rather than something about a state of mind, such as: 'Be more cheerful'. If you come up with something negative, for example: 'Stop phoning an ex-lover late at night', turn it into a positive change, such as: 'Phone a friend when I am feeling down'.
- Your 'one change' might seem small, in comparison with the needs, but remember *one* small change can set up lots of other positive changes that will lead to a fulfilling relationship.
- Be wary of huge changes, as there is the danger of going for the opposite of your current behaviour. This preserves the problem, and you will end up playing the opposing role in the same drama.

Here are the answers that Sandy and I created together.

What I have learnt along the way:
1 *I never really knew my father.*
2 *I am resourceful.*
3 *With help, I can overcome big obstacles. (She had counselling to get her drinking under control.)*
4 *I can be generous.*

One change I should make:
Help out at a local theatre society that works with disabled and able-bodied children.

What I need:
1 *To get to know a man before falling in love.*

What I should avoid:
1 *Controlling men.*
2 *Men who idolise me and will put up with any behaviour.*

Love Stories in Action

Our society gives very mixed messages to single people. On one hand, it celebrates the virtues of independence and self-sufficiency, but on the other, constantly reinforces the importance of settling down. This is why most fairy-tales, myths and legends finish with a wedding. Even plots like 'Overcoming the Monster' has the hero marrying the princess – to underline his transformation from boy to man. So don't apologise for really wanting to be in a relationship but wholeheartedly embrace the project.

Identify Your Personal Plot

There are two ways of approaching this part of the exercise:

Firstly, look at books, films or stories that have really moved you. For example, my recent favourites include: *The Shipping News* by Annie Proulx (Rebirth: Bereaved man and his family leave New York for the land of their forefathers, a remote frozen part of Newfoundland), *The Curious Incident of the Dog in the Night-time* by Mark Haddon (The Quest: Fifteen-year-old boy with Asperger's syndrome sets off on a journey to find his mother) and *The Promise of Happiness* by Justin Cartwright (Rebirth: Daughter comes out of prison for art theft and her family emerges from the shadow of the crisis). As a therapist, it is not surprising that my tastes reflect my interest in change and people discovering something important about themselves. However, until I did this exercise myself, I had not been aware how my favourites had such similar themes. What do your favourite stories say about you?

Secondly, look at your own life. Imagine that you are going to write your own autobiography. What would you call it? Which of the Seven Basic Plots would dominate? What major events would be covered? Imagining that these events would be given a whole chapter, what would that chapter be called? You might even like to get a few pieces of paper, put the title of your autobiography on the first and then write out the chapter headings. What kind of stories do you tell to yourself and about yourself?

Understand What These Stories Say About You

Below are the Seven Basic Plots and some suggestions about what this plot might be trying to teach you – especially if your autobiography, or one of the chapters in it, conforms to this story-line.

Overcoming the Monster

The most important question to ask yourself is: Have I overcome all the monsters? In many movies using this theme, there are often several minor monsters before the main adversary. For example, in *King Kong* the heroine is threatened by several dinosaurs before facing her greatest threat: Kong at the top of the Empire State Building. Real-life problems often come in packs too and we need to work our way through destructive coping strategies to reach the real enemy underneath. An example would be Kate, thirty-seven, who tackled a nasty drink problem: 'I would do stupid, dangerous things like go out drinking, fall asleep on the tube and be woken by the guard at the end of the line. It would be so late that the underground had stopped and I'd be forced to get a taxi home.' Kate undertook a treatment programme and made great progress. 'That's when my old eating disorder came back with a vengeance and I'd start stuffing myself with cheap cakes from the corner store,' she explained. 'The problem had started when I was a kid – I'd peel the wallpaper off my bedroom wall and suck on it – and as I told my therapist the story, I couldn't stop crying.' She was finally ready to talk about the abuse she suffered at the hands of her older brother. If this is your plot, celebrate your past achievements – and the monsters slain – but be realistic about the challenges ahead.

Rags to Riches

The problem with this plot is that the hero or heroine can be waiting to be lifted up – normally by a prince or princess – rather than finding a way to lift themselves up from the shadows. Even in movies like *Flashdance* (a welder wants a place at an exclusive dance academy) where the heroine is developing a skill to gain recognition, the plot-line glosses over the sheer number of hours needed and there is normally a love interest who opens the door to success. (In *Flashdance* the welder's boss uses his contacts to get her the crucial audition.) Talent shows, like *The X Factor* and *Pop Idol*, work on the Rags to Riches plot too. However, the producers always gloss over that the winning contestants have been taking singing lessons since they were five years old, so that the audience can relate to the 'ordinary' boy or girl who finds fame. This might make good TV, but misleads people into waiting to be discovered. If this is your favourite plot, ask yourself: What can I do to make things happen for myself? Am I repeating old patterns – same job, same friends, going to the same places – but expecting new things to happen? How can I change?

Quest

This is a very positive plot-line. The hero or heroine has a clear goal, expects obstacles and set-backs, but is not put off. Unlike Voyage and Return – see below – he or she learns something important during the quest and the reader/audience feel that they have deserved to reach the goal. If your favourite books and movies use this plot, congratulate yourself as this suggests that you are a positive and upbeat person. If a chapter of your autobiography fits this plot, look back at what skills, qualities and strategies helped you reach your goal. Ask yourself: how can I use these in my search for a partner?

Voyage and Return

When swapping disastrous date stories with friends, you are often conforming to this plot. In other words, you have been to a strange world and seen strange things but decided to return home. Although you might have learnt something from the experience, it is usually superficial. For example, don't wear high heels when dancing with short men. Don't worry, if this seems to be your autobiography or a couple of chapters, as everybody goes through this stage in the journey from adolescence to adulthood. The secret is to turn 'Voyage and Return' into 'The Quest' and to learn something important from your experiences. So think back to one of your date stories – particularly one that is critical of the other person – and ask yourself: What does this story say about me? For example, in the dancing-with-a-short-guy story: Do I make snap judgements on superficial qualities without knowing the real person? Are you attributing someone else's bad behaviour to a character flaw, but the same behaviour in yourself to particular circumstances. For example, when someone else shouts, they are short-tempered; when you shout, you are provoked or temporarily in a bad mood.

Comedy

Hollywood has used this story so many times that we know within minutes who will fall for whom. The interest is in seeing how they overcome the obstacles and find true love. However, few movie-goers stop and question the shape of this plot – which shows just how deeply ingrained it is into our subconscious. So how exactly has the comedy plot influenced our picture of love? The answer is best summed up with a line from *A Midsummer Night's Dream* – one of Shakespeare's most-performed comedies: 'The course of true love never did run smooth'. In other words, we have been trained to expect problems but know that 'love conquers all' (Virgil, 70–19 BC). The result is we believe that not only can we fall for someone totally unsuitable but that love will smooth over the problems, resolve our differences and provide a happy ending. Worse still, we can put up with bad behaviour from a new lover – rudeness, abusive language or even contempt – because many couples in romantic movies start off hating each other. If this is your favourite plot or your previous love affairs have followed the first part of the comedy plot, ask yourself: Do I expect too much from love? Love might be magical but it cannot magic away problems.

Tragedy

When we have had a few drinks, it is easy to become melancholy and view ourselves as a tragic hero or heroine. In the words of one

167

of Shakespeare's tragic heroes, King Lear, we feel 'More sinned against than sinning'. In other words, we might have done something wrong – like sleeping with a married man or woman – but actually we are the victim of a more serious wrong. The whole world is against us. Although this strategy can make us feel better in the short term, it can also stop us from properly acknowledging our mistakes, our own part in our misery, and learning something beneficial for the future. So what should you do if your autobiography seems to conform to this plot? In stories, the tragic hero or heroine ends up dead or alone because they have become gripped by their animus and ultimately cannot see anyone else's point of view. So look at the exercise below. In some cases, I find people with tragic autobiographies have cast themselves in too black a light. An example would be Molly, a 28-year-old single mother with a twelve-year-old son. When she was young she had babysat for the kids of her father's best friend. 'I had always been very close to this man – he'd been like an honorary uncle – and I'd been having a bad time at school, he listened and you can guess the rest. Well, it broke my father's heart when he found out – I tried to keep my pregnancy secret, I guess I was in denial. Dad had been in the Navy with this guy, they went right back, and it ruined their friendship. The man and his wife ended up getting divorced too. How could I have been so selfish?' I had to remind Molly that she had been underage and slowly she accepted that not all the blame was hers. Eventually, she changed her plot to 'Overcoming the Monster'. Would this be helpful for you too?

Rebirth

This is another positive plot as it involves someone changing and casting off dark shadows. However, unlike 'Rags to Riches', the hero or heroine does the majority of the work themselves. So if you enjoy this plot in books or films, or you see your autobiography as being under a dark shadow, how can you use the lessons and reach your own rebirth? Time and again in rebirth stories, the hero or heroine is very isolated. Scrooge has no friends and keeps his nephew at a distance. Mary in *The Secret Garden* is an orphan sent to a remote mansion on the Yorkshire moors. Look at your own life: why are you isolated? What could be done to change it? The other common thread through Rebirth is seeing the problem through fresh eyes. For Scrooge it is the visit from the three ghosts and for Mary it is the arrival of spring. How could you find a fresh perspective on your life? Remember you are not looking for someone to turn your life around but provide the impetus for you to do it yourself.

Rebalancing the Animus and Anima

1 *What is the bigger picture?*
   - Start with your own natural reaction to an important event in your life. Does it tend towards the animus or the anima?
   - If tipping towards animus, look at whether the short-term benefits of being self-orientated (for example, getting your own way) might be outweighed by the benefits in the long-term of considering others (maybe, better co-operation from colleagues). If tipping towards anima, although there are short-term benefits in always putting others first (for example, it makes you feel good about yourself or keeps the peace) what are the longer-term downsides (perhaps, being taken for granted)?

2 *Work outwards*
   (This is only for people tipping towards the animus, if you tip towards the anima go to number 3.)
   - What are the needs of other people? How are they impacted by your behaviour?
   - What about the community in general?
   - What would be the consequences if everybody behaved like you?

3 *Walk a mile in someone else's shoes*
- Imagine you are a friend or a family member who is close enough to be affected by your behaviour.
- What would be their opinion of your behaviour?
- How do they feel?
- Still putting yourself in their shoes: how would you judge your own behaviour?

4 *What could you do differently next time?*
- With your fresh perspective, think about the changes that you would like to make.
- If you are stuck for an idea, try the opposite of your normal approach.
- This is bound to help you experience the opposite part of your psyche.

5 *Afterwards, analyse the changes*
- What felt good?
- What felt uncomfortable but manageable?
- How could you build on this for the future?

The First Step:

Escaping the Single Trap

The Seven Key Lessons

1 *Do not punish yourself.* Our selfish individualistic society is making it harder to both embark on and maintain relationships.
2 *Like attracts like.* Becoming more open and honest will attract partners with these qualities too.
3 *Forgive your parents.* Although your mother's and father's decisions and parenting style play an important part in forging your attitudes to life and relationships, they in turn are the product of their own upbringing too.
4 *Embrace and learn from your feelings rather than distracting or numbing yourself.* Many of the most difficult relationship problems come from trying to ignore or take short-cuts round more simple ones.
5 *Unhook the legacy of one relationship before embarking on the next.* Otherwise one relationship's problems will cast a long shadow over the next, and shadows on top of more shadows can turn into black despair.
6 *Love is not a cure-all.* Our culture, stories and the media feed us unrealistic myths. This leads us to expect too much from our partners and from ourselves.
7 *Become more balanced.* Problems lurk in the extremes, the middle way is the most successful way.

Step Two:
Finding Lasting Love

Chapter Six

Take a Fresh Look at Dating

The aim of this book is to not only make you look at yourself with fresh eyes, but also to question how you have been searching for love. For most people this means dating, but is this the best way to find a life partner? Often the emphasis is on meeting as many people as possible, in the shortest time possible, and nearly always in an artificial setting. People will try the latest craze, for example, dinner in the dark (where the waiters wear night goggles and the lights come on only at the end of the meal), and for a short time all hope is invested in this new twist. It is rather like the latest diet, and in the same way that few people question whether dieting is the best way to lose weight, few people ask if dating is the best way to judge whether two people are truly compatible. In the meantime, dating becomes more deeply ingrained into our culture – until we imagine this is the only way to meet someone. However, dating is the product of a specific time and a specific set of circumstances.

The History of Dating

Up until the 1920s, a system named 'calling' was at the core of courting for middle- and upper-class men and women. Calling on someone was primarily a woman's activity, as they controlled social life. A hostess would decide on which days she would receive callers – when she was 'at home'. Just like dating, calling had a complex set of rules, covering everything from the time between an invitation and a visit (a fortnight or less) to how long someone should stay, what refreshments should be served and what entertainment was acceptable (probably the daughter of the house playing the piano). Even lower-middle-class families could afford maids who would answer the door and inform a gentleman if the lady of the house was 'at home' or not. *Ladies' Home Journal*, a bastion of American respectability, approvingly reports how a group of factory girls clubbed together to hire the parlour of a local widow – so they had a chaperone and somewhere to meet men.

The pressure for change came from above and below. Most working-class homes were drab and overcrowded, so courting couples would escape into the excitement of the streets. At the other end of the social scale, upper-class women would meet men outside the home as an act of rebellion against their mothers who controlled courtship. As Lady Bracknell informs her daughter in *The Importance of Being Earnest*: 'An engagement should come on a young girl as a surprise, pleasant or unpleasant, as the case may be.'

Like many social innovations, the term 'dating' comes from America – along with many of the rules. While 'calling' happened in private, at home, under the watchful eye of the family, this new way of courting was in the outside world – in the semi-anonymity of public spaces. So dating not only shifted the balance of power from parent to child, but also from women to men. While the domestic sphere belonged to women, the public sphere belonged to men; so an invitation to date was literally an invitation into his world. With 'calling', a hostess would issue an invitation, guests did not invite themselves; however, with dating, women were left waiting to be asked out.

By 1914, the term 'dating' had even reached the conservative *Ladies' Home Journal*. This was a time of huge cultural changes for single women in America. As recently as 1907, unmarried women had been warned never to eat in a 'public restaurant' with a man – even a relative – as it laid them 'open to being classed with women of undesirable reputation by the strangers present'. However, by the 1920s, Radcliffe girls, from the Ivy League college in Massachusetts, were given a list of approved restaurants where they could dine with a man. Even then, in some places it was only acceptable before 7.30 pm.

Gradually dating began to be codified into entertainment where the young couple 'went out' and 'spent money' – rather than just spending time with a member of the opposite sex, as had been the case with 'calling'. Commentators in the new young women's magazines would warn about men who just wanted to come over to their readers' houses and hang around. However, the new emphasis on spending money gave a lot of power to the person picking up the bill: the young man. The rise of the automobile also gave young people mobility and privacy, and further limited mothers' ability to control their daughters' courting.

Although we tend to think of dating as one homogenous way to meet the opposite sex, there were two contradictory fashions – both dictated by the social situation of their times. The first was called 'Competitive Dating'. The twenties in America were seen as a time of abundance and that was particularly the case with men. Young people would date competitively. The anthropologist Margaret Mead chronicles 'dating and rating' in *Male and Female* (1949), her study of American colleges. Dances, the primary way of meeting the opposite sex, had complicated rules about cutting in. The greatest fear was getting stuck with the same partner all night. If nobody tapped the man on the shoulder and asked to dance with his partner, he had two choices: taking her back to a group of her friends or continuing to dance. He could not just abandon her on the side of the dance floor. The social stigma of spending the whole evening with just one partner was so great that many women would fake a headache and ask to be escorted home. Beth Bailey, in her book *From Front Porch to Back Seat* (Johns Hopkins University Press, 1989), tells the story of one young man stuck with an undesirable dance partner who waved a single dollar bill behind the lady's back to bribe his friends to cut in. On realising what was going on, the young lady showed her strength of character by telling him to make it five and she'd go home. At Radcliffe College, 'date widows' – women who were serious about a man back home – would meet up on Saturday night to read letters from their beloved to each other and show off keepsakes. Girls who went steady were only marginally less pitied; at least they had *one* man to date. With competitive dating, the woman or man with the most partners was considered the most successful and therefore the most envied. In some colleges, women would agree not to accept dates on certain nights so they could study, safe in the knowledge that another competitor was not out with a popular man. Ultimately, competitive dating was not about courtship or even enjoying the company of a certain girl or boy, but being seen to have a date.

The second type of dating was called 'Going Steady'. After the Wall Street Crash of 1929 the era of abundance was over and commentators complained about the shortage of marriageable men – in other words, men financially secure enough to take a wife. Abundance had probably always been an illusion. Hostesses had needed to work hard to guarantee more eligible men than women; meanwhile, colleges – which set the trends for all young people – had always enrolled more men than women. The Second World War further underlined the advantage of a steady date and young people settled into a form of intense monogamy, even though they were still in their teens and few expected to go the distance from 'steady' to marriage. Previously, the most popular young people had hundreds of different dates, but by the fifties the attitudes had completely changed. A 1953 survey at the University of Wisconsin found that 36 per cent replied that 'popular students in their high school had gone steady', 33.4 per cent that 'popular students often dated the same person' but only 8.7 per cent that 'popular students had played the field'.

In 'going steady', boys had to call a certain number of times a week and turn up on date nights – how often he would phone and which nights out depended on local custom. There was also a complicated system of exchanging class rings and other symbols of unending love. Going steady had the advantage over 'dating and rating' in that both sexes could relax after a few intense weeks and were guaranteed a partner for special events. However, the pairings would be so fixed that anyone who missed the rush could basically forget about dating for the rest of the academic year. To modern eyes, 'going steady' would seem claustrophobic. Although boys and girls could go out with same-sex friends on non-date nights, they would still be expected to tell their steady partner. Fifties parents were not keen on these new arrangements. How could their sons and daughters make good long-term choices if, unlike 'dating and rating', they had such a narrow experience of the opposite sex? However, under the disapproval of fifties parents was an even greater fear that 'hot monogamy' encouraged necking, fondling and probably much more. Interestingly, they believed lots of dates with strangers, and little time to get intimate, guaranteed their daughters' safety – very different from parental fears today.

It is important to put dating into this historical context. Firstly, to show that there was no golden age of courtship; each system had its advantages and disadvantages and even if we wanted to turn the clock back, we are no longer those people. Secondly, history disproves socio-biological theories that men and women are inherently stereotyped: biologically driven to hunt or be hunted. The truth is that courtship has always been a product of the circumstances of each era.

What about Dating in Great Britain?

Although most people imagine that youth culture began after the Second World War, there were some signs as far back as 1905. In the book *Youth in Britain Since 1945* (Wiley-Blackwell, 1997),

William Osgerby reports how a nineteen-year-old semi-skilled youth in a Manchester iron foundry could earn one pound a week, surrender twelve shillings to his parents and spend the remainder on clothes, gambling and the music hall. However, the decline of heavy industry and depression meant that the majority of British youth had little or no disposable income and certainly courting, unlike dating in the USA, did not revolve around money.

Oral history provides a good insight into how our grandparents and great-grandparents met. The Hall Lane Community Centre in Armley, Leeds, undertook a project in the 1980s in which young people asked senior citizens about life in the early part of the twentieth century. Armley used to be a mill town and the line between starving and surviving was very thin. As one respondent explained, when it came to impressing the boys, girls needed plenty of ingenuity: 'We hadn't got nice dresses. This girl's mother was a dressmaker and so we got some pieces of material she had kept, stitched them to the bottom of our coats to show so much round the bottom, but we daren't take our coats off.' The young single people in Armley would congregate on a local hill-top, for what they called the 'Bunny Run': 'You used to go up there if you wanted to connect with a female. And there used to be a regular track: over the hill, down the other side, turn round, over the hill, down the other side.' Another man stressed the respectability: 'There was never any whistling or swearing or scrapping. You promenaded up and down and ogled the girls and struck friendships up, and then arranged to go dancing.' Some of the girls could be quite persistent, as one respondent discovered: 'I've been doing the prowl up there, and I'm walking down Town Street and I had a drink at the Travellers and next news I had company, and I had a hell of a job to get shut of this lass.' The Bunny Run is summed up by a fourth respondent as 'parading, mixing and saying "How do you do?"' Although customs and names would have differed, this is British courting boiled down to the essentials.

Unlike in America, the state considered it important to super-vise young people and therefore sponsored youth clubs. Unlike scouts and guides, these clubs were informal with no uniform or declaration of allegiance. The National Association of Girls' Clubs was founded in 1911 and the National Association of Boys' Clubs in 1925. The strict division of the sexes did not last and even from the beginning each staged open evenings as an alternative to 'pavement flirtations'. By 1944, the National Association of Girls' Clubs had added 'Mixed Clubs' to their name and in 1961 renamed themselves the National Association of Youth Clubs. The fare offered was basic by today's standards: sporting equipment and record players. Often the girls would dance while the boys watched, but youth clubs provided a relaxed, low-risk opportunity to meet the opposite sex. The social impact can be gauged from the sheer scale of attendance. Government research in 1969 found 69 per cent of male and 71 per cent of female twenty-year-olds were or had been a member.

The main focus of young romance in the fifties and sixties was the charabanc to the seaside (often organised by church, factory or youth club), the palais de dance (where you would normally meet someone inside) and the cinema – but this was normally for established courting couples. Even in the 1970s the American idea of a 'date', paying to take someone out, had not truly taken root. 'I met my husband-to-be back then, we were seventeen and all hung around in a loose gang,' says Christine who is now in her late forties. 'One night, waiting for the bus home, my best friend and her boyfriend started having a row and disappeared; I can't remember how, but Tony and I started kissing in the shelter. It was a bit of a surprise but really nice. Afterwards we sat holding hands and smiling. We didn't talk about it, but we sort of knew that we'd see each other soon. I think there was a group of us going swimming that Saturday. One thing led to another, we'd become boyfriend and girlfriend and the gang thing faded slowly into the background. Since my marriage ended, I've found dating very awkward. I thought it was me, but then I realised: I'd never done this before.' Her friend Joanne agrees that dating seemed alien when they were young: 'It was something that happened in

American TV comedies. The boyfriend made small talk with the father, smoking a pipe, while his date got ready upstairs and then he presented her with an orchid. Things like that just didn't happen in Luton.' In fact, dating did not truly establish itself until the eighties consumer revolution. The final piece of the jigsaw was probably cable and satellite which provided round-the-clock US chat shows, comedies and movies explaining the complexities of the dating code: the humiliation of being stood up by your prom date, the importance of being homecoming queen and finally conspicuous consumption.

Why Is Dating so Demoralising?

Contemporary dating's roots are still firmly planted in 'going steady', the fifties American code. In fact, the ideas are enshrined in the popular modern dating guide, *The Rules* (Thorsons, 1995). Ellen Fein and Sherrie Schneider's laws include: don't talk to a man first (or ask him to dance); don't go Dutch on a date; let him take the lead. Unfortunately these rules are hopelessly out of step with a world where a woman can be president of a multinational company, sail round the world single-handed or fight alongside men in Iraq. Attempts to update dating – like Rachel Greenwald's *Find a Husband After 35 – Using What I Learned at Harvard Business School* (Ballantine Books, 2004) – suggest that a woman turns herself into a product to be marketed and sold. We live in a sad world if the only options for women are either passively waiting to be asked out or scheming and game-playing.

Meanwhile, the decision to have children is being deferred from late teens or early twenties to late twenties and beyond, which further reinforces 'going steady'. Joanna, a thirty-year-old who works in the publishing industry, had a long-term boyfriend in her early twenties. 'Looking back, I suppose we were quiet serious and I often wonder what life would have been like if we'd married – but the timing was wrong. We were not ready to make the ultimate commitment and we drifted apart.' Joanna and her former boy-friend had acted 'as if' married – like the fifties American teenagers – even though they were not financially or emotionally ready.

Yet at the same time, modern dating has developed a completely schizophrenic approach: by adding 'dating and rating' into 'going steady' and running both systems in tandem. Going out with lots of different men or women – just like with 'dating and rating' – remains the ultimate proof of desirability. 'I like the attention from men, it makes me feel good about myself,' says Dominique, a 28-year-old systems manager, 'even the bad dates provide something funny to tell my friends at work. In fact, sometimes I think I enjoy talking about it afterwards more than going out itself.' No wonder we are confused by modern dating – it is pulling us in two contradictory directions.

Two further trends have made dating even more precarious. The first is our belief that we are time-poor. With 'not enough hours in the day', we make almost instant decisions about our date or the stranger at a party. As it is impossible to judge both character and emotional compatibility, we fall back on what society, friends and the media value: youth, looks, status, possessions. Worse still, these standards are getting tighter and tighter; the list of acceptable brand names shorter. Often we can discount someone, based not on our own intrinsic taste but on what people in general might think.

The second trend is abundance. Up to fifty years ago most people paired up with someone who lived nearby, the search limited by how far they were prepared to walk or cycle. In many rural areas, the choice might be very small indeed. The car widened the net, but our parents probably still married someone from the same town or a neighbouring one: a larger but still manageable choice. The internet and cheap airline travel means there are literally millions of potential partners waiting to meet us. Not only does abundance make it harder to choose, but allows us to discard on the flimsiest of pretexts.

Why a Successful Date Does Not Necessarily Mean a Successful Relationship

In the eighties, researchers at the University of Ontario in Canada looked at what made the difference between loving someone and merely liking them. The team – Seligman, Fazio and Zanna – believe that we respond to two different qualities in a potential partner: extrinsic and intrinsic. Extrinsic rewards centre around what someone can do for us, but has nothing to do with personality – their in-built qualities. In *Pride and Prejudice*, Elizabeth reveals an extrinsic quality when she answers her sister's question about when she first fell in love with Mr Darcy: 'I believe I must date it from my first seeing his beautiful grounds at Pemberley.' Elizabeth is, in fact, teasing her sister, because the main attractions are Darcy's intrinsic qualities: his character. In this case, Elizabeth loves his loyalty to friends, generosity of spirit and good judgement. Seligman, Fazio and Zanna divided the intrinsic and extrinsic benefits for student couples who had been dating for less than twelve months (average time six months) by asking them to complete the following sentences. 'I spend time with my girlfriend/boyfriend *because I* . . .'. This brings out intrinsic qualities. 'I spend time with my boyfriend/girlfriend *in order to* . . .'. This brings out extrinsic qualities. Although falling in love is a notoriously difficult experience to pin down, it is probably the moment that extrinsic qualities become intrinsic. In other words, extrinsic reasons make us *like* someone but intrinsic qualities make us *love* them; we *like* someone because they give us a lift to work, we still *love* our partner even if he or she is ill in bed and can do nothing for us.

The team at the University of Ontario were interested to discover if making someone aware of the extrinsic benefits of being in a relationship would make love between courting couples more or less likely. So they randomly divided the students into two groups. The control group just completed the intrinsic/extrinsic sentences and left. The second group stayed for a discussion where the extrinsic benefits of the relationship were pointed out. The next day, all students completed a test that measured how much they *liked* their boyfriends/girlfriends and how much they *loved* them. The students who had discussed extrinsic benefits scored highest on the liking scale and lowest on the loving scale and, in a third test, were less likely to see their girlfriend/boyfriend as a potential long-term partner. In other words, the more the practical and social advantages of a relationship were highlighted, the less likely people were to fall in love. Unfortunately, dating highlights these superficial and extrinsic qualities. 'On paper, he was definitely a great catch. Good job. He took me to great restaurants. My parents approved,' explains Teresa, who is thirty-eight. 'I kept telling myself time was running out and I enjoyed his company. My best friend thought I should shape up because she would have him in a heartbeat. So the relationship kept going for another six months, but I found that I was forcing myself to return his calls and finally ended it.'

In fairy-tales, princes and princesses disguise themselves to find someone who will fall in love with the real them, not the castle and the jewels. Myths endure because they tell us something important. In this case it is: everybody wants to be loved for themselves. Otherwise, if love is based on extrinsic qualities, what happens if someone richer or more beautiful comes along? Originally, we empathised with the ordinary man or woman whose virtue – an intrinsic quality – was rewarded by discovering that their beloved had, in fact, royal blood. However, our abundant culture has turned us all from frogs into princes and princesses, paranoid that someone will take advantage. As the team at the University of Ontario discovered, the more potential rewards we are given for someone falling in love with us, the harder it is not only to believe their motives but also to decide if we are in love ourselves.

Dating is also incredibly stressful. Firstly, there is the worry about whether someone will accept, next where to go, then how the two of you will hit it off and whether there will be a second date. When people are tense or feel judged, they are more likely to act out of character or start playing games. 'My mates always said the best strategy was to be cheerful and chatty,' says Brian, a 32-year-old conservation worker, 'but that's not me. After a couple of embarrassing dates where I made myself look a prat, I decided that tragedy trumps chirpy and stopped putting on an act.' Brian has now been married for three years. However, some people are so determined to impress that they lie or omit vital pieces of background information. Dissembling has become so widespread that it is now common practice to Google someone for a background check before the first date.

Fiona came into counselling after her disastrous four-month relationship finally collapsed. 'He led me to believe he was a lawyer – and he certainly had all the chat – but he was really a glorified conveyancing clerk. I'd been suspicious for a while and one night when I stayed over, I found an opened letter on his chest of drawers and learnt he was several thousand pounds in debt.' However, as the counselling continued, Fiona admitted that she had been less than straight too. 'OK, I did not tell him that an old boyfriend had been stalking and threatening me, I thought it would put him off.' Unfortunately, how a relationship starts plays a big part in how it will continue. After protecting ourselves from rejection by deceit or playing a brighter, better version of ourself, it is almost impossible to suddenly become open and honest – vital ingredients for a successful long-term relationship – sometime further down the line.

By the very nature of a formal date, and the planning involved, the big moment will be a few days or weeks into the future. In the meantime, there is plenty of opportunity for the imagination to run riot. 'I don't believe in that "the one" stuff, but I do start imagining a holiday together or what present he might like for Christmas,' says Maria, forty-five. 'If I'm honest, I have this picture of the perfect man. He will be older and his wife will probably have died, the children will be old enough not to resent me but young enough not to be too tied up with their own children and available to enjoy lunches in London or learning to horse-ride together.' She is self-aware enough to laugh, but in the run-up to a date Maria is busy rewriting her fantasy. 'When we finally date, it is nearly always a disappointment because he's shrunk two inches and I've forgotten that he talks about little other than the Jaguar Cars Appreciation Society.' Perhaps her date was nervous, and therefore had not noticed Maria's lack of interest in cars; alternatively, he could have been a bore. A second date would tell Maria more, but as she admits: 'By this stage, I'm so disappointed that I've switched off.'

The Perfect Partner

Contemporary culture encourages us to concentrate on what we *want* from a relationship. Somehow, if we can just articulate these desires, often in minute detail, we will be one step closer to finding that perfect partner and living happily ever after. Lydia is in her thirties with a young child, but has become disillusioned with the men that she attracted: 'They are all losers in some way. They are attractive but they would drink too much, smoke too much dope or have money problems. In effect, they can't look after themselves.' Determined not to make the same mistakes again, Lydia has drawn up a tick-list of requirements for her perfect man. I've added her explanations in italics:

☐ Aged 38–48. *('Ideally, he should be four years older than me.')*
☐ Unconventional. *('The father of my child had had a very ordinary childhood, so we could never really understand each other.')*
☐ Has a chequered past but now sorted. *('I'm bored easily and can find "normal" relationships claustrophobic.')*
☐ Travelled.
☐ Has read *Stone Junction* by Jim Dodge. *('If you don't like this book – which is really hippie and full of magic realism – you don't pass the test.')*
☐ Creative.

- ☐ The film *Gummo*. *('You don't have to have seen this film but it is another test. How else can I know that you can cope with my darkness?')*
- ☐ Left-field music tastes. *('I like contemporary jazz and funk.')*
- ☐ Spiritual but not religious.
- ☐ Good tattoos.
- ☐ Not possessive.

At first, I thought that Lydia was joking but she was serious. In fact, she suggested that I include her email address in the book in case someone could tick all the boxes. So I asked whether any of the items were negotiable. 'Perhaps the good tattoos; I can put up with a couple of dodgy ones. But if someone has none at all, I think we'd be too different to click.' Lydia's list reveals a lot about her. So much, in fact, that I started wondering if she was projecting herself onto this perfect partner. If this perfect man exists, he would be almost her twin and the two of them could live in perfect harmony. It sounds great, but what about the reality? Twenty-five years as a marital therapist has shown me that being too similar is almost as bad for a relationship as too different. These twin couples become like brother and sister or good friends, and all the passion disappears. In effect, we need difference to keep the relationship alive, interesting and growing. Difference is like the grit in an oyster shell, probably annoying for the oyster, but it produces something incredible: a pearl. So I wonder if the perfect partner is actually good for us. Perhaps what we *want* and what we *need* are two different things.

This idea is taken a stage further by Linda Hirsham, a retired professor of Philosophy and Women's Studies at Brandeis University in Massachusetts. The most common item on many women's list of wants is a financially successful husband. However, Hirsham believes that successful women should marry men with no career prospects! She came to this conclusion after research into the newlyweds' column of the *New York Times*. In 1996, at the time of their marriages, these women were doctors, lawyers and Wall Street executives, but ten years later they had either scaled down their careers or completely bailed out in order to raise a family. Her conclusion: these women had married above themselves. This is because the partner who earns least will need to sacrifice their career to child care. Her advice to women is to marry an artist (in the broadest sense of the word) – he will be interesting, stimulating, and provide a contrast to the soulless corporate world. However, most important, he will be in no position to blackmail you into looking after the children, as the family will not be able to live on his income alone. In addition, he will probably be self-employed and can fit his work round the demands of raising children. Meanwhile, your career can still flourish. Hirsham's beliefs are controversial but they illustrate how tick-lists are seldom the best way to chose a mate.

Latest Trends in Dating

It goes without saying that the internet has revolutionised how we communicate and meet people. However, despite all the chat rooms and social networking, the majority of young people – who grew up with the internet – still find boyfriends and girlfriends at college, through friends, in bars and at parties. In effect, the traditional way. Meanwhile, it is the thirty-plus age groups who have colonised the dating sites. There are two reasons for this: firstly, many of their peers have settled down and social life revolves around couples. Secondly, they are in a hurry and internet dating sites sell themselves on their sheer number of members and the promise of a quick match. However, searching for a soul mate in this way can be soul-destroying. 'You have to go into this with your eyes wide open,' says Erin, a 38-year-old divorcée, 'there are a lot of fakes, married men and weirdos. I quickly found that a lot of men lie. They knock a few years off their age and add them to their height. It's a bit like drugs in sports – everybody does it – so you join in to level the playing field.' Anyone who has done internet dating has their share of both funny and horror stories. There are tales of promising men or women who got away, but very few that end happily ever after. 'I think there is a new form of urban myth: the couple who met internet dating and get married and have a baby,' complains Erin. 'So when a friend has sworn by a particular site, for just this reason, I've questioned them about the names and whether I could meet them for tips. However, they end up being a friend of a friend of a friend. Do they really exist?'

I can reassure everybody that these lucky people do exist. I met just such a couple at the home of a friend in Toronto. Over dinner, I had plenty of time to discover the secret of their success. So what had they done differently from everybody else? Firstly, they were 'internet dating virgins' and had only been online for a few weeks. (In fact, Isabelle, thirty-five, had not put up a photograph when she started exchanging emails with Lewis, also thirty-five.) This newness allowed them to be open-minded and not rule someone out on fairly arbitrary grounds – like not having a photograph. Secondly, Lewis had been more interested in the favourite books and films section than looks or age: 'I was amazed how many people left the books section blank or had put down *The Da Vinci Code*.' Thirdly, the two of them spent weeks sending long messages before meeting. 'The greatest number of words you could send in one message is only 2,000 words. I know because we often tried to exceed it.' When Isabelle finally posted a picture, she was used to being frank with Lewis. 'My only recent picture was one taken by a professional,' Isabelle explained. 'I'm an opera singer and this was taken in full make-up, perfect hair and flattering lighting. The sort of head-shot that you send to prospective employers or put in the programme for a concert. I don't really look like that in real life. So I told Lewis that he could have a picture but not to get his hopes up.' In effect, Isabelle and Lewis had managed to meet up unburdened by the usual cynicism, game-playing and white lies that normally accompany internet dating.

However, the greatest benefit of meeting online is also the greatest problem: the sheer number of people. With so much choice, you need to come up with quick ways of narrowing your search. Women complain that men want someone at least ten years younger: 'If I went along with that idea, I'd be dating men who were fifty or even fifty-five,' complains Erin, 'but I want to meet men around my own age.' Men's complaint is that women only go for tall men. 'I'm five foot six inches tall,' explains Ben, who is thirty-six, 'but even women five foot nothing to five foot three want a minimum of five foot eight.' Even searching on common interests, rather than superficial qualities like looks, is problematical and can rule out a good match. For example, Nathan and Jane have been married for ten years and enjoy teasing each other about their respective tastes. 'He reads these brick-sized books with violent death on every page and he complains that I read boring books, which might win literary prizes, but nothing actually happens in them,' say Jane. 'I enjoy ridiculing his music – normally progressive rock dinosaurs that you thought died a million years ago – but he gets his revenge when he finds me bopping around the kitchen to pop songs on the radio. What is most important is that we laugh and cry over the same things, which I guess is harder to discover in a few emails.' Jane has a point: narrowing your search might cut down the sheer number of messages, but it is only a short step from filtering for practical reasons to believing that your beloved must fulfil a tight number of criteria and simply closing your mind to anyone else.

If you progress from exchanging messages online, to phoning and then meeting in a pub or coffee shop, the virtual world still casts a shadow. Your date will not only be trying to decide if there is a connection but comparing you to all his or her other potential dates. Susan, forty-seven, used lonely-hearts columns back in the mid-eighties and following her divorce has embraced internet dating: 'I always used to feel that I was auditioning rather than dating, that I should be tap dancing past while my date held up a score card for personality, looks and presentation. However, even in popular publications you would only get a handful of letters – now the possibilities are endless. Sometimes I wonder if we give each other a chance before we shout "next".' The volume of people hooking up via the internet has encouraged another new twist: sampling several people at the same time. Susan explains: 'I was surprised to discover just how acceptable this has become. There'll be people that you're flirting with online, maybe someone else who you're texting and you could be "seeing" two guys or more – in the flesh, so to speak. Not that you tell any of the guys – as you don't want to put them off – but they sort of expect it and, anyway, they will probably be doing something similar too. Hopefully, you progress to something more serious and be ready for the "shall we stop seeing other people?" conversation. I always think this sounds terribly American, but maybe there's no better way to put it.'

The other benefit of new technology, which can also be a curse, is the ability to gather vast amounts of data and rank items. Several dating sites offer the chance to rate other members and create charts of their most popular members. Even when there are no such features, internet dating also allows us to measure our own popularity – every time we log on. 'There is nothing better than finding your in-box full of mail,' explains Erin, 'it's a real ego boost – especially after a rotten day at work.' Unfortunately, people resort to underhand means to boost their popularity. These include shaving years off their age – especially if they have just crossed a significant birthday – or posting pictures several years out of date. 'One of the things that has to be negotiated on a first date,' explains Megan, forty-two, 'is how many lies there are on your profile. I'm still thirty-eight – and holding – as many men automatically filter anybody over forty.' But what happens if you meet up and start dating? Megan used to try to keep up the pretence but kept contradicting herself. 'I once started a story about my fortieth birthday party and passed the point of no return before I'd realised my mistake. So I've tried making white lies the first topic of conversation and slipping it in halfway through the first meeting – either way it is always awkward.'

There is another issue with internet dating: the sheer amount of time that it can swallow. 'You have to be careful or you are online all evening,' explains Susan. 'I'll promise myself that I'll just check my messages and before I know it, I've been at the computer for a couple of hours. It's sort of addictive – so I ration myself.' However, when she had had a tough time at work, she would 'reward' herself with a couple of hours of flirting. 'It really gives you a lift that some guy that you really fancy has "tagged" your profile, and a text from a potential date after a tough meeting, where nobody is prepared to listen, can help power you through the afternoon. But I've decided to come offline for a while. I realised that I might be "meeting" lots of guys but I wasn't getting to know any of them. For the first couple of days, I felt rather jittery – perhaps Mr Right had sent me a message – but I held my nerve and I've been surprised at how calm I feel. I can finally concentrate on my work and friends again.' It is important to realise that internet dating can be a mood-altering quick fix – just like alcohol, caffeine, chocolate and other substances that are fine in moderation but cause problems in excess. If you are concerned that your internet dating has got out of hand, take the questionnaire in the exercise section.

The Battle of the Sexes

Dating has always pitched man against man, with the most beautiful woman in the room as the prize, and pitched woman against woman for the attention of the most eligible man. One would have hoped that sexual equality would allow men and women to understand each other better and meet with open hearts. Unfortunately, relations between the genders seems to be getting worse rather than better. Take, for example, the arrival of books offering dating tips to men. In the past, the advice had all been for women seeking men. This is because historically men have been allowed to pursue women ardently and openly, while women have been expected to pursue men ardently but covertly. The second is much harder and therefore women have needed more help. Unfortunately, men are now being encouraged to try covert strategies too. A recent bestseller, *The Game* (Canongate, 2007), provides men with a multitude of ruses for picking up women. In interviews, the author, Neil Strauss, has defended the duplicity, complaining that women have all the power in dating – the same justification that female authors use for their tricks. As a relationship counsellor, I am fascinated that both camps feel the other is in charge – especially as couples in crisis have the same complaint. Time and again, both husband and wife report that their partner has all the power and that they are powerless. My job is to unpick the game-playing, help both parties understand their strengths and vulnerabilities, communicate better and finally learn to co-operate. The same approach can work with courting, but first we need to look again to find alternative, less stressful and judgemental ways to meet. In this way, we can be not only relaxed and open but, most importantly, make better choices.

Summary

- Dating belongs to a certain age and a certain set of circumstances. It is not automatically the best way to meet someone today.
- Stress makes us act out of character, tell white lies and indulge in tricks to make us seem more desirable.
- Game-playing is not a good foundation for a long-term relationship.
- Dating encourages snap value judgements and ticking boxes. Online, this process is speeded up and the problems are amplified.
- The 'Battle of the Sexes' is making it more difficult for us to find love.

Exercises

Examine Your Personal Tick-boxes

This next exercise requires a lot of personal honesty. However, if you can be truthful, you will be able to approach your search for love in a completely new way.

Part One: Compile

- What are all your requirements for a partner? Write each one down and be as specific as possible. For example, don't just write 'the same age' or 'younger than me', put in the full acceptable age-range.
- Here are some prompts to help you. What about height? Hair colour? What physical characteristics (for instance, weight, muscular build, size of breasts)? What profession? What salary? What interests? Where does this person live? What about their past? What about their class? What about their family? What about the opinions/requirements of your own family?
- Next, look at reasons why you have turned down people who have shown an interest in the past. For example: he was wearing a cheap watch, or she had a common laugh. Be honest about your prejudices. Whom would you never date?
- Factor in past relationships and bad experiences that make you wary of dating someone with similar tastes or traits. Some of these might seem petty to other people but, if you are honest, are deal-breakers for you. When I did this exercise with Connor, thirty-two, he admitted: 'I always check out the music collection – especially after I dated this girl who had nothing but artists who were famous for one terrible novelty record. I didn't even know that most had even brought out albums until I found them in her home. Not only did it make me seriously question her judgement, but worse we'd always fight about what we'd listen to on long car journeys.' On a more serious note, Phoebe's previous boyfriend had been a bully. 'He never

attacked me, but I had the sense that he might if he didn't get his own way. So I tend to be nervous of big men and especially those with loud voices.'

- Is there anything else to add? Even if it makes you look shallow, put it on your list.

Part Two: Compromise

- Having compiled your list, go back and study it. How likely is it that someone will meet all these criteria? When you say: 'I never meet any eligible men' or 'I never meet any nice women', do you really mean 'I never meet anyone who ticks *all* my boxes'?

- Are there items which, on reflection, seem too restrictive? If so, strike them off your list.

- Next, think back to previous relationships: were there any issues which seemed like stumbling blocks but which subsequently you overcame? For example, Phoebe did not like people smoking in her flat and refused to date smokers. However, she had got to know Jamie at work and he had sneaked his way into her affections before she knew it. 'We found a way round; he agreed to go outside for a cigarette and after six months he cut down to only smoking on Saturday nights if we visited friends who smoked or went out to a club.' What else could you cross off your list?

- Imagine that your prospective date is a reasonable person. On which items might it be possible to find a compromise? For example, Connor could agree to have his choice of music on alternate car journeys, or listen to nothing and just chat. Is there anything else on the list that might be negotiable?

Part Three: Challenge

- Look again at your most deeply held convictions. These might seem sacred 'must have' items but are you, in reality, just bowing to received wisdom?

- Does money truly trump every other quality? Is the height of your partner really that important? Are there other ways of being attractive rather than the obvious movie-star or model looks?

- What items on your list could you move from prerequisites to preferences?
- At this point, hopefully, your list will be more about your prospective partner's character – intrinsic qualities – than habits, looks and circumstances – extrinsic matters.

Ultimately, it is better to have a short list than a long and unrealistic one. If you are thinking that I'm asking you to 'settle' for just anyone, be reassured it is about keeping an open mind. In this way, you will not rule out someone at the first hurdle who – if you suspended judgement until you knew them better – could turn out to be a great partner.

My Dating Audit

The idea of this exercise is to compare how you have met the people who have been significant in your life up to now, to take stock and to re-examine your current search for love.

1 Make a list of all the men or women who have been significant in your love life. By significant, I mean anyone that you dated for six months or more. Think back again and add anyone that you might have dismissed with the benefit of hindsight but who, at the time, seemed significant. This exercise works best with as many names as possible on the list.

2 Go back down the list and write beside each name how the two of you met. For example: at work, friend of friend, through mutual interests, sporting activity, at a party, blind date arranged by friend, internet date, just got talking etc. Be as specific as possible.

3 Return down the list and rate the relationships that ensued with marks from one to five.

4 Beside each name, add your general state of mind and attitude to dating when you first met. Once again, this will only work if you are truly honest with yourself. Rosemary, forty-four, put

the following beside her names when we did this exercise together: 'really just wanted someone to talk to', 'curious', 'I was more interested in learning my new job than dating', 'escape', 'sexy', 'he looked interesting and I wanted to get to know him', 'bored', 'I was sort of seeing someone else, so actually it was the last thing I needed'.

5 Next, look for patterns. Have you tended to meet people in one particular way? Is there a difference between how you met the past lovers who scored highly and the relationships that scored lower marks and lasted a shorter amount of time. What impact did your state of mind, when you met, have on the subsequent relationship?

When Rosemary compared the scores for the relationship and her state of mind, the ones that scored best happened when she had an open mind. 'Escape' turned into a social-dating scenario – where she liked her partner's social circle more than him. 'Bored' went nowhere. 'I'd just come out of a long-term relationship and I think I was a bit too desperate to be liked,' she explained. 'Sexy' did provide a lot of passion but ultimately not a lot more and she gave this relationship an average score. Her most successful relationships were: 'I was more interested in learning my new job than dating', 'he looked interesting and I wanted to get to know him', and 'I was sort of seeing someone else, so actually it was the last thing I needed'.

6 Make a comparison with the beginning of your dating career and the last two years? Have you changed your method of meeting people? Why has this been? Is there anything you can learn from your past successes? What changes would you like to make?

7 Finally, I want you to look at your current feelings about dating. Below are a series of statements about dating. Please do not think about your reply – just put the first thing that enters your mind:
• When I get ready for a date, I feel . . .
• The next day, after a date, I feel . . .

words that come to mind when you
iences and the experiences of your

upbeat and fun, keep on dating in the
gative, destructive or depressing, it is
break from dating and concentrate on
k. (Otherwise, like Rosemary's low-
u will probably meet someone who
ate problems – like boredom – rather
undations for an equal partnership.)
look for love but use the alternative,
pach outlined in the next chapter.

ting Habits

questions and total up the number

1 Do you feel increased tension and excitement when there is a possibility of a new online hook-up?
2 Do you find yourself looking forward to going online?
3 Do you plan your life around going online?
4 When you're out socialising with friends, do you find yourself thinking about what you might be missing online?
5 Do you ever have text conversations with a potential hook-up even though you are out socialising with friends?
6 Is your online flirting and hunting a reward for the stress that you endure?
7 Do you find that after making a conquest, you can begin to lose interest and start searching for someone else?
8 Does the flattery of strangers – even though you suspect it might not be sincere – still make you feel better about yourself?
9 Can life online help you forget about other problems?
10 Do you sometimes only truly feel yourself when you are online?

11 Do you disguise or tell white lies about the amount of time you spend online?

12 Have you ever chatted up someone online that you don't really fancy or someone that other people might find disgusting?

13 Do you find yourself repeatedly on your favourite dating site longer than you expected?

14 If you wake up in the middle of the night, will you go and check your messages?

15 Are you afraid that life will become unbearably dull and boring when you get older and fewer people find you attractive?

16 Has a friend, family member or work colleague expressed serious concern about the amount of time that you spend online or your dating habits?

17 Would you instinctively understand someone who said yes to most of these questions?

Scoring Your Answers
This questionnaire is designed to get you thinking rather than provide a point where you pass – and have no problems – or fail and should take action. However, you should be concerned if you answered 'yes' to more than four or five questions.

Understanding Your Score
I've adapted this questionnaire from those used to assess people with addictive personalities who have developed a cross-addiction. (It is common for someone to give up, for example, alcohol, only to repeat the patterns with prescription drugs or high-caffeine drinks.) One of the pioneers in this field was Dr Richard Heilman, who worked at the Hazeldean Foundation in Minnesota. His breakthrough was looking at patterns of behaviour rather than just the amounts or frequency of use of mood-altering substances or pastimes. He identified eight characteristics: *Preoccupation* (tested in questions 1–5), *Use alone* (not relevant), *Use for effect* and *Use as medicine* (tested in questions 6–10), *Protection of supply* (tested in questions 11 and 12), *Using more than planned* (tested in

questions 13 and 14), *Higher capacity than others* (tested in questions 15–17), and *Memory blackout* (not relevant).

What Action To Take

First of all, I think there should be a disclaimer. There is a big difference between abusing alcohol, drugs or sex (which have a serious health impact on the sufferer and causes distress to their families) and spending too long online or compulsive dating. However, I believe that this behaviour can be counter-productive to your search for a committed partner. So what should you do? It is probably time to take a break and consider different ways of meeting people. (There is more about this in the next chapter.) Anyone who has had a serious addiction problem, and scored highly on this test, should consider getting advice from their doctor or returning to an appropriate programme.

Chapter Seven

The Art of Mixing

In my work as a marital therapist, I always start by taking a history of my client's relationships. Over twenty-five years, I have heard hundreds of stories of how couples fell in love. Despite the grip of 'love at first sight' and romantic notions of falling for strangers celebrated in books, films and songs, most people know each other casually, or even distantly, before going out together. Here is just one example: 'I'd heard a lot from friends about David – and his weird sense of humour – before I met him,' says Sharon, a 32-year-old account executive. 'I found his trick – of putting two straws up his nose to drink his cocktail – absolutely disgusting, but somehow he grew on me. After bumping into each other at mutual friends' parties for about six months, we decided we were meant to be together.'

Work has been another low-risk way to meet people. 'We got to know each other over the office internal email system,' explains Elizabeth, thirty-eight, who has been married to Henry for five years. 'He used to send out these really funny messages and although I didn't know him – he worked in a different building – I joined in one of the jokes. At one point, we must have exchanged a dozen emails across the day and then he appeared at my desk with a coconut low-fat latte, my favourite, and introduced himself.'

Other couples have a shared interest. Mike, the 38-year-old divorcé from Chapter Five who met his partner while ballroom dancing, explains: 'I asked her for a salsa, and later in the evening we had a quickstep and I stayed to chat to her and her friends. It was all very relaxed and at the end of the evening I asked for her number. I had no nerves calling a couple of days later and arranging to go dancing – because we'd got on so well. It's great to have something in common and we are thinking of entering an amateur ballroom-dancing competition together.'

The key advantage of meeting someone casually – as a friend of a friend, through work or sharing a hobby – is that all the defences are down. You are not meeting a potential life-partner but chatting for thirty seconds while waiting for the lift. You are not fantasising about a picnic on the beach with the stranger at the bar, but sharing the minutes to a meeting because someone did not photocopy enough, or learning to speak Spanish together. Under these circumstances, your subconscious can get to work on whether there is a true match – without your conscious brain criticising: too fat, too poor, too not-me. Better still, the stakes are so low that there is no need for game-playing and you are more likely to be yourself.

What I'm suggesting, in effect, is a return to the roots of British courting: parading, mixing and saying 'How do you do?'. Don't worry, it does not involve hanging round windy hill-tops, but finding the modern equivalent of mixing. At parties, it is not looking for a partner but for an interesting conversation – which might lead to a recommendation for an art exhibition and getting talking to someone else at the gallery. It is about joining a poetry class, not to find a potential date, but because you love words, and then going to a classmate's coffee-shop performance and being introduced to someone from his or her workplace. It is about volunteering to join the 'blue skies' think-tank at work, being sent off to the Basingstoke branch and sharing a taxi from the station with someone. Mixing is about being open to new ideas, new opportunities and ultimately new people. This is how it works in practice. Andrew, in his mid-thirties, and Iliana, in her late twenties, have been married for two years. They met shortly after Iliana moved into a new flat in London and needed paper to line the drawers of her wardrobes. She could find nothing in the nearest department store so asked at the till. Andrew overheard this conversation and suggested another shop nearby. 'I could have kicked myself that I let her get away,' he explains, 'I should have offered to show her where it was.' 'I have to admit that I thought he was very attractive,' said Iliana. Fortunately, fate threw them together ten minutes later. 'I had bought the paper and was heading back when I saw Andrew on the pavement. So I walked up and thanked him,' she explained. 'I wasn't going to let her get away a second time and invited her for a cup of coffee,' he added. They went carol-singing together, he helped decorate her flat and slowly they became a couple. What is crucial about this story is that neither of them was looking for a date. Iliana was out shopping; Andrew was just being helpful. Even after their first coffee, they did not start dating but rather 'hung out' together.

Seven Skills for Effective Mixing

The good news is that not only will these seven skills help you meet more people but they will also undo some of the bad habits acquired through dating. So what are they?

1 Riding the flow.
2 Six degrees of separation.
3 Becoming open-hearted.
4 Flirting.
5 Taking a risk.
6 Do as you would be done by.
7 Becoming philosophical.

Some of these skills are immediately obvious and others will need more explanation. They work best when they become second nature and, to this end, I've devised a series of exercises at the end of the chapter.

1 Riding the Flow

Have you ever been so wrapped up in something that when you finally looked at your watch, time had just evaporated? Psychologists call this total immersion 'riding the flow' – not only is it extremely pleasurable but your mood is expansive, tolerant and creative. Even better, we forget ourselves and are therefore less self-conscious and less likely to be self-critical. Not only is this the perfect state of mind to meet a partner, but the chances are increased dramatically: happy people are a pleasure to be around.

So what is the difference between an activity that keeps us busy and riding the flow? The founding father of the flow concept is Mihály Csikszentmihályi, a psychology professor at Claremont Graduate University in California. He believes that flow peaks when 'challenges are met by skills'. The most obvious arena is work and, as previously discussed, work is a great place to meet a partner. However, research in ten European countries shows that people get more satisfaction from activities outside work. The most common examples would be sport or exercise, which provide plenty of challenges. Alternatively, the satisfaction could come through leisure activities like joining a choir – anything that is taken seriously and demands a level of skill. Another type of leisure activity which meets Csikszentmihályi's concept of challenge is volunteering. Indeed, when researchers looked at the motives for people volunteering in London, over a third of respondents said 'it gets me out of myself' and two-thirds explained 'I really enjoy it'. Unfortunately, our most popular leisure activity, watching the TV, seldom provides flow as it requires little commitment or challenge and no skill.

So how do you find your own personal flow?

- It must be something that you find personally rewarding and which maintains your interest. This cannot be stressed too much. Although, for example, a woman might find more potential partners in a car-maintenance class, if she is not keen on learning about engines she will be checking out the guys rather than riding the flow. Therefore, she is more likely to tick boxes and less likely to get to know her classmates. Even somewhere less likely to provide heterosexual men, like a reading group, is a better option. In the flow, a woman will make relationships and it does not matter that these are other women. Market researchers have consistently found that women who marry have more female friends than those who remain single.

- Set yourself small realistic goals. It is better to aim at learning twenty French words a week, than to speak French in time for your holiday. While a goal achieved sets up flow, aiming too high and being overwhelmed only sets up failure and depression.

- Make certain that your goals do not conflict. It is unlikely that you will succeed if your ambitions are both to earn more money and to improve your backhand at tennis. In fact, researchers at the University of Michigan found that people who have goals that are money-orientated or about social recognition are significantly less likely to be happy.

- Seek to help others rather than just look after number one. Surprisingly, you will reap the personal benefits. The University of Michigan research shows that volunteering is the second greatest source of joy, after dancing, and a good way of meeting people, making friends and ultimately finding a potential partner. The amount someone 'participates in personally and culturally valued goals' is the best predictor of happiness – better than personality (how extroverted and outgoing) and resources (wealth and access to opportunities). Remember, happy people are attractive people.

Tip: As your aim is to find a partner, look for ways to flow with other people. If hours disappear when you are playing the piano, instead of playing alone, accompany the local amateur operatic society. If you enjoy squash, don't just play your regular opponents, join a league. If you are a keen gardener, rather than just cultivating your own patch, join a conservation group and help manage a forest. If you cannot think of something to fire your imagination and provide flow, see the exercise section.

2 Six Degrees of Separation

When I discuss my work with single people, they always complain about how difficult it is to meet people. I have to suppress a smile, because these conversations often happen at parties where we are literally surrounded by people. Maybe none of our fellow guests are suitable partners, but each one of them has friends and acquaintances who might be perfect. In fact, according to the sociologists at Duke University in North Carolina, most people have 750 acquaintances by name or sight. When you consider that each of them will have a similar number of friends too, before long it is possible to believe that everybody is connected. Frigyes Karinthy, a Hungarian author and journalist who lived between 1887 and 1938, claimed that we can link ourselves to any other human on earth using no more than five intermediaries, one of whom is a personal acquaintance. The idea was tested in a famous sixties experiment by an American social psychologist called Stanley Milgram. He mailed random people and asked them to forward a parcel on to a stockbroker in Boston. All the recipients had to go on was a name and a city. The idea was that they would redirect the parcel to someone who might forward it closer to the final recipient. The average number of times that the parcel was forwarded was six. In the nineties, the idea was also taken up by American college students in the game 'Six Degrees of Kevin Bacon' where any film actor, from any period of history, is linked by appearing in the same movie as Kevin Bacon or someone who had been in a movie with him. In fact, most actors do not need six intermediaries, which suggests we might all be closer than we imagine.

But what does all this mean for mixing and finding your ideal partner? Firstly, the more friends and acquaintances, the greater chance of meeting him or her. Market researcher John T. Molloy interviewed 2,500 couples coming out of marriage-licence bureaux in the USA and wrote the book *Why Men Marry Some Women and*

Not Others (Warner Books, 2004). He discovered that women about to marry knew significantly more people – in fact, 90 per cent had between seven and fourteen good women friends. Molloy also interviewed women with no proposal in sight and discovered that they had statistically fewer friends. Secondly, six degrees of separation underlines just how important it is to take every opportunity to talk to people. A stranger could be one of the links to your significant other, and even if they are not, the practice will also help build your confidence. To this end, I've created an exercise called 'Working the Six Degrees in Your Favour'.

Tip: To demonstrate just how powerful this concept can be, look back at your previous partners. How many times did you meet someone who was a friend of a friend? Even if you met by chance, at a bar, club or on the internet, did you have acquaintances in common? Calculate how many degrees of separation there were between you and each of your lovers. My guess is that it will probably be just two or three.

3 Becoming Open-hearted

What is the best predictor for whether two people will be attracted? When I put this question to friends, business contacts and acquaintances, there was a clear consensus: looks. When searching for single people to be interviewed for my book, I would be told: 'she or he is very attractive/presentable' as if this is the sole key to finding a partner. My contacts always sounded slightly bewildered that their friend had not been snapped up. Yet if you look round your own circle of friends, you will find ordinary and even plain people who are never short of dates and gorgeous ones who seem doomed to remain single. So what's going on?

Fortunately social psychologists have always been fascinated by what attracts people to each other and the results go completely against our preconceptions. The key predictor is not looks but the *sheer amount of contact time*. A classic study in the 1950s studied friendship patterns of students on a large university campus. At the beginning of term, the apartments were assigned randomly. At the end of term, the researchers looked at who became friends or partners. The strongest predictor was not personality, nor looks but the location of the apartments. Another test which studied sexual attraction assigned college students their seats in class by alphabetical order. Once again, students who sat closest were most likely to become couples. On one hand, the importance of proximity should not be a shock. If we don't meet someone we can hardly be attracted to them. But on the other hand, romantic books and films are built on the premise of the handsome stranger. In other words, we expect to be attracted to the unknown but are most likely to fall for the known.

Social psychologists have found a second key predictor of mutual attraction: *similarity*. By this, they mean that we are most comfortable with people who are like us because this confirms and validates our view of the world. Although we might occasionally like a challenge – perhaps for a fling or a short-term infatuation – ultimately we choose someone similar in one or more of the following ways: attitudes, personality, demographic characteristics and lifestyle. Similarity and proximity mutually reinforce each other because time spent together increases the perception that someone is like us and therefore the chance of being attracted and ultimately of falling in love.

So how do you move from a spark of interest for someone that you see on a regular or semi-regular basis to a relationship? This is where my third skill for effective mixing comes in: becoming open-hearted. Contrary to many people's expectations, personality is more important than looks in attracting a partner. The evidence comes from research into 1,000 freshers (first-year students) at the University of Kent who were asked to rate qualities in possible mates. The results were:

1 Kind/considerate
2 Socially exciting
3 Artistic/intelligent
4 Easy-going/adaptable

When the team followed this up with in-depth questions, where respondents were asked to pick just one quality for an ideal relationship, friendship came out top for both men (12 per cent) and women (13 per cent). Honesty came second for both women (11 per cent) and men (7 per cent). The only significant differences between the genders was that women stressed companionship (7 per cent) while men preferred kindness (5 per cent) and that men put attractiveness in their top five qualities (5 per cent) while women hardly rated it at all (1.5 per cent).

So how do you come across as open-hearted?

- *Smile*. This will not only make you seem warm but approachable too.
- *Maintain good eye-contact*. People who cannot look us directly in the eye are considered to be lying or trying to hide something.
- *Be positive*. We like people who are positive because they make us feel good about the world and, most important of all, ourselves. Someone who criticises, even if it is just something inconsequential like the decor, might be perceived as clever, intelligent or funny but we are always wary. Deep down, we fear they will be equally cutting about us behind our backs or, worse still, that the criticism is an indirect attack on our tastes or our personality.
- *Appear interested*. This includes nodding the head, repeating back key phrases so the person speaking knows you have been listening ('so he stepped right out in front of you') and, most powerful of all, identifying feeling ('you must have been horrified').

Although everybody is happy to sign up to being open-hearted, unfortunately buried beneath our surface bonhomie is often something very different. While researching this book, I have been surprised at just how quick we are to judge. It might not be socially acceptable to make sweeping statements about someone based on their ethnic background, religion or sexuality, but we are happy to judge 'all unattached men' or 'all single women'. Charlotte, thirty-eight, was very forthright about her lack of choice: 'It's only the losers left.' When I questioned whether that damning phrase could really apply to every unattached man in London, she softened her stance – but only slightly. 'OK, but I am very suspect if a man is successful and not in a relationship. I don't want to have to do all the work or all the nurturing.' As she had such a low opinion about single men, I wondered if single women were equally 'suspect'. 'Your average woman is better versed in chat, understanding and empathy so, no I don't think the same rules apply to women on the singles scene,' she concluded. Unfortunately single men in their thirties are not so forgiving and make similarly dismissive judgements on single women in their thirties. Simon is thirty-six and single, but having achieved his childhood ambition to travel the five continents and finished his training to become a photographer, is ready to settle down: 'I've been surveying the market and I think I will probably go for a younger girl. Women in their thirties have a lot of mileage and baggage. They have been jilted a lot and are often embittered, so need a lot of work to soften them up. I often find myself thinking: "I don't know if I'd bother."' Both Charlotte and Simon would have described themselves as open-hearted. (Simon said: 'I've got a lot to offer and I'm honest with myself and other people' and Charlotte: 'I'm intelligent and I have a kind heart.') However, it took only a little probing to discover a judgemental side which undermined their chances of finding a partner.

Tip: John Gottman, emeritus professor at the University of Washington, has studied how couples interact for over thirty years and claims to be able to predict with 90 per cent accuracy which newlyweds will remain married and which will divorce four to six years later. He stresses the importance of positive strokes: compliments, thank yous, reassurances, recognition of the other's viewpoints. We imagine that one unpleasant gesture – like criticism or complaint – can be cancelled out by one positive stroke. However, Gottman's findings suggest that our instincts are wrong. Couples that stay married will balance one negative with five positives, while couples that divorce can often have ten negatives to one positive. So, to appear open-hearted, it is important to increase your ratio of positives to negatives. This does not mean becoming unbearably cheerful or making up compliments, as this can come across as false, but communicating more effectively. Most people feel hundreds of positive emotions about their friends and work colleagues every day: 'it's nice to see you' or 'I really admire the way that you handled that'. Unfortunately, we keep most of these thoughts to ourselves. So try telling people your internal positives rather than keeping them secret. For more on this subject see the exercise 'The Power of Acknowledging'.

4 Flirting

If the core of the British way of meeting potential partners has always been 'parading, mixing and "how do you do?"', the first two skills ('Riding the flow' and 'Six degrees of separation') were parading, the third ('Becoming open-hearted') was mixing in its purest form. The fourth skill covers 'how do you do?'. Today, we call it *flirting*. If you have been out of the singles game for a while, this can be particularly daunting. Even if you are an experienced flirt, this recap will be helpful. In essence, there are three key ingredients to successful flirting: encouraging body language, easy-flowing conversation and confidence. So taking each in more detail:

Encouraging Body Language
- Leaning slightly towards someone – although not too close so that their personal space is invaded – shows interest.
- Keep an open posture, as crossing your arms will make you look defensive.
- Nodding signals not just encouragement but demonstrates involvement in the story that you're being told. However, be aware that we normally nod in pairs. Three nods suggests that you wish to interrupt.
- Blinking can also set a romantic mood. We blink every two or three seconds and increasing the rate will increase your partner's

too. Conversely, slowing down a blink to a third of its natural speed can be sexually attractive as it mimics a wink.

- Mirroring – where you match your body posture to someone else's – can amplify any intimacy that is growing between two people.
- Babies love the game 'peek-a-boo' – where you hide your face behind your hand and then suddenly appear from nowhere. They will play it over and over without ever seeming to get bored. Adults who are interested in each other play a very similar game: looking at someone, then looking away and back again. They also use props like menus to disappear behind and then suddenly appear.

Easy-flowing Conversation

- Value small talk. It is a good way of warming up for a more interesting conversation and provides a breathing space to relax and get a general impression of each other. So make a list of opening subjects that are non-controversial. For example: weather, recent news story, celebrity goings-on and TV programmes.
- After being introduced or the first burst of conversation, how do you keep the words flowing? The secret is to offer small snippets of self-disclosure that can seed a longer conversation. For example, don't just say that you're a teacher, but give the age group or the subject that you teach. (This gives the other person two possible avenues for more questions, observations or personal self-disclosure.)
- When using your small talk topics add extra conversational hooks. For example: 'At least the rain will bring on things in my allotment' or 'I love the hot weather but my dog prefers to lie in the shade.'
- Look for areas of conversational connection. Even if you do not have an allotment or a garden, you could be interested in food miles or organic production.
- Echo the other person's language. If he is a teacher and calls his pupils 'kids', use the same word as this will help increase your

connection. If she is a businesswoman and refers to her 'firm', don't subsequently call it a 'company' as this will put up a conversational barrier.

- Don't block topics. For example, if you meet a dog owner, telling the story of how you were bitten by a dog as a child is not going to build rapport. A rant against dogs fouling the pavements will not help either. Instead, build on the topic by asking questions – 'what kind of dog?' – or bridging to another subject: 'do you take your dog on holiday with you . . .' followed by 'where are you going this year?'
- Never underestimate the importance of asking questions. Everybody likes talking about themselves and their interests. A good listener will always be appreciated. So as well as offering your snippets of self-disclosure, be ready to take up other people's too.

Confidence

- We like confident and outgoing people, so hold your head up both literally and metaphorically. If this is hard, make a list of *three* things under each of the following headings: parts of my body that I like; positive aspects of my personality; past achievements; past compliments; and my potential.
- Check your language in case you are unknowingly running yourself down. Examples would be: 'this is probably not a good idea . . .', 'it's only me' or 'it's not important what I think'. Listen to your friends and see if they make similar mistakes and compile a list of phrases to be avoided.
- Be upbeat. For example, if someone asks 'what do you do?', don't waste this opportunity by saying 'I'm only a . . .'. Even if you do not like your job, talk about the aspects that you do like: 'I'm a salesman and you get to see some really beautiful parts of the country.' When you are interested and excited, your face muscles become more animated and more attractive.
- Confidence is not about being perfect. It comes from knowledge and experience, and through achieving small goals. The good news is that by working your way through this book you will

already have increased your knowledge about yourself and about courting. Adopting the seven skills of mixing, and in particular the exercise 'Taking a Risk: a Step-by-step Approach', will build experience and provide small achievable goals.

Tip: Become a people-watcher. At parties, restaurants and in bars, look at how people interact. Here are a few things to concentrate on: What encourages someone to cross the floor and talk to someone else? What behaviour or posture repels rather than attracts? What body language shows that two people are engrossed or that they are bored? When is it appropriate to self-disclose and what information should be kept back? How do confident people behave? A note of caution. The aim is to critique your own technique, and check whether you are not unwittingly putting people off, rather than to become a seductress or a smooth charmer. Such tricks provide a quick ego-boost but are no foundation for a serious relationship.

5 Taking a Risk

Embracing the seven skills of mixing has a cumulative effect on your prospects for finding true love. If you have been in the flow, taken on board the networking opportunities of six degrees of separation, met new people with an open attitude and indulged in some low-grade flirting, someone or even several people will emerge who you'll begin to think of as more than a work colleague, an acquaintance or a friend. So how do you decide which prospects to pursue and which to discard? When long-term couples are asked how they knew their beloved was someone special, they often answer: 'we just sort of knew'. The journalist and writer Malcolm Gladwell would put this down to intuition. In his bestselling book, *Blink* (Allen Lane, 2005), he both celebrates and warns about thin-slicing: judging a whole experience by a few moments' exposure. He tells the story of the expert who took one look at an ancient statue – and despite the documentation and scientific tests proving authenticity – rightly declared it a fake. His instinctive response was repulsion and he knew something was wrong. When it comes to dating, many people decide if they are interested in someone when that person walks through the door – before she has even opened her mouth or he has taken his coat off. It saves time and cuts the crowd down into a manageable size.

However, Gladwell has examples where thin-slicing went spectacularly wrong. Coca-Cola decided to change the recipe for their soft drink on the basis of a taste test where their new sweeter formula scored higher appreciation scores than the traditional brand. However, the launch of the new Coke was a complete failure and Coca-Cola had to re-introduce the old recipe – at huge cost to the company. What happened? The people in the trial had been asked to just *sip* the new recipe and on that basis the sweeter formula did taste better. However, we don't just take one sip of a soft drink. We drink a glass or a can and under these circumstances, the new Coke tasted too sweet. Applying this to finding love, we tend to thin-slice and imagine that we can judge compatibility and lasting passion on just shaking hands and thirty seconds of conversation. In others words, just sipping the relationship is one experience, living with someone – drinking the whole two-litre bottle – is quite another.

If thin-slicing can let us down, what is the alternative? The conventional answer is facts and figures. Coca-Cola had spent a fortune on market research and the museum that bought the fake statue had analysis that seemed to prove that the surface could only have aged over hundreds or thousands of years. Gladwell quotes one of the museum's curators: 'I always believed scientific opinion more objective than aesthetic judgement.' In dating, this approach is 'how many of my boxes does he or she tick?' In fact, Lydia, whose tick-list I included in the previous chapter, had lost all trust in her own judgement and even wondered what it would be like to have an arranged marriage: 'I doubt that my parents could make worse choices than I've made for myself.' Another example of the scientific approach is Oliver, thirty-nine, who drew up a questionnaire to take to a speed-dating event. 'I gathered a huge amount of information about the women, but at the end of the evening all I had was lists of ages, jobs, interests, favourite movie stars and whether someone was a day or a night person. In fact, I was more confused than ever.' So how do you find a middle way between snap judgements on one extreme and being overwhelmed with masses of information on the other? This is where *taking a risk* enters the equation.

When adopting this mixing skill, the first job is to reconsider people that you already know but have dismissed on possibly spurious grounds. John T. Molloy, who interviewed the couples coming out of marriage-licence bureaux, found that 20 per cent of the women had not liked their intended when they first met him. However, something had made them reconsider and take a risk. Here is an example from my case book which illustrates the benefit of this approach: 'David had been the boyfriend of one of my closest friends, so I knew him well from dinner parties and outings to the theatre,' says Caroline, a 38-year-old communications manager. 'His split from my friend was painful, but amicable, and to help David through the lonely times I would still invite him to my parties. People said we would make a good couple, but to be honest he was short, a little overweight and losing his hair. Not my type; I didn't fancy him. What can I say? Still, he was a good listener, fun to be with and we had similar values. One Sunday afternoon, he was sitting in the courtyard outside my flat. I'd had a barbecue but everybody else had gone home and suddenly I had this thought: "What would it be like to love David?" Almost instinctively, I started stroking his arm. It felt good; he gave me a kiss. The rest is history.' Caroline and David are now married and have two children. 'The funniest thing of all is that today, I find him really attractive,' confesses Caroline. The second way of taking a risk is to suspend judgement for longer and give your unconscious time to breathe and decide. In Molloy's sample of brides-to-be, there was another group who had been neutral about their future husband and stopped dating him after one or two dates. However, these men had not given up, and six months or so later had phoned up again and the women had relented. They had, in effect, taken a risk on a fresh look and liked what they had seen.

So how does *taking a risk* work in the context of mixing? If you have been thinking about someone in a new way, it is probably time to see more of them. This might be officially seen as a 'date' or possibly just an extension of your normal routine: for example, going for a drink together after work or class. Of course, you are going to want to make a judgement about your compatibility and whether to progress this relationship further. However, I would suggest that you follow these guidelines:

- *No introspection on the 'date'.* Far too often we become paralysed by too much analysis. Just enjoy the moment.
- *Let the experience brew.* Straight after, it is fine to have a top-line impression – 'that went rather well' – but try to avoid making a judgement on compatibility and instead sleep on it.
- *Allow memories and thoughts to bubble up to the surface overnight.* Remember when you saw a great movie or TV programme or maybe read an interesting book, you keep thinking about it days and sometimes years later. The ideas or characters return unbidden. In contrast, the majority of what we see or read – however enjoyable at the time – is almost instantly forgotten. The same process happens with 'dates' and is a good way of sorting the life changing from the merely pleasant.
- *Ultimately, your unconscious will tell you if there is a true match.* But your unconscious can only talk if you are prepared to listen – and that is impossible if you are too busy analysing. By waiting until the next morning, you will have avoided the snap judgement but will have not had enough time to be overwhelmed by information. Most importantly, you will have taken a risk and have stretched your normal window of decision making.

Tip: Don't be in a hurry when it comes to finding a lifelong partner. In fact there is a lot to be said for falling in love slowly. There is less chance of projecting your ideal partner onto some poor unsuspecting man or woman (who subsequently makes you angry because they fail to live up to your expectations) or becoming a victim of a hyperactive imagination (where you misread neutral or polite gestures as interest and fall for the wrong man or woman). Most importantly, don't be overwhelmed by first impressions. When Ellie, thirty-one, saw Kieran, thirty-six, for the first time she almost sneaked away: 'To be honest I did not fancy him at all. However, it would have been rude to just disappear so we had a coffee and agreed to see an exhibition in the gallery. I was impressed straight away by how he automatically fell into my pace. He was very knowledgeable and as we went round the paintings, he would guide me with a light touch in the small of my back. It was very gentlemanly but suddenly I felt this charge of desire.' If you feel ready to take a risk, and increase the number of people with whom you mix, there is a step-by-step approach in the exercise section.

6 Do As You Would Be Done By

In the name of finding love, our behaviour is often anything but loving. We frequently judge on the most superficial grounds, condemn whole tranches of the population and lie or bend the truth. However, we expect others to consider our character and personality, not just our looks, weight and bank balance. Moreover, we demand honesty and transparency. In effect, there is one rule for us and one rule for everybody else. How can love – which thrives on equality – stand a chance? This is why the sixth skill draws on ancient wisdom: 'Do unto others as you would have them do unto you' (Bible, Matthew 7: 12) or 'What you do not wish upon yourself, extend not to others' (Confucius, a Chinese philosopher who lived between 551 and 479 BC) and 'This is the sum of duty; do naught unto others what you would not have them do unto you' (*Mahabharata* – ancient Sanskrit text of Hindu mythology and philosophy). This idea is expanded further in the exercise 'Looking in the Mirror'.

One of the most important areas for 'Do as you would be done by' is asking someone out. We need a level playing field so both sides understand the particular pressures and pitfalls of asking and refusing. If men knew the problems of women (who have been traditionally supposed to wait to be asked) and women knew men's fears (looking foolish), we would be kinder and treat others as we would like to be treated ourselves. So how would it work? These are the new rules of 'seeing someone':

1 Both men and women have an equal opportunity to ask each other out. After all, everybody aspires to an equal partnership and this should be in place from the very beginning.
2 With both genders asking out and being asked out, and therefore understanding the fear of rejection, the policy should be, generally, to accept an invitation.
3 First outings should be small events: just going for a coffee together, rather than concert tickets and meals in expensive restaurants.
4 By keeping the first outing quite short, it is easier to say 'yes' and expectations are kept low too.
5 Afterwards, if you promise to call or contact, it is your responsibility to do so.
6 Alternate paying. Whoever suggests the outing pays, as this will get round any discrepancy in salaries.

Tip: You've finally plucked up the courage to ask him or her out, but the answer was: 'thank you, but no thank you'. So how do you deal with a refusal? Brush it off! There are thousands of reasons why he or she might have declined your invitation. It could be that he or she is already involved (in which case make a note to research availability next time) or maybe sees you as a friend (you can never have too many friends) or perhaps has made a judgement that you are not his or her 'type'. In many cases, the refusal is as much about your target's circumstances, personality and tastes as it is to do with you. So be positive (I had the courage to ask and it will be easier next time) and know that you cannot be successful all the time (the more people I ask the greater the odds of an acceptance). But what about your internal chatterbox which keeps running you down and ruining your confidence? The more you listen, the worse rejection feels until it reaches catastrophic proportions. Instead of letting the voice carry on unchecked, write everything down. Do not censor anything, just keep taking dictation. Then go back and cross off anything that is wrong, pure supposition or needless exaggeration. This will cut the chatterbox voice down to size and help preserve a sense of proportion.

7 Becoming Philosophical

If you have taken on board the ideas in part one of this book (working on your emotional heritage and unloading the baggage from past relationships), and adopted the other skills of mixing (thereby changing the way that you search for love), your chances of finding a partner will have increased dramatically. I would like to write that you will be guaranteed to find a loving and rewarding relationship – but life is never that simple. I wish this was not the case. As my partner would tell you, my greatest fault is that 'I want it all and I want it now'. If that's how you feel about finding true love, but fate, your god or the universe is throwing up obstacles, what do you do? Firstly, you need to ask yourself: Have I got more baggage to unpack? Secondly, have I truly embraced mixing: am I getting out enough with a relaxed and open attitude? Thirdly, and this is where the final skill of mixing comes in, you need to be philosophical.

Although we think of philosophy as being something studied at universities and dominated by dead men with beards, it is in essence about making sense of the world around us. Its goal is wisdom, truth and happiness. In other words, philosophy is not just for academics, but a tool for a better everyday life. So what would a philosopher make of the dilemma of not being able to find love? First of all, Socrates (470–399 BC) would applaud you for all the work that you've done so far on yourself. He believed that 'the unexamined life is not worth living'. Next, we should stop lashing out in every direction with frustration. As Aristotle (384–322 BC) said: 'Anybody can be angry – that is easy, but to be angry with the right person, and to the right degree, and at the right time, and for the right purpose, and in the right way – that is not within everybody's power and is not easy.' In the search for love, we should heed the warning of French philosopher Blaise Pascal (1623–62): 'Man's unhappiness springs from one thing alone: his inability to stay quietly in one room.' Pascal believed that our fear of unhappiness is so great that we flock to the slightest thing if it promises diversion. Unfortunately, diversions follow the law of diminishing returns and soon become boring. So instead of ricocheting between excitement and boredom, we should sit quietly, look deeper and listen harder. In this way, we might discover something or, in this case, someone, who is more than a passing diversion.

But perhaps Stoic philosophers like Epictetus (AD 55–135) have the ultimate answer: 'Make the best of what is in your power, and take the rest as it happens.' The idea is expanded by Prajnānpad (1891–1974), who introduced Freud and psychoanalysis to India: 'What is done has become the past; it does not exist now. What will happen is the future and does not exist now. So? What exists? What is here and now. Nothing more . . . stay in the present: act, act, act.' How do we embrace Epictetus and Prajnānpad, and use their wisdom to ease our path through mixing? We have to accept the things over which we have no control and concentrate on what we can influence: our own behaviour. This means embracing all seven skills of mixing and following, in particular, the exercise 'Taking a Risk: a Step-by-step Approach'. Sometimes when we stop trying to control – and when we least expect it – love comes to us.

Tip: Try reading some philosophy. André Comte-Sponville is a professor of philosophy at the Sorbonne in Paris and has written several good books for the general reader. Alain de Botton is another gateway into philosophy; his best-known book is *The Consolations of Philosophy* (Hamish Hamilton, 2000). I would also recommend reading about Buddhism, which is just as much a philosophy as a faith, so try: *Eight Steps to Happiness* by Geshe Kelsang Gyatso (Tharpa Publications, 2000).

Summary

- Most successful couples know each other before going out together. They meet through casual social connections, hobbies or work and are therefore less likely to play games or be defensive.
- Mixing is a new approach to looking for a partner. Rather than intense periods of searching – like at a party or on the internet – followed by long 'switched-off' periods of working and general living, mixing allows you to be forever meeting people but in a low-key way – with judgement suspended – so that your unconscious can check out if there is a true match.
- Looks are not the most important ingredient for finding a partner. Contact time, similarity and personality are all key.
- Both men and women need to be kinder to each other, less dismissive, and to avoid making sweeping generalisations. If we do not judge, it is likely that others will return the favour and be less judgemental about us.
- Take your time to get to know someone rather than judging on first impressions. This is not 'settling' but rather waiting for second impressions and thereby not ruling out someone too soon. Instead, give yourself to the moment and let the magic unfold naturally and in its own time.
- Looking for love brings out the philosopher in us. At one end of the scale, some people are passive and leave it up to fate. At the other, they take too much responsibility and view not having a partner as a sign of personal failure. Mixing provides a middle way between these two extremes.

Exercises

Unblocking the Flow

It is fine for people who have all-consuming hobbies, challenging jobs or a drive to help in the community. What if you find your work uninteresting, have not played sport since leaving school and are not creative? The following exercise will help you get started:

1 *Remember your childhood.* Children love to play, it is how they discover their skills and their creative abilities. Unfortunately, as we get older we begin to censor ourselves. 'I will never play football for Manchester United' or 'dance a solo for the Royal Ballet'. What would you have done if only you had had the opportunity, the encouragement or the self-belief? If you find it hard to remember, ask your parents or look at old home movies. When I did this exercise myself, I remembered my childhood desire to have a puppy which ultimately led to getting a collie/spaniel cross and joining a dog agility club.

2 *What makes you angry?* There is passion in anger and creativity too. It may be that there is nothing for young people in your area. Perhaps the suffering of animals or cancer patients gets you going. Research which charities are looking for volunteers.

3 *Switch off your television on three consecutive evenings.* The TV not only swallows hours of our spare time but acts like a tranquilliser and stops us thinking. Although the first evening will probably be uncomfortable, these are the withdrawal symptoms – stick with it. (Try not to use other distraction tactics – like going into internet chat-rooms.) By the second evening, you will be calmer and other ways to occupy yourself will suggest themselves. Even if these do not seem very promising, do not be discouraged. Even something physical, like

scrubbing the kitchen floor, can occupy the body and allow the unconscious to throw out some good ideas. By the third evening, you will probably have some ideas to research – follow these threads of interest and see where they go.

4 *Think outside the box*. Don't be put off by big ideas. In fact the bigger the better. At the dreaming stage, you can do anything. So don't shut down a potential avenue by getting all practical, allow your imagination to float free. Wait until your passion is firmly established before looking at how to turn an idea into a reality. OK, you will not be playing for Manchester United but you could train to be a referee or coach a youth team. Want to get into the movies? Although you are unlikely to cause Nicole Kidman any sleepless nights, you could register with an agency that provides extras for film and TV productions.

5 *What is stopping you?* Write down all the excuses and look at them rationally. Are they true? Am I exaggerating? Should they really stop me from pressing ahead?

Working the Six Degrees in Your Favour

We all know the importance of friends but just how much they affect our well-being is underlined by a research project in Chicago. Participants who named five or more people with whom they had discussed intimate matters over the past six months were 60 per cent more likely to feel 'very happy'. Firstly, if you feel good about life and yourself, you will attract other positive people and be less likely to indulge in comfort dating. Secondly, your friends have friends and they have friends: a network of opportunity.

• Do a friendship audit. Look back over the past six months and calculate how many people you spoke to about 'intimate matters' – by this I mean sharing your hopes, disappointments and fears.

Write down the names. These will be the front line in your support network.

- Is there anybody else who you would feel comfortable talking to on a truly intimate level? If the answer is yes, tell this friend about your search for a partner and how this makes you feel. They can provide emotional support – or 'bonding' social capital (look back at Chapter One for more on this concept).
- Are there any friends who could provide emotional support, but circumstances, lack of time or a falling-out has meant that you have not seen or spoken to them for six months? How could you re-establish contact?
- Having increased your 'bonding' social capital, turn to your 'bridging' capital. These are normally people with whom you have less in common but, because they are highly sociable, know lots of other people. In this way, they act as a bridge to increase your circle of acquaintances.
- Can you think of anybody who fits this description? If so, it is probably worth strengthening your connection – by, for example, inviting them to your next barbecue or inviting them to join a group of your friends on a night out. Don't worry that you are 'taking advantage' because these social connectors enjoy introducing people to each other.
- What about your close friends, do they know anybody who 'knows everybody'? In other words, someone with a lot of bridging capital. If so, ask for an introduction. These people are vital for quickly working the six degrees of separation in your favour.

The Power of Acknowledging

Twenty-five years of couple counselling has shown me that there is nothing more powerful in turning round a difficult situation than the *power of acknowledging*. It not only shows that you are open-hearted, but helps open up the heart of the other person too. So how does it work? Lizzie, forty-two, has been dating Thomas, forty-five, for twelve months and they came into counselling because they could not decide whether to live together. Their relationship was complicated because both had children from a previous marriage and Lizzie had a twelve-year-old autistic child. 'He has a mental age of about three or four which means that he is hard work and I can't give Thomas the attention that he seems to demand. I don't think he understands just how exhausting it is for me, day in day out. There is no let-up.' Thomas kept his eyes fixed on the floor and muttered: 'I do know what it's like.' For a while, each partner kept on repeating their basic case – with more and more supporting evidence. Eventually, I threw up my hands: what did they want from each other? 'I just want Lizzie to understand how hard I've tried,' said Thomas. With a little prompting, Lizzie did acknowledge that Thomas was patient, kind and supportive, and went on to list examples and occasions when she'd been particularly grateful. Thomas, in turn, acknowledged how much Lizzie had achieved with her son. Obviously both had known deep down that the other appreciated them, but they needed to hear it! Finally, Lizzie and Thomas were ready to negotiate with open hearts and soon found a formula for living together. Here are the ingredients for acknowledging:

- *It has to be neutral.* Rather than said angrily, sarcastically or with strings attached.
- *It works best with examples.* Instead of just 'thank you for being helpful'–which is a good start–try something more detailed: 'I really appreciated the way that you rallied round when I lost my passport.'
- *It is often heard loudest when least expected.* For example, on a car trip a couple of weeks later: 'I know that you hate hospitals so it was really nice of you to come and visit my mother with me.' This makes us feel our kindness has not been forgotten and therefore we feel doubly acknowledged.
- *It identifies unspoken feelings.* In difficult situations, communication can be improved by acknowledging the feelings behind the words or the mood. 'I guess you're angry?' or 'Are you sad?' Don't worry if you do not guess correctly, because your friend,

date or colleague will be happy to provide the correct emotion and instead of lurking unexpressed all the feelings will have been acknowledged.

Acting 'As If'

This is the best piece of advice that I have ever received. But first, let me give a bit of background. I once interviewed a woman whose daughter was found face down in a neighbour's pond. The child was resuscitated but did not have a heartbeat for forty minutes and was left severely handicapped. Her mother blamed herself, as she had left her daughter in the care of a nanny. It is hard to think of anything worse and I asked this woman how she kept going. 'Of course, there are times when I want to lock myself in a small dark room and scream and scream. Except my daughter needs me and I have another able-bodied child, a husband and a business. People are counting on me. When I think I can't go on, I remember this wonderful woman who shared her secret with me. "Act as if you can cope. At first it will be just that – an act. But after a while, you will find yourself acting less and being more. Suddenly, one day you will find that it is no longer an act and you can actually cope." '
I remembered this advice when I was at an important crossroads myself.

As I explained earlier, my first partner died when I was thirty-five. Five years later, I had just begun another relationship but was held back by the memories that haunted me. My new partner was patient but ultimately became fed up with competing with a ghost. I was given an ultimatum and told to choose: who did I love more? My new partner obviously did not want to continue to play second fiddle. But how could I wipe out the seven-and-a-half years that I'd spent with my first partner? It seemed an impossible dilemma. At this point, I remembered the 'act as if' trick. So I decided to walk round my house and act as if I loved my second partner the most. I was amazed by what I discovered. In each room, beyond the toilet and bathroom, there were pictures of my first partner and none of my second. I had honestly not realised the imbalance. So still acting as if, I took down the majority of the photos. I didn't need them to remember my first partner. The strange part of this story is that I felt better inside too – less haunted.

So this exercise is simple. Next time you find yourself facing an obstacle ask yourself: how would I behave if I had confidence in my abilities? Once the picture is firmly in your head, imagine the first step and act as if . . .

For example, if you find yourself despairing that you will never find a partner, picture yourself walking down the street hand-in-hand with him or her. How would you behave if you believed this person existed? You would leave your home and try to find him or her! Acting as if, you will find your beloved, you will start going out more and accepting invitations to friends' parties that previously you might have turned down. By acting confidently, you will behave confidently and somewhere further down the road you will cross over into being confident.

Taking a Risk: a Step-by-step Approach

If you fancy someone, it is incredibly hard to start a conversation. In fact, the more interested you are, the less likely you are to make a move. That's why this is an exercise that builds slowly.

Week One: Talk To Someone Who You Might Not Normally Talk To

- This could be a work colleague, a distant acquaintance (like your postman or -woman) or a stranger in the bus queue.
- These are not people that you fancy, but this just gives you an opportunity to practise small talk. In this way, when someone truly interesting appears, you will not be tongue-tied.
- Try to ask open questions. Where should I change for . . .? How are you today?
- Open questions start with: 'who, why, what, how, where, when'.
- Sometimes a yes/no question will allow a moment of rapport,

especially with acquaintances, that can be built on – but always have a follow-up question ready. For example, 'Did you have a good weekend?' can be answered yes or no. However this can be followed by 'What did you get up to?'

- The aim is thirty seconds of casual chat.
- At the end of the week, and subsequent weeks, reward yourself with a treat – like a favourite food, an indulgent activity or buying yourself a little something.

Week Two: Set Off Five Minutes Earlier

- With more time to do things, you are more likely to chat to someone.
- Take time to look around.
- When we are less focused on what we expect to see, we are more likely to notice opportunities.

Week Three: Take Up an Opportunity that You Would Previously Have Turned Down

- For example, if you belong to a choir, but rush off because you have to get up early for work, go for a drink with the other members.
- A friend wants you to accompany them to a work-related drinks party – accept. Alternatively, take a friend along to your work-related 'do' instead of turning it down because you hate hanging around on your own.
- Afterwards reward yourself.

Week Four: Look Carefully at the Profile of the People that You Speak To

- My clients often speak to the same type of person. For example, Graham – who had trouble getting over a girlfriend who dumped him – felt most comfortable with elderly ladies.
- Do you only talk to people in certain circumstances?
- Add extra types of people or places to your profile.

Week Five: Go Somewhere that You Have Never Been Before
- We tend to go to the same bars or follow the same pastimes with our friends.
- Suggest somewhere different.
- New situations bring new people into our lives.
- Don't forget to reward yourself.

Week Six: Try Something New
- Sign up for a class.
- Try that hobby you have always wanted to do.
- Become a volunteer.

Week Seven: Make the Commitment to Keep Looking
- In just the same way successful salesmen are always looking for a lead, you should always be looking for opportunities to mix with new people.
- Keep expanding your circles of acquaintance to become bigger and bigger, and to include more and more people.

It is important to stress that none of these activities is primarily about looking for a partner, but more about improving your mixing skills. Firstly, you will be relaxed when talking to someone who might later turn out to be a potential partner. Secondly, you will be out meeting people rather than waiting for Mr Right or Miss Wonderful to parachute into your living room.

Looking in the Mirror

This exercise has been specifically designed to help with the mixing skill 'Do as you would be done by' but will also make you become more open-minded and less ready to judge others.

When people complain about their partner – he never listens, she runs me down – they are often guilty of the very same thing themselves! So phrases like 'single men are losers' or 'women in their thirties are bitter' tell us as much, if not more, about the person complaining as about their targets. This is because relationships are like mirrors – we see the things we don't like about ourselves in the behaviour of others. Except, rather than admit to our own failings or cutting our nearest and dearest a bit of slack, we find it easier to rail against others. Certainly Simon, the 36-year-old who thought women his own age were bitter, had more than a hint of bitterness himself: 'Being single, I've put more into my friendships and often been let down.' Another example would be a conversation he had with a woman that he slept with: '"You're carrying a bit of weight," she said. "But you do find me attractive?" I joked but she came straight back: "I put up with it."' (Interesting how women feel it OK to make digs at a man's weight but would be horrified if a man did the same back.) Meanwhile, Charlotte, the 38-year-old who thought single men losers, had spent the first half of our interview stressing how far she had travelled – and it was impressive – but it did suggest that deep down she still felt that she had something to prove.

So without stopping to think, write down your three main criticisms about the men or women that you have dated or the singles scene in general?

1

2

3

Now imagine looking in the mirror, could any of those criticisms be levelled at you. Even in a small way? If so, what changes could you make?

I know this makes for a very sobering exercise. In my twenties, I worked for a medium-sized company and found one of the new recruits really irritating because he was pushy and rather full of himself. One day, when he'd made me particularly angry, I counted to ten and then asked myself why I had such a strong reaction while my colleagues had no such problem. That's when I realised who he reminded me of: me. It was a shock, but from that moment on I was not only more forgiving but found him much easier to manage. If we can forgive the faults in others, maybe we can begin to extend the same favour to ourselves? It's tough but worth the effort.

Be Philosophical

Whether we realise it or not, everyone has their own personal philosophy that underpins their search for love. These philosophies are central to our view of the world and ourselves, in fact so central that they are often unspoken, unexamined and untested. This is a pity because a well-balanced personal philosophy is the key to a happy and fulfilled life. What is yours?

1 You're waiting to hear about a perfect job, but they are taking longer than expected to let you know. Do you . . .?
   a) Phone all your contacts to find out what's going on.
   b) Do nothing: if it's meant to be, it's meant to be.
   c) Wait patiently: I'll find out soon enough.

2 You've a new boss at work and the two of you don't click. You feel picked on, stressed and unhappy. Do you . . .?
   a) Start looking for another job.
   b) Hope the problems will sort themselves.
   c) Speak to someone in human resources.

3 Your last relationship ended three months ago and your confidence is in pieces. What is your attitude?
   a) Get back out there: I'll show him/I'm better off without her.
   b) How could he/she?
   c) It'll take time to get over my wounds but I'll make it.

4 You went out with a new prospect whom you really liked. She or he promised to call but you've waited five days and heard nothing. Do you?
   a) Phone him or her.

    b) Keeping checking for messages, texts and emails almost hourly.

    c) Think: I've better things to do.

5 You've been seeing someone for six to nine months and although it started well, there are problems and you're anxious that the relationship is about to collapse. Do you?

    a) Get in quick and end it first.

    b) Worry and try desperately to please.

    c) Accept that it might end and then start finding ways to sort it out.

6 When it comes to a holiday in an exotic or unknown destination, which statement best describes your attitude?

    a) I get peace of mind by researching the place in advance and tie down all the details so I know exactly what to expect.

    b) Leave the arrangements to the friend with whom I'm going on holiday.

    c) The adventure is part of the fun.

Mostly a)
Control freak. There is nothing more unsettling for you than not knowing. You would much rather be doing something – anything – even if it's wrong. Deep down, you feel that love is a test that you either pass or fail. However, you need to grasp that we cannot control every single aspect of our lives. Once you can truly accept this truth, both intellectually and emotionally, you will be free to enjoy life more. Next time you feel compelled to act, put everything on hold for forty-eight hours. In most cases, you will find there was no need to do anything.

Mostly b)
Passive acceptance. You hate to rock the boat and would rather do nothing than risk making the wrong move. On a positive note: you have truly accepted that you cannot control every aspect of your life. Well done. However, you often cling so tightly to your expectation of

how something should turn out that you fail to notice other opportunities or new doors opening. Finally, stick up for yourself. It is often the first step to solving a problem, rather than just side-stepping it.

Mostly c)
Embracing the unknown. When faced with uncertainty, you do your best and let the rest go. In effect, you have learnt to live with the three most difficult human emotions: I call them the triple A: anxiety, ambivalence, ambiguity. This is a hard path to tread and if you feel yourself panicking, talk over your problems with a friend. Sometimes it takes an outside eye to know the difference between what can be changed and what is beyond our control.

Chapter Eight

The Rhythm of Relationships

The good news is that you have been out mixing and either seen someone in a different light or met someone completely new. You have been out together on a few occasions and everything seems promising. But how can you tell if this is 'just friends' or the makings of a lifetime love affair? Fortunately, there is scientific research into just this question, plus useful work on the honeymoon period of love and the natural rhythm of relationships. This knowledge will not only help you progress at the right pace but decide if this new man or woman is the right person for you.

The First Steps in Making a Relationship

What makes the difference between budding love thriving or withering? Researchers John H. Berg and Ronald McQuinn at the University of Mississippi took thirty-eight student couples who had been on *five* dates and gave them a detailed questionnaire and then repeated it four months later. Berg and McQuinn were particularly interested in the differences between couples who continued to date and those that split up and whether it was possible to predict which group a couple would fall into. Being social psychologists, rather than romantics, they saw relationships in a very functional way: a balance between the benefits of dating and the costs. So they measured not only liking and loving but the rewards of the relationship – which they explained as 'the extent to which your dating partner has helped with problems and projects, and the number of favours exchanged'.

The results were very interesting – all the couples were unsure about whether they would keep dating. Nobody 'just knew' they were destined to be together. This is something, with the benefit of hindsight, that we retrospectively award to our relationship. The most important difference between continuing and non-continuing couples was the amount of self-disclosure at five dates. In other words, people who were more open and honest – rather than just putting on a front or being defensive – were the most romantically successful. Human beings are very good at sniffing out a fake and we just do not trust someone who is closed off.

The second difference is a surprise. The continuing couples argued more than the non-continuing ones. Common sense would dictate that conflict would drive people apart. However on further reflection, the findings are fascinating. How well long-term couples handle conflict is the single best predictor for relationship success – and it seems the ability to constructively disagree is just as important at five dates as five years. The non-continuing couples were probably swallowing or ignoring the conflict, which fits well with the pattern of low self-disclosure, and storing up problems that would ultimately drive them apart.

The final important finding from Berg and McQuinn is that the rewards of the relationship were not important to any couple at five dates but became much more important at four months. Why should this be? Berg and McQuinn theorise that it takes time to know someone's needs and the more needs that are met, the more rewarding the relationship.

So how can you use this research?

- Although self-disclosure is good, make certain it is a balanced exchange.

- Avoid pouring out your heart while he or she listens. Instead, share a little information as this will encourage him or her to disclose too.
- Remember this research is based on five dates and disclosure takes time. So do not expect to achieve everything on your first outing.
- Berg and McQuinn illustrate that it is OK to disagree with your date or to have different tastes. For example after a film, you could debate its strengths and weaknesses, rather than feeling that the two of you have to agree on everything.
- Hold back on the impressive trips or offering to paint the outside of the house until you know each other. Otherwise, it can seem like an attempt to bribe.

In the same way that it is counterproductive during mixing to judge too quickly, it is equally important to move slowly through the first steps of making a relationship. In effect, there are three types of outings or dates: *Getting to know you* (assessing if there is any connection), *Fun outings* (enjoying each other's company and checking compatibility) and finally *Courting* (the beginnings of a lasting relationship). It is impossible to get to the third type of outing without moving through the first two. Unfortunately, many potential relationships are crushed because one half is in too much of a hurry to court. 'I just like to know where I stand,' says Ingrid, who is thirty-two, 'I haven't got time to waste with men who are not interested in a commitment.' When I ask how she can judge, she becomes a little coy but after some probing admits: 'I will float the subject of marriage, perhaps a friend has got engaged and I will see how he reacts. Although I'd never ask directly for his opinions on marriage.' It might seem casual, to the person dropping the 'M' word, but seldom comes across this way. Jerome is also in his thirties and rarely sees anyone past the third or fourth date. 'I sometimes think that woman are obsessed with commitment. Sure, I want to settle down, have children, the whole nine yards, but I want it to be with someone who loves me, not with a woman who seems desperate to commit to – if I am being brutally honest – almost anyone,' Jerome explains. 'I can almost time when the conversation will turn to settling down, marriage, babies or whatever. It is such a turn-off. I'm still getting to know her and she's measuring me for a morning suit.' On one occasion, he was really keen on a girl that he had met at work. They had been out the night before, but when he arrived at the office Jerome was thinking of calling her. 'I sat down and logged on for my emails and found that I had two from her. She had left a message on my voice mail; I was still thinking of calling when the phone rang. She wanted to meet me on the third-floor lobby – straight away. When I arrived, she shoved a piece of paper into my hand and disappeared. It was a poem dedicated "to my soul-mate".'

Obviously the time needed to progress from 'getting to know you' to 'courting' will change from couple to couple – but as a rule of thumb: it is somewhere between five and ten outings. Around the middle of this period, sex begins to loom large. When to make love is a complex issue. On one hand, good sex is an important ingredient for a successful long-term relationship and you need to test whether the two of you are compatible. However, on the other, sex can easily overwhelm a budding relationship.

Sex and the New Relationship

The 1960s sexual revolution gave women permission to enjoy sex just as much as men – something that has improved relationships no end – but had the side-effect that some women reversed an old trick. Today I am more likely to counsel women who offer sex as a way of starting a relationship than those who withhold it. Our new understanding of how the brain works – from PET scans, MRIs, endocrinological studies and galvanic skin-response tests – offers some support for this strategy. Male oxytocin levels (the bonding chemical) are lower than women's, except for one moment: ejaculation.

However, there is a big difference between sleeping with some-one and laying the foundations for a lasting relationship. Both offering or withholding sex starts a relationship off with game-playing and is detrimental in the long term. You can trick someone to be interested, but only temporarily; eventually he or she will cotton on and wake up disillusioned. The secret of knowing when to agree to sex, and when to pass, lies in a proper understanding of how two people bond and working with the process.

So What Are the New Rules for Sex at the Beginning of a Relationship?

When getting to know someone, it is difficult to discuss when to become physically intimate. These guidelines should provide clarity:

1 When two strangers meet, their subconsciouses will start checking whether there are complementary needs or the skills to make each other complete. Give this process plenty of time and do not rush into bed too soon.

2 Sex is so powerful that it can short-circuit this delicate match-ing and bond two people who are not necessarily compatible or have different agendas. Wait until at least the fifth or sixth date.

3 Trust your instincts – rather than the opinions of your friends – they are there for a purpose.

4 Remember that sex means different things to different people. For one partner, great passion in the bedroom might be a sign of falling in love forever and ever. For the other partner, wonderful sex could be an end in itself.

5 If you suspect you and your partner have fundamentally different attitudes – especially if he or she arrives shortly before making love and leaves soon afterwards, or cannot find the time for proper courting – test the waters by withholding once or twice. This will soon provide clarification and avoid long-term misery.

6 Never discuss your sexual relationship with previous partners, however much he or she asks. Giving in will only encourage jealousy or sexual competitiveness.

Fear and the New Relationship

As I discussed in Step One, some people get trapped in dating patterns that handicap their chances of making lasting relationships. If you recognised yourself in the examples, you will probably be anxious about the progress of your new relationship. So this is a good place to give a little reassurance. If you have been following my programme and looked at the legacy from your childhood, under-taken a relationship detox and worked on yourself – before looking for a partner again – you will probably be making better relationship choices and attracting more promising potential partners. Although there is a lot to celebrate, you also need to be aware that old habits do not disappear overnight. If you feel yourself slipping, the next section provides advice on how to get back on course again.

Over-committed

If, in the past, you have been the person who puts all the energy into making the relationship work while your prospective partner – after the initial burst – seems rather nonchalant and sometimes even uninterested, you will be anxious not to fall into the same pattern again. The following checklist will allow you to monitor your progress:

- I have not put myself permanently 'on call' to satisfy the needs of my new love interest.
- I have considered my needs as well as his or hers (and not seen the two as the same thing).
- I have tried to keep my fantasies of 'every after' under control and enjoyed today rather than worried about the future.
- I have not put myself under unnecessary stress by thinking: 'this

is the most important relationship I'll ever have' or 'this is the one'. There is also no artificial pressure or ticking clock, for example: 'I must be in a relationship by the time I'm thirty' or 'I must have someone for my sister's wedding.'

- If there has been a problem, I have not shouldered all the blame and thought: 'If only I'd behaved differently.' Ultimately, both partners have to take responsibility for the happiness and health of a relationship.

There will be wobbles and the odd slip back into old ways but as long as you strive for the goals above, your relationship will grow from strength to strength. If your new partner appears to be cooling or engineering time alone, don't panic. Take a deep breath and take stock. Firstly, accept that everybody needs their own personal space – even you. How could you use a free evening in a profitable way? Secondly, be aware that the more that you chase, the more your partner is likely to run.

Occasionally, when people stop being over-committed, and swap emotionally unavailable partners for someone with real potential, the shock of their love being returned is so great that they panic and long to disappear. Surprisingly enough, this is a positive development. Finding a balance between freedom and commitment is something that successful couples share, rather than one person fighting for independence and the other for togetherness. If, despite my reassurances, your new relationship still feels claustrophobic, the next section will be helpful.

Blowing Hot and Cold

If your past relationships were red hot while you were pursuing but cooled once you had won someone over, how do you break the pattern? If you have taken the courtship process slowly and not overwhelmed your beloved with attention, presents and commitment too soon, you will be in a strong position. Your beloved will have realistic expectations of your budding relationship and you will be under less stress to deliver. However, there will still be moments of doubt or when you simply want to be on your own. What should you do?

- It is normal to be anxious and sometimes overwhelmed with feelings of claustrophobia. Beyond the first heady moments of falling in love, no couple want to be together constantly. If you spend weekends together, build breaks and time apart into your general routine. When you need to be alone, it is generally better to get out of the house. Shutting yourself off behind the TV or computer will be perceived as rejecting. This is why, traditionally, sheds, allotments, dogs, golf and fishing have been so popular. They all offer an acceptable excuse for a short break from togetherness.
- Look back at your previous relationships and identify the point when you panicked and fled. Before you reach this point, have a quick discussion with the new man or woman in your life. This does not have to be a very heavy conversation but you should put your cards on the table.
- Give feedback on the relationship so far, some basic facts about your issues and finish with a short warning. For example: 'I'm really enjoying getting to know you [no need for extravagant protestations of love as you are not trying to win him or her over], however I think that you should be aware that in the past I've got cold feet, often for no real reason [there is no need to go into childhood issues about abandonment, abuse etc.], so if I seem distant sometimes, please be patient and please feel free to discuss it with me.'
- Give honest feedback and explain what particular behaviour contributes to your claustrophobia: 'I appreciate it when you offer to cook supper on Sunday night but sometimes I need to get home and get things ready for the next week.'
- Be aware that your date/prospective partner will probably have concerns about commitment too, so be ready to listen to what he or she has to say.
- Never underestimate how much confessing to a feeling can release the tension. For many people, this is the single most

important way to cut down their fears. Beforehand, your heart will probably beat faster but afterwards you will feel surprisingly lighter – maybe even liberated. In addition, honesty empowers your prospective partner. He or she knows about the issues and will not mistake cold feet for something worse and either give up or, worse still, pursue.

- Cut yourself and your partner a little slack. If you begin obsessing about your new lover's failings, ask yourself: am I expecting too much; am I using his or her faults as an excuse to move on to another relationship. Although we might hope for the perfect lover who will transform our lives and solve all our problems – with no conflict and no heartache – he or she is just a myth. As the wit and author Quentin Crisp (1908–99) said: 'there is no great dark man'. However, there are lots of good people with whom we can rub along very nicely, and in the process lose some of our and their sharp edges. So don't mistake the momentary discomfort of growing together as a fundamental flaw.

- If you still find yourself wanting to flee, step back for a moment. What are the good things in the relationship? What qualities does the other person possess? Have you overreacted? Remember, you are deciding whether to *continue to court* rather than *making a lasting commitment*.

With all fears about commitment, the first line of defence is to get the problems out in the open. But how does it work in practice? James, forty, and Emma, thirty, hit a barrier early in their relationship. 'I felt completely overloaded. I had a difficult patch where I had to fight for every freelance contract,' explains James. 'At the same time, I felt I was expected to help boost Emma's career and be her mentor too. I remember walking through Leicester Square on a sunny afternoon and there were all these people enjoying themselves. They seemed without a care in the world. I knew I could cope with my own problems but not Emma's too. One thing led to another and I sank lower and lower, until I started questioning whether we should even be together.' Fortunately, they communicated well: Emma noticed that James had turned sullen and James was honest about his feelings. 'I don't think I can sort out your career and keep my own on track. I just don't have the energy,' he told her. Emma was furious and hurt: 'What makes you think I'm asking?' In effect, James had assumed – in this case wrongly – that he was Emma's full-time cheerleader. Although the couple had a nasty argument they had learnt a lot about each other. Often our new love's needs, expectations and demands for commitment exist only in our own fevered imagination. The only way to discover the truth is to be open and talk.

Déjà vu

Sometimes a new lover can start to behave just like your old lovers. It is not only depressing to repeat the same arguments, but can make you seriously question the viability of your new relationship. So have you fallen for another identikit partner or is just déjà vu magnifying your problems? Philippa, twenty-eight, had dated a man who had been unfaithful: 'He became very friendly with a girl at the office where we both worked and eventually he admitted he had feelings for her. After a lot of soul-searching, I decided to fight for him. Although the other girl backed off, the magic had gone and we drifted apart. I was very hurt and felt a complete fool. No man was worth that sort of knock to my pride.' Six months later, she started dating Darren. 'It was going really well and we spent most weekends together. However, one Friday morning, he phoned and said he didn't think he would be able to make it back that evening. His job, in TV production down south, was over-running. Although I was upset, at least he'd had enough respect to warn me – because I hate last-minute cancellations. We agreed to speak later and see what time he finished. I didn't hear anything. I tried phoning but his phone was switched off. Probably, he was stuck in the edit suite. After work, I dropped into the pub not far from home – where we'd both met. My older brother, who runs the place, told me that Darren had been in. I thought: great, he's back home, we can go out after all. So I called his mobile, but it was still switched off. I kept trying all night and still nothing. I felt so betrayed. What else could it be but another woman?' As it turned out, Darren had been offered a ticket to a football match and, knowing what Philippa's reaction would be, pretended to be still down south. Déjà vu had made Philippa assume the worst, rather than waiting to get the facts. They talked over their problems, and Darren agreed not to hide behind white lies and Philippa to be more flexible about changing plans – if there was a good reason.

If you find yourself overreacting to something your partner says or does, stop and think: does it have an extra punch because of something that happened in the past? With intractable problems, I normally reckon that 20 per cent is about today and 80 per cent about your childhood. So look back and unhook the bits that belong to the past. For example, Justine (who we met in Chapter Four, with her habit of falling for bad boys) decided to stop trying to police how much her boyfriend drinks: 'I might have felt responsible for my dad's behaviour when I was a girl, but my boyfriend is an adult and he can make his own decisions. It certainly makes life less stressful for me.' Although the problem had not changed, Justine's way of approaching it had changed – with a knock-on effect on the atmosphere in the house. 'I stopped panicking every time he opened the fridge and with it less of an issue, he drank less. I also began to see that although my boyfriend sometimes drank too much – unlike my dad, he did not have a serious problem.' If our partner's behaviour is making us unhappy, our first reaction is always to try to get them to change. But in the rush, we forget about our own contribution, our own history and how we might be projecting past problems onto our new relationship. By behaving differently, the chances are that our partner will react differently too. So if you suspect déjà vu, step back and ask: in what other ways could I approach this problem? If you can't think of anything different, ask your friends or try the opposite of your normal tactics. Anything that breaks the old cycle, makes you see your partner as an individual and stops past relationships overshadowing what is happening today.

The other key to breaking old patterns is hanging on a little longer. Often when we are arguing with our partner, we think the relationship is in trouble, but actually fights are a sign of hope. This is particularly the case with déjà vu. If most of our big problems have their roots in the past, today's fights are a way of solving, by proxy, those long-standing issues. Even if you suspect an identikit partner, in 90 per cent of cases it is better to hang on and give yourself time to try to solve the problems. Certainly until your relationship has reached the first crucial milestone.

The Three-months Test

On one hand, trying to define a relationship too soon is like pulling up a plant-cutting and checking its growing roots; but on the other, just wishing and hoping for the best can lead to a dead-end relationship. Margi, thirty-two, has been with her boyfriend for three years. 'He had a nasty divorce and his motto is "once bitten twice shy". I understand about the marriage thing, but he won't even promise we'll be together forever. I catch myself telling friends that "marriage isn't all it's cracked up to be" but sometimes think that the only person I'm fooling is myself. Part of me thinks "I deserve to be with someone who wants the same things", but I love him and we've had a lot of good times together. Why throw that all away?'

Although one of my central messages is 'don't judge too quickly', the moment of truth cannot be put off indefinitely. In my opinion, three months is an important milestone. How does your relationship measure up?

- Have you both stopped accepting 'dates' from other people?
- Can you openly label each other as boyfriend or girlfriend?
- Does conversation flow like wine?
- Can you relax in each other's presence?
- Do you *like* yourself when you are with your new man or woman?

- Are you both interested in the particulars of each other's lives?
- Who is putting the most energy into developing the relationship? Who calls? Who suggests outings?
- If it seems that you are doing the majority of the work, step back and give him or her room to take the initiative. Sometimes it is better to let a relationship fold than put increasing amounts of energy into preserving it.
- If your partner has been making most of the running, what happens if you let down your defences and suggest something that progresses the relationship? For example, meeting family, or taking a short break together. (Hopefully the relationship will move forward, but sometimes the first signs of commitment can make a prospective partner panic and retreat.)

How to Spot if Your New Love Is 'Too Good to Be True'

It is around the three-month point that cracks can begin to appear in what, up to this point, might have seemed a perfect relationship. The temptation is to ignore the warning signs and enjoy the passion and the romance – but that would be a big mistake, because some potential partners are dangerous.

Although most of my advice is applicable to everyone, this next point is specifically for women. Stockholm Syndrome was named after a bank siege in the capital city of Sweden in the 1970s where kidnappers and hostages bonded to such an extent that afterwards one woman became engaged to a gunman, while another launched a legal fund to pay for the robbers' defence. This is an extreme example of what is becoming an increasingly common phenomenon: smart women who become willingly trapped in relationships with bad, dangerous or abusive men. So how does it happen and why should you be on your guard?

On the surface, Stockholm Syndrome Man is wonderful. He makes dramatic romantic gestures (like buying wildly expensive presents), he is impulsive ('let's drive down to London, as I know this wonderful little restaurant') and he enjoys breaking the rules ('who cares what people think?'). While many men fight shy of commitment, Stockholm Syndrome Man is the complete opposite, as Michelle, twenty-eight, discovered when she first met Alex, in his late thirties: 'On our second date, he announced that he'd never met anybody like me, I was the love of his life and he was teasing me about what to call our second child,' she remembers. Naturally, she was flattered and began to entertain similar feelings. 'He followed it up with flowers, a stuffed hippo and a weekend in the Cotswolds.' Stockholm Syndrome Men do not so much kidnap women but ambush their emotions. 'I was on an incredible high,' explained Michelle, 'it seemed almost too good to be true.' Indeed it was. While it is normal to fall quickly in love, most people hold back until they are certain. By contrast, Stockholm Syndrome Men are not afraid of a quick commitment. They make unrealistic promises, have a whole future planned out after a handful of dates and some even move in during the first month. Alex's grand gestures made Michelle feel like she was in a romantic movie, so she ignored behaviour that would normally have made her suspicious. 'On our way to the Cotswolds, he kept blowing his horn and accusing the driver of the car ahead of being a creep. At the hotel, the room wasn't quite ready and he made a terrible fuss. He was rude to the girl on reception but I didn't like to say anything because he was being so generous.' Although Michelle recognised that Alex had a temper, and hated not getting his own way, she never thought his fury would be directed at her. After all, he had told her she was his princess and nothing was too much trouble. What Michelle did not realise was that Alex had started the classic Stockholm Syndrome pattern: fear and reward.

Not every Stockholm Syndrome Man becomes violent towards their partner. Some just throw things or get into fights with other men. In this case, Alex spent a night in a prison cell after another man in a night-club looked at Michelle in what he considered to be a 'funny way'. The goal is to make the woman on guard and therefore easily controlled. Ultimately, all Stockholm Syndrome Men become emotionally abusive. 'Because Mike really loved me and wanted the best for me,' explains Josie, thirty-two, 'he would be honest about what he thought.' However, this included insults about her flabby arms, the small roll of flesh round her stomach and her taste in clothes. Gradually the remarks got more personal and Josie became more self-conscious. 'For some reason, you believe criticism but put compliments down to flattery,' says Josie, looking back on how Mike gradually destroyed her confidence. 'He had been to a good university and enjoyed dropping names into the conversation and then explaining, as if I was five years old.' Worse still, he started dissecting Josie's behaviour in public and telling her she was stupid or knew nothing. So why didn't Josie just leave him? 'If he went too far, he'd be really sweet: breakfast in bed, turning up at the office to take me out for an expensive lunch, jewellery. I felt that was the real him and if I tried harder it could be like that all the time.' Mike was exhibiting the second classic Stockholm Syndrome behaviour: alternating fix and withdrawal.

The bad behaviour in public begins to isolate the woman and, like the hostages in the bank, they are cut off from the outside world. Certainly Josie decided it was too much trouble taking Mike on office outings and, as she explains: 'He always claimed we were happier, just the two of us.' Slowly Josie gave up all her outside interests – like horse-riding – as Mike would insist on coming too and hanging around with a long face and taking all the pleasure from her hobby. He had an issue with her family too. After a call from her mother, Mike would launch into twenty questions, picking away at the conversation for criticism – real or imagined. So Josie would only phone her family when he was not around: 'He thought mum took advantage and didn't understand the "special nature of our love".' Mike had put in place another key ingredient for a Stockholm Syndrome Relationship: the enemy. The common foe intensifies the bond between captor and victim. Worse still, with nobody outside to question what is 'normal', women trapped in Stockholm Syndrome Relationships put the problems down to their own behaviour. Indeed, Michelle felt Alex behaved badly because: 'I didn't do enough to make him feel safe, didn't make enough sacrifices.' She even felt she was lucky to have someone who put up with her – as by this time, she felt inadequate and worthless. 'If a small voice inside told me anything else, he would ridicule me, tell me I was crazy. Nobody else would want me.' She was truly Alex's prisoner.

So what drives these men? Although a few consciously set out to capture women, most genuinely think they are great guys. Through their eyes, they are very romantic and passionate (but it can get out of hand and become fisticuffs), and their strong sense of entitlement is just an extreme version of our society's self-centredness (I'm in a hurry, so it doesn't matter if my poor parking holds up everybody else). The problem is that these men have an almost pathological inability to understand anybody else's viewpoint or the impact of their behaviour. This makes them permanently right and everybody else permanently in the wrong.

How Do You Spot a Stockholm Syndrome Man?

- Give him the waitress test. Does he whine, complain, torment and generally treat her like dirt?
- What about his ex? Does he tell stories about a mad, angry, stupid or ungrateful woman?
- Does he give reassurances that you didn't ask for? For example, he never gets drunk or would never actually hit a woman.
- Is he proud of bad behaviour? Like claiming to be a 'butt-kicker' at work or doing 'crazy' things like hanging around outside a girl's apartment all night?
- What about his friends? Stockholm Syndrome Men have only acquaintances or a handful of friends who are just like him.

I have yet to come across a woman employing the techniques of Stockholm Syndrome. However, there are other personality traits which are superficially attractive, but deadly for relationships, that are exhibited by both men and women:

The Lure of the Narcissist

Greek myth tells the story of Narcissus, a handsome sixteen-year-old who rejected the love of the nymph Echo. As a punishment for his cruelty, Narcissus was doomed to fall in love with his own reflection in a pool of water. Unable to consummate his love, he pined away and died. Myths survive because they tell us something important about us today. In this case: loving yourself too much can prevent you from loving someone else. In the seventies, psychoanalyst Heinz Kohut took the idea one stage further and identified Narcissistic Personality Disorder to describe patients with grandiose self-importance who fly into fits of rage at every knock to their self-esteem. This might sound suspiciously like the behaviour of the average spoilt celebrity, but narcissism is slightly more complicated. Freud, the founder of psychoanalysis, considered narcissism a natural part of all of us. He stressed the difference between primary and secondary narcissism. The first is a natural stage of a child's development: when the baby learns a clear sense of their own identity, to love themselves, before learning to love anyone else. While secondary narcissism is the self-love which prevents meaningful relationships with others. The American Psychiatric Association believes that about 0.7 per cent to 1 per cent of the population are sufferers from Narcissistic Personality Disorder and that the majority of them are men. According to their diagnostic manual, five or more of the following would suggest that your new man or possibly woman is a sufferer:

1 Has a grandiose sense of self-importance.
2 Preoccupied with fantasies of unlimited success, power, brilliance, beauty or idealised love.
3 Believes that they are special and should only associate with special, high-level people.
4 Needs excessive admiration.
5 Has a sense of entitlement.
6 Exploits others.

7 Lacks empathy.
8 Envious of others or thinks they are envious of him.
9 Haughty, arrogant behaviour.

Narcissists spend a lot of time and money on their appearance. On the surface, they are very confident and, as previously discussed, confidence is very attractive. Narcissists' relationships – like everything else about them – must be the best: more intense, passionate and rewarding than everyone else's. For this reason, they throw all their considerable energy into conquering their prospective partner and convincing them that this is the love of the century. It is little wonder that narcissists find it easy to attract prospective partners. Except they are incapable of giving real love and use relationships to inflate their own egos. Ultimately, these are hollow men and women and are best avoided.

So when assessing your relationship at the three-months stage make certain that you consider all the evidence and are not blinded by superficial qualities, overly extravagant gestures or someone playing a role to please you. As the old saying goes: if something seems too good to be true, it normally is. Unfortunately, by this stage in many relationships something has often entered the equation which makes rational thought very hard.

What About Love?

A book about finding a partner would not be complete without a proper discussion about love and how it influences our behaviour. Unfortunately, few of the founding fathers of psychology have examined love. However, there is one honourable exception. Starting in the mid-sixties, experimental psychologist Dorothy Tennov set out to try and understand how falling in love could be the source of both supreme joy and intense misery. She undertook 500 in-depth interviews and discovered that men and women, from all cultures, described the experience in the same way. Despite the obstacles to overcome and the fear of love being unrequited, 95 per cent of her respondents still called love 'a beautiful experience'; 83 per cent felt that 'anyone who has never been in love is missing one of life's most pleasurable experiences'; 42 per cent described it as 'living on top of a cloud'. To differentiate between the magic of falling in love and the settled everyday love of a long-term couple, Tennov coined the word 'limerence' (*Love and Limerence*, Stein & Day, 1980).

Although romantic novelists, poets and songwriters talk about love, they are really describing limerence. As we will see, there are some key differences between love and limerence:

- Under the spell of limerence, everything about our beloved is special. Tennov quotes one of her respondents, Terry: 'Anything that she liked, I liked; anything that belonged to her acquired a certain magic. Her handbag, her notebook, her pencil. I abhor the sight of tooth-marks on a pencil; they disgust me. But not her toothmarks. Hers were sacred; her wonderful mouth had been there.' In a long-term relationship, the pencil covered in toothmarks would probably end up in the bin rather than the centrepiece of a shrine.

- Despite the power of limerence to infuse everything with a romantic glow, two-thirds of men, and three-quarters of women, could identify their partner's character defects or bad habits. However, these problems are happily overlooked or down-played. Tennov quotes one respondent: 'Yes, I knew he gambled, I knew he sometimes drank too much and I knew he did not read a book from one year to the next. I knew it, but I didn't incorporate it into the overall image. I dwelt on his wavy hair, the way he looked at me, the thought of him driving me to work in the morning.' These feelings are very different from those experienced by established couples for whom wavy hair does not trump coming home drunk.

- Under the spell of limerence, it is impossible to stop thinking about your beloved. In extreme cases, students drop out of courses and we all know work colleagues who get nothing done because they are either daydreaming about their beloved, writing sexy emails or chatting on the phone. By contrast, married couples are perfectly capable of working, running a house, and enjoy a social life both independently and together.

- It is impossible to be limerent with more than one person at a time or even have eyes for anyone but your beloved. 'I went to a friend's stag weekend and we ended up in a lap-dancing club,' explains William, twenty-eight. 'There were some pretty girls and all my friends were cat-calling and laughing. I could accept that one girl, for example, had nice legs, but I judged them too long and her ankles were ugly. I just kept comparing every girl unfavourably with Holly.' By contrast, 90 per cent of established couples regularly fantasise about someone else during lovemaking – according to psychotherapist and author, Brett Karr, who gathered the responses of 19,000 British adults for *Sex and the Psyche* (Allen Lane, 2007).

- Most powerful of all, limerence makes us feel that we can cope with anything. Financial difficulties fade into the background; so what if our job is boring or our mother domineering? Hand-in-hand with our beloved, we can conquer the world; obstacles are something to embrace: an opportunity to prove or strengthen our feelings for one another.

Limerence is a heady, almost addictive force. There is just *one* problem. It does not last forever. At the bottom end of the scale, full-blown limerence lasts for about six months. This is normally when the love has not been returned. A good example is Owen, forty-eight, who fell for a much younger colleague: 'Her look when we passed each other in the corridor would send me into ecstasy: perhaps she felt the same way too. I longed for her so intensely that the only relief was fantasising about a possible life together: sharing croissants and coffee in a long garden that leads down to a river or touring the churches and galleries of Venice together. However, the relief was just momentary because my fantasies made me long for her even more.' Unfortunately, his colleague was engaged and

Owen had enough of a grip on reality to know that she was unlikely to want to visit galleries anyway. Even though Owen's colleague remained oblivious, his limerent feelings remained strong. Fortunately, they did burn themselves out after a while.

Limerence is even more of a problem when it has crystallised for one half of a couple in a short-term relationship, but the other half has drifted away. 'It really was the perfect love,' moans Ryan, twenty-eight, 'we were both mature students at university, had tons in common and spent all our spare time together. We would work side-by-side in the library, so we knew if the other was going to the coffee shop and could co-ordinate our breaks. Real soul mates; I thought we'd spend the rest of our lives together.' Their break-up came as a real shock to Ryan: 'I hadn't seen it coming, but in retrospect she had been studying alone more and more – but I thought it was because exams were looming – and then she had to go home for the weekend. At the time, I put it down to missing her mum.'

Unfortunately, limerence makes us downgrade the differences between us and our beloved (because we are so keen on achieving union with them). It makes us overlook any potential conflicts and interpret anything – however contrary to everyday experience – as positive for the relationship. This is probably why Ryan misread the signs and felt so let down. After his girlfriend left him, he spiralled into depression: 'I couldn't concentrate. I skipped lectures and failed to hand in a crucial essay on time.' If you too are suffering from the fall-out from limerence, see the exercise section for more advice.

If limerence seldom lasts for less than six months, what is the top end of the scale? In my experience, limerence normally lasts somewhere between eighteen months and three years. Fortunately, the 'blindness' lessens towards the second half of this period and reality intrudes. Slowly but surely, a couple can assess whether there is a long-term future for their relationship. It is at this point that couples begin to develop what I call loving attachment. The good news is that loving attachment, unlike limerence, can last for a lifetime. (For more information on how to nurture and protect loving attachment, see my book *I Love You But I'm Not in Love with You*, Bloomsbury, 2006.) When I explain about limerence, some of my clients are rather disappointed. Reciprocated limerence is wonderful, one of life's joys. Why can't it last forever? Firstly, it would not be practical to be forever sitting around mooning over our beloved. We'd never get round to raising any children and mankind would probably still be living in mud huts. Secondly, under the influence of limerence, we make many bad relationship choices. We convince ourselves that wholly impractical people will make perfect partners or throw ourselves into hopeless and painful affairs. Yet without a burst of limerence, I doubt that two people would ever launch themselves into the adventure of a shared life. How else would anyone be crazy enough to trust a complete stranger with their future? So if you are currently under the influence of limerence, surrender to the experience and enjoy every moment. The fact that it will not last forever should make every moment of bliss that little bit sweeter.

The Eighteen-months Test

If three months is the moment when casual going-out becomes a full-blown relationship, eighteen months is when that relationship turns into a committed partnership. The crazy peak of limerence, when you cannot eat, work or think straight, has passed but there is enough bliss left to smooth over the tensions of moving in together. Scientific evidence backs up my theory that this is the crucial window of opportunity. Long-term tracking by the University of Texas has found that an eighteen months' to three years' courtship is the optimum period for a happy marriage. Social biologists discovered that dopamine, phenylethylamine and oxytocin, the three hormones responsible for love and bonding, are at their height for eighteen months to three years too. The final piece of evidence comes from John T. Molloy's research into couples leaving American marriage-licence bureaux. He also identifies eighteen months as the time courting couples are most likely to become engaged. In his opinion, by twenty-two months the chance of a proposal begins to dips slightly. Then over the next year and a half, the odds diminish gradually. After three-and-a-half years together, however, the odds of a couple making a lasting commitment begins to plummet.

So answer the following questions about your relationship:

1 If someone attractive shows an interest would you tell him or her that you're already seeing someone?
2 Would your boyfriend or girlfriend do the same?
3 Is your lover the person to whom you tell the ins and outs of your day?
4 Do you enjoy just hanging out together without some structured activity – like going to a movie or dining out?
5 Could you discuss and book next year's summer holiday or discuss plans for Christmas?
6 Does the way that your lover talks about the relationship match with his or her actual behaviour?
7 Do you both want the same things out of life?
8 If you had an emergency – for instance, if your house was broken into – would your lover be the first person you phoned for emotional and practical support?
9 If you had good news, would your lover be the first person that you would call?
10 Do you generally put each other's interests first?
11 Can you confide your inner secrets, fears and dreams?
12 Would your lover protect you against a personal attack from his or her family?
13 Can you co-operate and organise a major event together – like a touring holiday or a big party?
14 Would you describe your beloved as a good person?

There is no pass or fail score on this test, but you should hope to be able to answer 'yes' to at least the first seven questions. From here onwards, each question reveals progressively important qualities about your relationship. When I discuss this test with clients, they expect support through adversity to be the key test. However, whether our beloved can truly share in our success is more important; often our partner fears that it will take us away from them. I've put co-operating even further down the list because successful relationships are all about teamwork, so this is another make-or-break issue. Moving on to question 14, I would be concerned if you answered 'yes' but added a rider, for example: 'as long as she has not had too much to drink' or 'as long as he controls his jealousy'. How likely is that to happen? What is the opinion of people who really care about you?

There are two more questions in the eighteen-month test:

15 How old is your beloved?
16 How many of their ambitions have they achieved?

If you want to get married, or to make a commitment for life, these two final questions are the most important. Let me explain why. The average age of first marriage in the United Kingdom is 30.5 for men and 28.2 for women. Our thirties are the prime period for settling down, because by forty-five, only 6 per cent of women and 9 per cent of men have never married. Age is also a crucial issue for women who want to settle down and have a family. However, contrary to popular wisdom, men have a biological clock too – which begins to tick around the age of forty-two. Men are not so worried about being able to father a child but whether they will still have enough energy to be an active father.

Moving on to ambition, rightly or wrongly, most men still expect to be the principal breadwinner and will not consider settling down and starting a family until they are established in their careers or have achieved their ambitions. Take Simon, the 36-year-old photographer who is finally looking for a partner: 'Previously, I wanted the freedom to do what I wanted, when I wanted.' He had been in a steady relationship between the ages of nineteen and twenty-one but found his girlfriend's love restrictive: 'It was all going round the shops on Saturdays and roast dinners with her parents on Sundays. I wanted to see jungles, volcanoes and sail south of the equator.' Men who have been to university – and therefore take longer to get established on the career ladder – get married later. Their prime window is thirty to thirty-six (towards the top end of this range if they take a second degree or undertake further training). In contrast, men who are not university graduates marry between twenty-eight and thirty-three.

Although a man or a woman might be determined to make their mark on the world, and worried that the demands of a clinging partner might hold them back, they have not taken a vow of celibacy. Charlie, thirty-two, has a successful career in the City which involves a lot of business trips – as he says: 'I have to travel light.' However that did not stop him falling in love: 'It was wonderful and horrible. I felt ill. I couldn't think of anything beyond her, she bled into everything else I did and it was all wonderful. It was magnetic.' Unfortunately, she wanted a family and they eventually split. As Charlie summed it up: 'Right girl but the wrong time.' It is easy to paint men like Charlie as 'lying bastards', but he insists that he is up-front about not wanting a serious relationship: 'Time after time, I thought everything was on the table but we still ended up in bars with her crying, "but I love you".' It is not just men who want a little 'uncomplicated' affection. I've had complaints from older divorced men who miss the warmth and companionship of a relationship but cannot find a woman interested in a committed relationship. Take Greg, forty-eight, who has been on the singles scene for three years: 'I'm amazed by all these predatory women in their fifties. Don't get me wrong, they're beautiful and they keep their bodies in amazing shape but they have their lives sorted: nice flat and car, good circle of friends, and they don't want it complicated by a full-time man. There was one woman, the sex was incredible, but the closer we got the more that she kept slipping away until suddenly she was gone.'

Another group that is single, dating but not truly available, is made up of people who are still embroiled in past relationships. 'I love the fact that Justin is a great father to his two young kids,' says Amelia, a 32-year-old divorcée with children of her own, who has been 'sort of dating' him for two years. 'However, we can never really plan anything, as his mobile will ring and he'll have to rush round to his ex for some "supposed" emergency like the downstairs toilet won't flush. I suggested that she called a plumber, like anybody else, and he didn't call me for a fortnight.' So remember, it is perfectly possible to answer 'yes' to all the questions in the first part of the eighteen-months test but find the relationship in jeopardy because of life-stage, careers or other commitments.

How to Turn Your Relationship into a Committed Partnership

There are many couples who take the eighteen-months test and find that they are not ready to make a long-term commitment. My message is 'don't panic'. There is still time to overcome the obstacles and turn the answers from negative to positive. It is easier for a man in love. He can cut through the confusion with a proposal. It's romantic and gets all the issues on the table. A woman in love has to be more tactical and engineer a conversation about the future. Although an ultimatum to 'marry me, move in together or else I'll move on' might seem straightforward and honest, nobody responds well to threats. Instead, make clear that you are the 'marrying kind' or 'need a proper commitment' and discover where both of you stand. It will be difficult but, by the eighteen-months point, your relationship will be robust enough to cope with a bit of conflict.

Hopefully, the conversation will go smoothly but if there are sticking problems, or he says something hurtful, be careful not to overreact. This is important for two reasons. Firstly, your future together does not want to become such a toxic subject that it is hard to bring it up again. Secondly, you may be so fearful of rejection that you have projected outright defeat onto a more nuanced position. So instead of rowing, sulking or storming off, return to the conversation the next day or when your beloved is in a good mood. The aim is to seek clarification. 'I'm not ready' can mean both 'no' and something more ambivalent.

Take Charlie and his 'right girl, wrong time': 'I wanted children but I needed two more years.' Unfortunately, he had not had this conversation with his girlfriend and she left without knowing the full picture. Another common word that can mean different things to different people is 'someday'. This can be a nice way of saying 'never' or it could mean a specific date.

Sometimes attempts to clarify a beloved's position is met with more blocking. If this is the case, try an old trick that I learnt as a journalist dealing with the police – who are notorious for keeping facts to themselves. It's called fishing. When someone claims 'I don't know', you guess a possible answer, for example: 'twelve to eighteen months'. Normally the other person will either agree or correct you. If you get a second 'I don't know' try fishing once more. For example: 'longer or less' can sometimes trigger a ballpark prediction. However, if your partner genuinely doesn't know, let the subject drop or you risk a pointless row. The other useful response to 'I'm not ready' is so simple that many people overlook it. Try asking: why? There could be a perfectly understandable reason: 'I'm worried about my student debts' or 'I'm saving for a deposit'. However, if you are still upset by his or her response, you need to make the following points:

- *Reassurance*. 'I love you but I'm disappointed because I was hoping to spend the rest of my life with you.'
- *Explanation*. 'I'm hurt because I thought the relationship was going somewhere.'
- *Reassertion*. 'Children/Marriage is important to my happiness.'

Sometimes a tactical retreat is better than keeping on repeating the same point. At eighteen months, there is still enough time and sometimes when one partner stops pushing that is the moment when the other partner changes his or her mind. I know this from experience. My first partner lived in Germany and was reluctant to move to the UK. At that time, I made my living in radio and could not speak good enough German to get a job there. One day, I got tired of nagging, so I said: 'I still want us to live together but I'm going to stop going on at you about it. It doesn't mean I've lost interest.' Nine months later my partner arrived with a removals van and eighty-seven boxes.

Sometimes when the cards go on the table at eighteen months, a couple will discover very different agendas. Here is an example from my counselling case book. 'I really enjoy going out, doing stuff with Ellis. The sex is great and she might even be the "one",' said Martin, who is thirty-four, 'except she already has her family and to be honest, much as I like her kids, I wouldn't want to miss out.' But what about Ellis, doesn't she have expectations? Martin looked down at his shoes and mumbled. It was obvious that Martin and Ellis had avoided this conversation. Martin wanted the benefits of a relationship 'for now' and although Ellis seemed to want a commitment, she was afraid to force the issue. Sadly, the couple separated. Generally, if there is no commitment by two years together, and commitment is important to you, I would suggest becoming less available or stopping seeing your partner altogether. (See 'Coming Down Off the Limerence High' in the exercise section.) In some cases, a retreat will change your partner's mind but be aware that he or she might also disappear.

Riding the Natural Rhythm of Relationships

When a couple are getting along fine, the temptation is to enjoy the moment and forget about tomorrow. There is a lot to be said in favour of this. We cannot live in the future or the past. All we have is now. However, many people who complain: 'can't we leave things just as they are' or 'why do we have to keep trying to define our relationship' are frightened of change. A relationship is a living thing and, like all living things, needs to be fed, nurtured and allowed to grow – otherwise it will die. The Byrds song 'Turn, Turn, Turn' – based on the Bible (Ecclesiastes 3: 1) – sums up this idea best: 'to everything, there is a season, a time for every purpose under Heaven' – and it is equally applicable to a successful long relationship as it is to planting and reaping. So what is the natural rhythm of a relationship and how can you use that knowledge?

In the late seventies, when gay relationships became visible for the first time, two psychologists decided to study them. Dr David McWhirter and Andrew Mattison (*The Male Couple: How Relationships Develop* – Prentice Hall, 1985) tracked 156 gay couples in California, between the ages of twenty and sixty-nine, over five years, and discovered that their relationships moved through six clearly defined stages. I have adapted McWhirter and Mattison's findings, in the light of twenty-five years' working with heterosexuals, to reveal the universal experience for all couples.

The first stage on the road to a committed relationship is called 'Blending'. Limerence is at its height and the two lovers want nothing but to be together all the time. When separated, they have a real physical ache and are forever thinking of each other, sighing, buying small gifts or boring their friends with tales of their beloved. Unfortunately, some people expect limerence to last forever. 'In the early days, I'd walk past her house, even if I knew she wouldn't be in, just to see her orange-painted walls through the window and imagine her eating breakfast there while we chatted on the phone,' says Thomas, a 32-year-old events co-ordinator. 'Life couldn't get better, so when she wanted to talk about the future my response was always: why change things and risk spoiling everything? Except slowly the magic wore off, we started arguing, until one day it seemed we had nothing in common any more. Friends said move on, but we had been so good together.' Fortunately, in counselling, Thomas and his partner were able to settle their differences, but only after accepting that they could not staying in the 'Blending' stage indefinitely. By eighteen months, a couple should be ready for 'Nesting', where building a home together becomes the central way to demonstrate love. This phase lasts for about a year and a half. Stage three is called 'Self-affirming', where partners remember personal needs which have been put to one side while forging couple needs. This is the point at which each half remembers that there is an 'I' as well as a 'we'. Stage four is 'Collaborating', when couples use their new sense of individual identity and the security from their shared love to launch a joint project, like having a child together. The timings here are more approximate – especially for couples who meet later in life – but generally 'Collaborating' comes somewhere around the fifth year together. Obviously, it is possible to have a child earlier but many couples who should be enjoying the bliss of 'Blending' or 'Nesting' are worried about issues that normally do not arise until much later. 'I love my boyfriend but I don't know if we have a future,' says Claire, who is twenty-seven and has been with her partner for twelve months. 'Right from when I can remember, I've always wanted children and I thought we'd discussed the idea in principle but now he doesn't seem so certain. I want to get married before I'm thirty, then wait a couple of years together before trying for a baby. Already this would make me past my most fertile years. If my boyfriend can't commit, I'll need time to find someone else. Should I offer him an ultimatum?' Instead of going with the natural rhythm of relationships, she is trying to jump ahead. No wonder she feels overwhelmed and unable to make a decision.

The fifth stage is called 'Adapting', which is from fifteen to twenty-five years into the relationship. These couples are busy adapting to the changes thrown at them, rather than dealing with internal changes within the relationship. These can be everything from children leaving home to ageing parents. Finally, comes 'Renewing' – from twenty-five to fifty-plus years, and the good news is that older couples are often the closest. At the beginning of a relationship, closeness is based on the promise of a future together, now it is based on the reality of a life shared together. The best is ahead of us. (If you would like to know more about the six relationship stages, I cover them in detail in my book *I Love You But I'm Not in Love with You*.)

A Happy Ending

Whatever the stresses and disappointments encountered while looking for love, finding a long-term partner will transform your life for the better.

Hannah, thirty-six, met Paresh, thirty-three, when he joined the company where she worked. Although he liked her immediately, she is ashamed to admit that she cannot remember her first impressions of him. 'It took Paresh three months to pluck up the courage to ask me out,' explains Hannah. 'Over that time, I'd got to know him as a member of my team and a great guy. But I'd never thought of him as anything but a work colleague until he started to get a bit flirty – which looking back was a bit of a clue! The turning point was when our company hired a boat for an evening cruise down the river. I found myself looking forward to getting to know Paresh away from the office, so I was dismayed when he walked up the gangplank with a lady at his side. I later found out that she was just a friend who had moved to the area. But I felt this pang of "never mind but what a shame".'

Things progressed and Paresh finally asked Hannah out for a drink but she had previous commitments. 'One week went by and the next week he was due to fly out to Singapore for work and then on to India to visit his parents. I remember giving myself a poke to pluck up the courage and ask him out before he flew off. On that first date, we were so at ease that drinks led to a very posh dinner. In the taxi afterwards, the driver was playing Kenny Gee so loudly that we could not stop giggling. He pecked me goodnight and then went off on his trip.'

However, their enforced separation turned out to be an advantage. 'For the next three weeks, we exchanged wonderful emails full of stories about childhood and tales about families. When he got back I was as excited as a child on Christmas Eve. We went out a few more times and finally had the most yummy kiss in his kitchen.' Early into their courtship, Hannah and Paresh house-sat for friends who had a place in Bermuda – on condition they walked an old dog and looked after a budgie. Hannah tells a story that illustrates their love but also shows how love helps people grow. 'I tended to the budgie every day, calling it "sweet budgie" and trying to coax it out of its cage. All to no avail. However, Paresh put his hand in and offered his finger, but the budgie would hastily hop to the other side of its perch. Paresh said that I reminded him of that budgie. He's a very tactile person and it was a bit of a shock at first for me and I would keep a slight distance.' This explains how long it took for him to get his first kiss. 'Anyway, Paresh started calling me "sweet budgie", so I called him "sweet budgie" back and the names stuck. After he proposed, on a mountain in India covered in tea plantations, the tuk-tuk that took us back into town had a sticker with two budgies on the windscreen.'

I like this case history because it illustrates both how ordinary and how extraordinary love can be. It also provides a happy ending for this book and, I hope, inspiration for your happy ending too. Just take your time, believe in yourself and be prepared to change. Love is out there waiting for you.

Summary

- In the same way that many potential long-term prospects get overlooked in the dating rush to judgement, many people want to rush straight into courting without giving the relationship time to grow naturally.
- Have a clear idea of what you want from sex in the relationship. If both of you are just enjoying the pleasure of each other's bodies – fine. However, sometimes one partner views sex as part of the journey to a committed relationship while the other views it as an end in itself.
- Sex too early in a relationship can bind two incompatible people together and override the delicate process where each person's subconscious checks if there is a true match.
- If there are problems in your new relationship, talk about your fears rather than ignoring them and hoping they will go away.
- Arguments when dating can be positive. The strong feelings invoked will lead to self-disclosure, promote honesty, bring issues to the surface and help a couple to truly get to know each other.
- Three months is a good time to stop and assess the potential of your relationship. However, make certain that you listen attentively, so that you hear what is said rather than what you want to hear.
- The ecstasy of limerence can blind people to the true character of their beloved and the relationship. Only when limerence has subsided – probably around eighteen months – can you begin to judge whether this is lasting love or not.
- Change is inevitable and relationships grow and change. Ultimately, it is better to accept the natural rhythm of the relationship and make it work for you.

Exercises

Coping with Relationship-anxiety Attacks

Why should we be frightened when someone loves us and wants the best for us? Unfortunately, there are two contradictory forces at play: we crave affection but we want to protect ourselves – and nobody can hurt us more than someone we love. So with one hand, we pull our partner close but with the other – just to be safe – we hold him or her back. We hope this strange dance will protect us from loneliness, rejection, being vulnerable and feeling helpless, but often it causes more pain. So what's the answer?

1 Accept that relationships can be scary and that everybody feels like this from time to time.
2 Look at your past to understand where your fears come from. Perhaps your parents got divorced or there was a painful early romance? What patterns has your childhood set up and how do they influence your behaviour today?
3 Understand that the best way to deal with fear is to confront it. The more that you shy away from something the more the fear grows.
4 Explain to your partner what circumstances throw up shadows from the past. In that way he or she will know when to tread carefully.
5 Keep a fear diary. Write down when you feel uncomfortable down one side of the page and provide a rational explanation on the other. For example, fear = 'he's late, he doesn't love me'. Rational explanation = 'traffic's bad'. Writing fears down stops them multiplying in your head and accesses the adult logical part of your personality.
6 Re-balance your life. Draw a pie chart which shows how you divide your time and energy between: relationship, work, friends, myself. Next, draw a second chart showing how you would like it to be. How can you make this future happen?

Coming Down Off the Limerence High

It is impossible to escape limerence until one of the following conditions has been met:

a) Consummation: the bliss of reciprocation is gradually either blended into a lasting love or replaced by less positive feelings.
b) Starvation: even under the spell of limerence it becomes harder and harder to interpret the actions of someone not interested into positive signs of hope. It is finally accepted that the object of limerence does not return the feelings.
c) Transformation: attentions are transferred to a new person. (This normally overlaps with Starvation, because someone at the height of limerence is unable even to consider an alternative partner.)

So if you find yourself trapped in limerence with someone who does not return your feelings, here are some tips on achieving starvation.

• Try not to indulge yourself with fantasies of how it could all come right in the end. Although this might provide a few moments of pleasure, it will only increase your pain.
• If you find yourself weakening, use a distraction technique – like doing some exercise or phoning a friend.
• Don't torture yourself. Put all the photographs and keepsakes in the loft. Find different ways to work that do not go past the favourite restaurant that the two of you shared together. Don't put on his favourite CD or read books by her favourite author.
• Disconnect your thoughts. When you find yourself thinking: 'I wonder if he would have liked this movie' or 'what would she have looked like in that dress' put up a mental STOP sign and think of something else mundane – like what to buy at the supermarket.
• Cut the links. If you have mutual friends, stop seeing them for a while. If you are honest, you probably decided to go out with them in the hope of either hearing about your beloved or getting them to pass on information about you.

- Forget closure. It is tempting to think 'if only I could understand why she is not interested' or 'if only I could get my own back on her then I would feel better'. However, these thoughts just preserve the links.
- Remember, starvation needs time. Six months on a strict regime should cure most cases. If you are still stuck, ask yourself: 'What is the benefit in staying where I am?' Common reasons for not moving on include: punishing yourself, punishing your beloved (when he or she hears how miserable I am then he or she will be sorry), fear of making a new relationship.

How to End a Relationship and Mean It

One of the hardest ways to finish a relationship is, what I call, the stuttering end. Instead of one clean break, the couple will give their relationship a second try and then a third. In the worst cases, I've met couples who have spent several years splitting and reconciling again. With each false dawn, the promises that it will be better this time are more extravagant, the disappointment more fundamental and the bitterness greater. Not only is the final end more painful but the recovery time much longer. So what causes the 'Stuttering End'? The problem is that the person instigating the break-up doesn't really mean it. In some cases, the instigator hopes that the drama of a threatened end will 'wake up' the other person, but this is a high-risk strategy. It is much better to work on the specific issue – for example, we don't spend enough time together. However, the main cause of the stuttering end is that the instigator gives a mixed message. For example: 'Although I don't love you any more, I don't hate you and maybe we could have a future in two, five, even ten years' time.' Most people would read that as goodbye, but someone desperate – especially if under the spell of limerence – will discount the negatives and build up the positives. Obviously, the instigator does not want to destroy their partner but letting the other person down gently can backfire. For example: 'You will always be in the bottom of my heart.' It might be true but someone under limerence will read this as: 'I don't really want to break up.' So how do you avoid the stuttering end?

1 *Don't ignore problems.* This is useful advice for any relationship – even happy ones. It is better to address issues as they happen rather than closing your eyes and hoping things will magically change.

2 *Be realistic about the prospects of fixing your relationship.* Although I have helped many couples fall back in love again, they have generally been together for five years plus and have a basic foundation of good times to fall back onto. The extreme stuttering-end couples, who have spent years in on–off relationships, generally have nothing in the 'happiness bank' beyond a burst of intense limerence at the very beginning.

3 *Have a good break-up.* Split up face-to-face and with enough time for the other person to ask questions. It might seem easier to break up remotely – by email or on the phone – but the other person will feel cheated and pressure to meet up. Out of guilt, because it is not fair to split up at a distance, you will probably back down. However, you might have unwittingly set a pattern where your ex-partner uses guilt to force a series of concessions or even reconciliations.

4 *Give a clear message.* Stick to the facts and be careful not to offer false hopes like 'maybe' or 'someday' or 'in the future'.

5 *Accept that your ex-partner will be angry and hurt.* He or she will probably heap all the blame on you but trying to justify yourself only prolongs the agony. One of the advantages of a break-up is that you no longer have to worry about what your partner thinks.

6 *Stick to your guns*. You might miss him or her but keep your doubts to yourself. Don't call and say: 'I was listening to the CD you gave me and thought of you.'

7 *Remain polite but distant*. Respond with a simple note to flowers and presents but keep focused on your message: it's over. If she phones, keep it short and sweet: 'Sorry, I can't talk now.' If he emails to ask what you have been up to, reply with the bare minimum: 'Shopping with my mum, you know, same old stuff.' Your ex-partner might be a pain but rows can provide enough drama to sustain someone who sees themselves as the tragically discarded lover.

8 *How realistic are the promises of change?* It is easy to promise to 'try harder' or to have a complete personality transformation but much harder to pull it off.

9 *Are you looking back with rose-tinted glasses or thinking 'if only . . .'.* Of course, your relationship would have been easier 'if only we did not live 500 miles apart' or 'if only she did not adore her family – they will have nothing to do with me'. What are the chances of these things changing?

10 *You can become friends but not just yet*. It is fine to aspire to being friends with your ex – they could even introduce you to someone special – but allow enough time to lapse for one type of relationship to end and for the other to begin. In the meantime, an invitation to your birthday party would be a mixed message. It might seem cruel, but it is in everybody's best interests.

Six Ways to Revitalise Your Relationship

This exercise works at any point in the development of your relationship, but it is particularly useful after an argument or a rough patch caused by the upheaval of moving from one stage to another.

1 *Look at each other more*. Couples in love spend 70 per cent of their time looking at each other when they are talking, rather than the usual 30 per cent to 60 per cent.

2 *Go that extra mile*. Unfortunately, we take the everyday gestures – like cooking or filling up the car with petrol – for granted. However, we notice the special things and being extra kind will encourage him or her to reciprocate.

3 *Stop editing your day*. We imagine that our partner is not interested in the minutiae of our lives but the less we hear, the less we care. So save up colourful incidents from your day to share in the evening.

4 *Enjoy casual body contact*. Cuddling on the sofa, stroking and kissing should be enjoyed in their own right, rather than just as a prelude to intercourse.

5 *Laugh together*. Private jokes and teasing can really feed a relationship. Alternatively, go to a comedy club or see a funny movie together.

6 *Pretend that you don't know each other*. Psychologists at the universities of British Columbia and Virginia discovered that we treat strangers better than our partners – as we hope that this will make them like us. So the researchers asked couples to interact as though they had never met before and found that their well-being rose significantly. So why not meet your partner in a bar or some other public space, pretend to be strangers and chat each other up? You will probably learn something new about each other and have a good laugh too.

The Second Step:

Finding Lasting Love

The Seven Key Lessons

1 *How a relationship starts is generally how it will continue.* This is why it is important to be relaxed and open when you first meet.
2 *Game-playing undermines the forming of a lasting bond.* It makes it harder to change into up-front and honest.
3 *Take longer to assess and nurture possible relationships.* First impressions are not always right, so keep an open mind.
4 *This is the era of the new relationship pioneers.* We are the first generation who can make our own choices, to our own ethics.
5 *If we truly believe in equal partnerships, this should be reflected in how the relationship starts.* Both men and women should be free to ask each other out.
6 *Choice might make for an uncomfortable ride, but ultimately this is liberating.* So although we might occasionally feel nostalgic for past types of dating, the best of times is now.
7 *A romantic life-changing adventure is just round the corner.* So travel optimistically and do not be in too much of a rush.

Acknowledgements

Thanks for the advice, help and support while I've been writing this book: Rachel Calder, Jenny Parrott, Richard Atkinson, Erica Jarnes, Natalie Hunt, Ignacio Jarquin, Gail Louw, Chris Taylor, Jamie MacKay, Vanessa Gebbie, Catherine Grace and all the clients and interviewees who contributed to my research.